# *The Accidental Caregiver*

# *The Accidental Caregiver*

How I Met, Loved, and Lost
Legendary Holocaust Refugee
Maria Altmann

*a memoir*

GREGOR COLLINS

Edited by Jessica Swift

Book Cover and Interior Design by Sara Dismukes

ISBN: 978-0-9858654-0-5

Published by Bloch-Bauer Books

www.TheAccidentalCaregiver.com

*To Maria*

*"There are only two ways to live your life:
One is as though nothing is a miracle.
The other is as though everything is a miracle."*

Albert Einstein

# CONTENTS

*January 30, 2008*
*Hollywood, CA*


Gregor: Yo.

Archie: What's up!

Gregor: I met a girl.

Archie: Huh?

Gregor: She's Austrian.

Archie: Who is she?

Gregor: I can't describe her over the phone.

Archie: Over 18?

Gregor: Barely.

Archie: How old?

Gregor: You're, um—you're breaking up. Have to run to an audition anyway. Call you later!

*So I went to that audition unable to shake this girl from my head. Meeting her was like being in Paris for the first time, or eating peanut butter and chocolate ice cream on an empty stomach. It was a game-changer: For the first time in my life I wasn't ashamed to admit to my friends and family I was in love and that I was powerless and unwilling to fight it. And though I didn't realize it then, I would never leave her. I was hers. Forever.*

*But even in those first magical moments in that Beverly Hills kitchen, there are things we would never know. We never knew we would spend the next three years together intimately—that we would be transported to Vienna in its heyday, and that we would be forced to leave it behind to escape the Nazis; that we would barely make it to Holland; then to England; then to Massachusetts; then to California—where we'd work, raise a family, and live out the rest of our lives in Los Angeles. And we would never know it would all end at her funeral, where I would be pulled aside and told I was the last great love of her life. No, we would never know the heights we would reach together before it ended.*

*But I'm getting ahead of myself. For one, I was an actor, not a caregiver, and, frankly, I needed an old lady like I needed a hole in the head...*

### October 31, 2007

I'm "Seventies Guy" for the tenth year in a row—tie-dye t-shirt, fluorescent-green bellbottoms, black combat boots. It's a lame costume, I get it, but I'm a virile 32-year-old man who understands that the prevailing point of Halloween is to meet women. When you're donning a massive mask, or a clunky one-piece suit that monopolizes your entire body, you're not only squandering prime opportunities to show these women what you look like on October 30 and November 1, but you're indubitably spending more time sweating in the corner and less time flirting on the dance floor. And in the wee hours of the morning with, presumably, a girl or two on your shoulder, who's really thinking about how much thought you put into your costume? Anyway. This is how I've felt about Halloween for most of my adult life. It's probably why I'm still single.

I'm an actor. I'm sort of like Blythe Danner or Tilda Swinton or Christopher Plummer, in that I've never had one person think I wasn't good at it. The only reason you haven't heard of me is because I haven't gotten my big break yet. Everyone says I'm going places. My agent and my manager do, my peers all do, and even my brother and mother do, who once both made me cry at an Olive Garden in Virginia because I couldn't tell them the precise date I was going to start making a living as an actor. That was a real low point for all three of us. But it's gotten better.

I'm coming off a starring role in an independent feature called *Night Before the Wedding*, set for a spring 2008 release.

After nearly a decade in Hollywood I finally feel my career taking off. I've paid my dues. I've done virtually everything there is to do behind the camera save craft service, hair, and makeup. I've been an intern, an executive assistant, a tape librarian, a production assistant, and a producer. I've even supervised a *Girls Gone Wild* Tour (Sorry, Mom, it was only partially true that I was working on a "nature" show in Key West).

Acting found *me*, which is why I knew I couldn't ignore it. It was early 2004. I'd spent the previous five years in reality television. My last job in reality was at *E! Entertainment* producing the red carpet segments for the Golden Globes and the Academy Awards. The gig ended, and the phone calls just stopped. I went from a busy producer to a busy sleeper, in a twelve-hour period. I was suddenly at a major creative standstill in my life, for the first time forced to confront what I could really offer Hollywood. Weeks—months of unemployment ensued. I grew my first beard ever (turns out it has a reddish tint), and I made a Double Kingburger from Fatburger magically disappear every other day. I was at my heaviest. *What the hell was I meant to be doing?* My best friend Archie suggested I try an acting class. I took his advice.

In my first class I performed one of David Mamet's first plays, *Sexual Perversity in Chicago*. When my partner and I finished what felt like torture, I was certain I was as ineffectual as an audience member sitting there watching it, and that I had no acting talent whatsoever. I couldn't wait to get out of that class. I was humiliated, sitting there facing a theater full of strangers judging me. Then the teacher, Darryl, asked me how long I'd been acting. I looked down at my watch and said, "Two minutes." He was shocked. "I would have guessed you'd been acting for years."

I strutted out of that class like I was already a movie star. I booked the first film I ever auditioned for—a comedic short called *Bagel Time*—and within six months I was guest starring on the soap opera *Passions*. It had come! After 28 years of stumbling around life as if it were a moon bounce at a kid's birthday party, I was suddenly standing firmly on solid ground able to proudly state my life's purpose: *to regale the world with my acting.* I had finally found something worth fighting for.

Sure, there have been ups and downs since *Bagel Time*, but, despite what you might think, nothing ever happens overnight in Hollywood. If Malcolm Gladwell's right—that it takes ten years or ten thousand hours to become "successful" at something—then I'm due any day now.

So this Halloween party. I picked up Archie, who was dressed as Indiana Jones (and just so you know he and I share the same Halloween philosophy), my friend Paul, who was dressed as some sort of head-to-toe vampire/zombie amalgam, and my friend Jeff, a priest with a choirboy stapled to his crotch. I know what you're thinking—the vampire/zombie costume went a little too far.

I met all three guys on the dating show, *Blind Date*. It was our first job in Los Angeles, and we became family. I was a tape librarian, Paul was—and still is—an editor, Jeff was—and still is—a producer, and Archie—a writer/filmmaker/executive producer—wrote the thought-bubbles above the two people who went on a filmed date. Archie and I became an unlikely pair—he was a 32-year-old, short, skinny, wisecracking Jewish guy from New York, and I was a 24-year-old, tall, muscular, reserved gentile from Virginia. Not much has changed in eight years. We're like Arnold and Danny from the movie *Twins*: He lures the girls in with his jokes, and I keep them around with my looks. Just don't tell him I said that.

The party was in the Hollywood Hills, way up at the tippy-top of a mega-mansion neighborhood called Mount Olympus, where the streets are as wide as an airport tarmac. The house could have been a Victorian estate in the south of England. It was teeming with the usual naughty nurses, dominatrices, Cat Women, and Cat Women Dominatrices. I danced with a busty blonde nurse who said she was a former Miss Hawaiian Tropic. She wrote her phone number in crayon on the back of a paper plate. I'm partial to brunettes—I feel like they're more into me, too—but I had so much fun with this blonde that she must have dyed her hair earlier in the evening. I never get my hopes up. For me, to find genuine friendliness and fun in a girl is extremely difficult out here. You'd think in a city called the "City of Angels" that finding an angel would be like finding a needle in a stack of needles.

## November 5, 2007

I had an audition this morning for an "under-five" on *Cold Case*. An under-five is a character in a TV show with less than five lines. It was for a cop. "Put the gun down, Banks" I think was one of my lines.

My agent's been pretty good about getting me auditions lately. That's not always how it is. In fact, I'm living a life of audition luxury right now: I've gone through a 90-day period without an audition, during which the only calls I seem to get are from West LA Dental, who must be hard up for money, because they call me from different phone lines to trick me into answering so I'll make an appointment. I can barely make my rent each month. An out-of-work actor's teeth are way down the priority list.

In this town, when it comes to auditions and acting work, if it rains it pours, and when it's cloudy it stays cloudy for so long you're ready to quit. You agonize through the slow times by working a day job that's at least tolerable and pays the bills, which for me right now is working at one of the largest catering companies in Los Angeles, Patina Restaurant Group. That's what we "starving artists" do—serve food that we can't afford to eat, to the people we'd kill to be. But it's the perfect day job. Most of the events are at night, leaving the days free for auditions, which is why so many actors are in the food industry. That, and the free meals.

Acting is tough. I've proven I can walk on set and give a director what they want, but for some reason I haven't figured out how to walk into an audition room with the same on-set bravado. It's frustrating. Casting directors say they want that *actor-in-shining-armor* to walk through the door so they can get to production, but they always seem to have the most unmotivated person reading opposite you at the audition. How am I supposed to show them what they can expect on set when I'm reading with someone who doesn't even care if I get the job?

Auditions are the most awkward two minutes of my day, and that I'm required to stun a complete stranger with everything I have to offer the world in 120 seconds is just unreasonable and irrational in my opinion. Some people—like, say, the funny fat guy, or the weirdo—can just walk in there without saying anything, and they're the guy. Casting directors understand who they are the second they see them. I'm not fat or weird, at least looks-wise. I need Clint Eastwood. I've heard he doesn't believe in auditions, he just sits down and has a nice chat, and either has a good feeling about you or doesn't. I wonder if that's actually true.

I've been lucky. Most of the projects in which I've been cast are a result of the director or producer having seen my work in a film or in a play, or have had some kind of hunch about my talent. That's what happened with *Night Before the Wedding*. David, the director who I met at Patina and barely knew at the time, walked up to me one day at a post-opera-party at the Music Center and said, "You're perfect for a part I just wrote." He had never even seen my acting. I could have been horrible. He sent me the script, and within a weekend I stepped aboard as the star/producer. It was my first lead role in a feature film, and David's directorial debut.

Acting is a numbers game. But I'm close. I may not be curing cancer, but what ultimately keeps me energized is knowing that I've found very few things in this life that make me feel more that I'm right where I'm meant to be than being in the moment with another actor.

It's just the in-between crap that sucks.


## November 7, 2007

I have a Skype session this afternoon. My mom, my brother and I like to do this every few weeks. It usually takes us a couple days of back-and-forth emails to get the times zones right, because my mom always gets confused. I swear sometimes she's convinced the time zones change weekly. My brother Christian lives in London, my mom in DC, and I'm in Los Angeles. Today we agreed on 1 pm my time, 4 pm my mom's time, and 10 pm my brother's time. Since we don't see each other in person more than once a year if we're lucky, we do this mostly so we don't feel guilty. At least that's my take on it.

Ever since that Olive Garden incident a couple years ago— the one where at least a dozen strangers saw me break down in tears over my bottomless bowl of salad and breadsticks—Christian has showed more interest in my career. He saw an early cut of *Night Before the Wedding* and wrote me an email: "Gregor, you are a really, really good actor." He had never complimented me on my acting before. And my mother has also gone out of her way to be encouraging, sending me links every few days to certain artsy guests on *Charlie Rose*. It's her way of saying, "I'm in your corner, Gregor." As for my dad, who's a writer, he's always understood and supported my creative endeavors. We all love each other, but we're not one big happy family who wear colorful sweaters and hang tinsel around a Christmas tree every year. We've never been that. I've wondered what that would be like. It's something I continue to be curious about.

### Mid-November, 2007

It's safe to say I didn't book *Cold Case*. It's been over a week and I haven't heard from my agent. The toughest auditions to book are the under-fives. The casting director sees, say, 30 people who look and sound exactly the same, reading the same four words the same way all day for two or three days straight. You can imagine how difficult it is to distinguish yourself, unless you go in there and act like a crazy person, which sometimes works. It basically comes down to the way you look and the way you sound, and of course you have no control over that. That's what ultimately makes this business so damn heartbreaking.

And as if not booking auditions isn't depressing enough, the girls out here are unreliable. Like this "blonde" nurse from the Halloween party. I figured I'd be secure and call her the next day. No callback. She's like a casting director. Out here having fun with a girl on a date doesn't mean anything. All it means is that it was only a night of fun. It may not snow here, but there are flakes year 'round. No one wants to commit to anything because there's always something better around the corner, someone "more connected" or more famous who can help further their careers.

I really don't understand girls. Maybe I would if I had a sister. I want to understand them. I understand my guy friends completely. But girls sometimes seem more like wild animals:

attention-grabbing from afar but when I get too close the claws
come out. I haven't found one I can have nonjudgmental fun with,
without being worried about those claws, and getting hurt. Isn't
that pathetic? I don't know if it's me, or them. Probably both.

Los Angeles is my girlfriend. It's my deep-tissue massage.
My memory foam neck pillow. And that makes me happy. All I do
is work. But that's only satisfying on the surface. Everyone is
running from some-thing. We all do one thing because we're
scared of another thing. I only bury myself in my work because
I'm frightened of what I'd do or who I'd be if I didn't. I can't help
that I want big things for myself, and the only way I see that
happening is to be selfish. I admit I'm so selfish I'd make Ayn
Rand jealous.

Sometimes cool things can happen out here, but ultimately
I'm living in a land of dreams, and in a land of dreams the
majority of people living in it will never achieve those dreams. So
you have a city swelling with sad sacks slumping around
wondering if it will ever happen. Well it won't. And maybe the
most discouraging thing about the entertainment business is that
there are talented people—more talented than the ones you see on
TV or in the movies—who you will never hear from. And they'll
be forced to come to terms with their worst nightmare: a life of
anonymity.


### November 22, 2007

I went on a date tonight with a girl in her 20's who has never
eaten a vegetable. Not *one* vegetable her entire life. I was so
stunned I asked her how she was still alive, and she started
making excuses and saying she eats fruit, but only apples, and
only "sometimes." She had no sense of humor about it, showing
not even a hint that she thought it might be strange or dangerous.
When I spoke passionately about how I could eat broccoli or
asparagus or mushrooms every meal for the rest of my life, she
looked at me as if I told her I just loved roasted vomit. I felt like
asking why her parents would allow her to grow up like that, but
I didn't. It wasn't worth it. I just smiled the rest of the night and
dropped her off. And she was wearing a hat, too—at night—which

is another red flag for me when it comes to women. I didn't even want to kiss her. The hot girls are always weird or crazy. Will I ever meet one who isn't?

### December 1, 2007

I have a good friend named Tom who's a fellow actor. A few weeks ago he answered an ad on Craigslist to be a caregiver for an old lady from Europe. He's been caring for her ever since. He can't stop bragging to me about her. This morning he texted me, "You *have* to meet this woman, she's amazing!" He's really having a good time with her. I'm happy for him.

### December 6, 2007

I'm so bored of catering. I should be the person being served. I should be the one dressed all spiffy and Hollywood-y, taking the tuna tartar on a crispy tortilla from *them*, not the other way around. I need something else. I don't know what, all I know is this is not what I envisioned the "dream life" would be. *Help*.

### December 9, 2007

Tom's in his second week raving to me about this old lady, and I feel like he's making me feel guilty for not being as excited as him. Why is he pushing her on me? He's now telling me the family needs another caregiver, because it's only him at the house 24 hours a day, 7 days a week. He actually wants me to consider coming on as a caregiver. When he was fishing for an answer I was noncommittal and sort of craftily changed the subject, which is one of my better qualities. A caregiver? I'd basically be saying, "Gregor, you know all you've worked for out here? All those blood, sweat and tears? Well get ready to flush it all down the toilet. For a 92-year-old lady." C'mon. This town is tough enough going at it alone.

## *Mid-January, 2008*

Being happy isn't when I'm at my happiest. I don't think I'm ever at my happiest, even when I'm happy. What does true happiness feel like anyway? Will I ever know? Why am I never truly happy? Is it me? The life I've chosen? The girls? How I'm wired? There's an emptiness inside me, a fear that nothing will ever work out and that I'll be a loser the rest of my life. The glamor in this business is a myth. It's not like that bullshit you've seen in ads or in movies or on *Extra.* It's dark. It's dreary. It's desolate. Empty business. Empty girls. Empty voicemail.

## *January 17, 2008*

> To: Kathryn.Grant@hotmail.com
>
> From: GregorCollins@yahoo.com
>
> Dear Mom;
>
> As you know I've been having a tough time out here recently, but I just wanted to write you to tell you I have made advances in having faith. I am learning to trust, even in the down times or times of seeming inactivity. I do feel loved and guided, and, though I don't know exactly what, I know my efforts will be rewarded sometime soon.
>
> -Your Youngest

## *January 17—January 29*

Same. Old. Shit.

January 30, 2008

*"And you must be Gregor."*

I'm sitting here in Tom's black Ford pickup truck on our way to
Maria's house. That's the old lady's name. I was tired of him
repeatedly going out of his way to bring her up and make me feel
guilty about not meeting her, so here I am. I'm struggling with
why Tom even wants me for this. I'm not exactly the picture of
caring, and I know absolutely nothing about pills or needles or
medicine. I warned Tom about that, and that I've only taken one
Tylenol my entire life, when I was eighteen. I don't even drink
caffeine. I've told him I'm waiting to hear from a director to see if
I'm cast in a film, even though it's not true, but it's an exit
strategy if I need it.

     I guess the only upside to a job like this is the potential for
consistent income. But what if I get an audition? Or what if my
agent calls me while I'm making her bed or feeding her breakfast
or whatever I'd be doing as a caregiver? Well, all auditions are
last-minute. There's actually no other way to audition in this
town other than to stop your entire life to go to one. Got a day
job? Casting doesn't care. Grandma's funeral? Maybe you can
make Grandpa's.

     Maria's neighborhood, Cheviot Hills, is an undulating
maze made up of a thousand confusing little entrances. Which is
why Tom drove. It's old money in this neck of the woods. The
homes are huge, and they feel lived-in, unlike some of the empty-
feeling Beverly Hills homes down the street that look more like
embassies. I've lived in L.A. eight years and I never even knew
Cheviot Hills existed!

     We pull into the Altmann driveway where an old, gold
Ford Taurus sits parked in the garage of a surprisingly bland and
modest house. Isn't this lady supposed to be "rolling in it?" At
least that's what Tom tells me.

     A tall, congenial man with a white beard suddenly swings
open the door to greet us before we can even get out of the car.
He offers me his hand as if I were an old friend. This is Maria's
middle-son, Peter Altmann. "It's sooooo good to meet you,
Gregor!" Wow. Warmth. You don't meet Peters in Los Angeles.
Turns out he's from Tacoma. No wonder he's so friendly.

     Tom is the head caregiver and has been living with Maria
for the three months he's held the job. The family relies on him
for his extensive medical knowledge. He confirms or challenges

what the doctors suggest or prescribe. He took care of both of his grandparents until they died, so when it comes to death, Tom's been there, done that. Chuck, Maria's oldest son at 68, lives here too but isn't here today.

Peter takes me on a tour of the house. It has a 70s odor to it. Vintage red corduroy furniture, old hardwood floors and faded wallpaper, muted-yellow kitchen floor tiles and an off-white, antique refrigerator that hums. Peter points out the medium-sized pool in the backyard, then to the grapefruit tree hanging over it but tells me his mother isn't allowed to eat them. I'm uneasy. Uneasy because Peter is talking to me like I've already accepted the job.

As the three of us are sitting in the kitchen chatting away, we hear creaky wheels rolling down the hallway. *Here she comes.* My heart is in my throat for some reason, like I'm about to go on stage on the opening night of a play. Peter puts down his glass of water and stands at attention, as if to welcome the President of the United States. *What does a 92-year-old woman even look like in person?*

My question is answered when a tall, busty one rounds the corner pushing her walker with the two tennis balls on the bottom. She's looking pretty sporty, wearing a violet blouse with a silk scarf draped around her neck, black dress pants and white tennis shoes.

She stops and straightens up like a squirrel, and curiously scans the room like a bunny rabbit. She greets Peter and Tom, then she turns to me with reddened cheeks and a smile as wide as the 405, and says, "And you must be Gregor." The concept of *love at first sentence* was not one I'd ever considered before—I mean, *hello,* I don't even believe in love at first sight, and sometimes don't even believe in love. But after today, I know with beautiful certainty that it absolutely, definitely exists.

Her accent is Viennese, which from what Peter tells me is different than a German one. Her inflection and choice of words are a blend of Julia Child and Dorothy from *The Wizard of Oz.* When she speaks it's like a rollercoaster whipping around a track—up and down and side to side—and then her sentences always ends on this impossibly delightful up note. She's a human songbird.

Peter pulls out his mother's seat for her and eases her into the chair. Once she's settled, she looks me in the eyes and says, "So, tell me about you." Then she sits there eagerly anticipating every word about to come out of my mouth. I could have sworn I was the most important person in the world in that moment. I tell her who I am, my connection to Tom and that he's been telling me a lot about her. Everything I say seems to her like it's the most interesting thing she's ever heard. I feel Peter intensely studying how I'm interacting with her, how patient I am, how I make sure to speak loudly and clearly.

The whole old-person business is new to me. I've had virtually no relationship with grandparents. Generally, elderly people who I'm familiar with don't have this youthful enthusiasm, and I don't think I've ever used the word "charismatic" to describe anyone over, say, 85. Until Maria.

What turned out to be my interview ended with a story about a condom. Maria said ten years or so ago she was driving with her 86-year-old friend Lily, when suddenly Lily screamed, "You have a boyfriend!"

Maria pulled to the side of the road and Lily pointed at a condom, or *preservative* as she refers to them, lying on the floorboard near her feet, minding its own business.

"Thank God it was unopened," Maria said as she comically clutched her chest.

Apparently one of her grandsons had borrowed the car that weekend and never realized the preservative he forgot to use or never had the chance to use was on the floor of the car. Eighty-six year-old Lily was convinced eighty-two-year-old Maria had a boyfriend she wasn't telling her about. I laughed and looked at Peter, who sat there frozen and red-faced.

Ten minutes later, Maria retired to her room for a nap. Peter pulled me aside, offered me the job, and I accepted. Screw it. I'm a caregiver. Off to my audition.

*February 4, 2008*

*"If you're having women problems, my advice is to just line 'em up and shoot 'em."*

I somehow made it through the Bermuda Triangle that is Cheviot Hills on my own today, walked toward the front door, and a man who turned out to be Chuck Altmann saw me through his office window. He looks like George Washington and he sounds like James Coburn.

I jumped right into action. *Okay. Pills. Maria takes pills every morning. Where are the pills?* I found them in the cabinet in one of those days-of-the-week containers I've never seen in person, and laid them out neatly on the kitchen table, as if I'm actually a certified caregiver. There are four, all different colors and sizes, and I have no idea what they do other than they go in her mouth with water, and then I have to wait at least ten minutes until I give her juice or food.

*What else did Peter tell me? Right, the paper. Maria reads the paper every morning.* As I ran to the front doorstep, Maria suddenly materialized in a lime-green bathrobe down the shadowed hallway in front of me, leaning on her walker, and time does what Einstein said it does: ceases to exist.

My heart snapped awake. There was a human being standing before me that needed to be kept alive, and I was the one responsible for that. *I'm a caregiver.* Yesterday my own life was it. Now there's another life that's more important than mine.

She squinted at me inquisitively. "Is that you, Kenny?" I inched closer so she could get a better look, and she was suddenly a light turned to the brightest setting.

"Oh, it's *you!* From afar you look so much like my grandson Kenny! How are you? Shall we have a soft-boiled egg together?"

I shimmied around her to open the front door, grabbed the *Los Angeles Times,* and stutter-stepped behind her until I had room to dash around and toss it on the table.

Maria's breakfast of choice: Soft-boiled egg, English muffin, Earl Grey tea. I made her a soft-boiled egg, something I've never done before except by accident. I got the third egg right (the first two were either too hard or too soft), and all my clumsiness made me think Maria was sitting there wondering, *With this new guy, is my egg gonna take fifteen minutes every morning?*

I placed the plate in front of her and sat down. She smiled and said "Thank you," then started on her egg. The yolk kept slipping off her tiny spoon, and she so valiantly kept scooping it back up, only for it to keep sliding off. I reached to help her and she finally landed the edible sun in her mouth, then thanked me abundantly for helping her. I honestly can't remember the last woman I had breakfast with.

After our eggs we talked about everything from her love of the greatest contemporary opera star, Plácido Domingo (I told her I see him at the Music Center during the occasional catering event. She was beside herself) and her general aversion to women (her advice: "If you're having women problems, my advice is just line 'em up and shoot 'em"). The range of topics was all over the place. I already feel like I've known this woman for months!

I was so engrossed in what she had to say that I almost forgot about her nap. "We need to go get some rest," I told her.

"We?" She inquired with a devious grin.

I helped her out of her kitchen chair—which I especially like because I get to feel her satiny soft bathrobe—and she led me to the hall closet, set her walker aside and opened the creaky cupboard. She picked out a sheet and a pillowcase, and as she finally spotted the nice, fluffy comforter she was straining to find, she said: "One sleeps so much better with a comforter, my love." *My Love.* It gave me chills to hear it.

On the way home it suddenly occurred to me that I had made it through this entire day without even thinking about acting, or that audition I didn't even nail anyway.

*February 6, 2008*

*"A Hungarian goes to the market..."*

In my first two days I've learned Maria's priority is to always ensure my stomach is never empty, and that I never leave or arrive at the house without access to food. I've always heard Jewish grandmothers do this. Is it because food was scarce during the Holocaust? I'm clearly a clueless gentile. Whatever it is, it's a good sign. I'm always hungry.

I've also noticed that every time Chuck walks out of his office and passes through the kitchen area—which is apparently going to be where Maria and I will hang out most—he stops to visit his mother to give her a kiss. On each occasion Maria greets him like a newborn baby. It's never just a, "Oh hey, Chuck," and then on to something else, as you'd expect it should be after seven decades. She stops whatever she's doing to unload a coating of doting. Chuck has voluntarily lived on and off with her for 30-plus years, which (sorry Mom) sounds like a nightmare. Tom tells me Chuck will not move out until she dies. That's his promise to her.

On one of his ambles through the kitchen, Chuck tells us he's off to his girlfriend Donna's house in Huntington Beach. They met on Match.com. He told me: "I wrote in my profile that I wanted a woman within ten miles of me and no pets, and I end up with a woman 45 miles away with 8 pets. That's internet dating for you."

This family is already everything I've wanted in life, and I haven't even been here a week. Every gesture, every word, is genuine and heartfelt. Not at all like the hollow, surface-y relationships I've sought, all under the guise of seeking love and acceptance. My own family shows a love and respect for each other. We're not dysfunctional in the traditional sense. But we lead separate lives all over the world. We're literally not as close as we should be. We can be ships passing in the sea, all extremely independent, which has caused me to lead a life where I secretly crave dependence. Well, the grass is always greener.

Already Maria never ceases to amaze me. Her sense of humor is unmatched. Not that this is even remotely the extent of it, but before I left today she told me a joke: "A Hungarian goes to the market, and says to a worker: 'I need some pepper.' The worker asks, 'White pepper or black pepper?' The Hungarian says, 'Toilet pepper.'"

*February 12, 2008*

*"You're going to become a chef and then
leave me for a restaurant."*

As I prepared to leave for work this morning I realized that I simply must carry around a little notepad everywhere I go, in order to document all the things that happen during a shift. Maria mentioned to me yesterday, "I'm an open book with you." If she's an open book with *me,* Dear Reader, then Maria and I are now officially an open book with *you.* I already can't wrap my brain around this woman. I've never met anyone like her. I'm constantly forgetting she's 92.

This morning I wrote down "Klimt-Mobile," which was coined by Peter and refers to Maria's 1992 Ford Taurus, bought for her that very year by her late husband, Fritz Altmann. Maria says her friends wonder why she doesn't go out and buy a Mercedes: "Just because I came into all this money people think I should go out and buy meaningless things." Apparently Maria stopped driving only two years ago, at 90, when she was just down the street and almost caused a major accident. She left the car on the side of the road, walked home, gave Chuck her keys, and said, "I'm done." Ninety! I can't get over that someone so "old" is so young!

Maria and I took a walk around the block after breakfast. It was a stroll down a quiet, shaded sidewalk where a young person and an old person's arms were locked together like a peanut butter pretzel, and the old person hobbled along telling enchanting stories of a world that made the young person want to wake up one morning and be standing in the snowcapped Mountains of Salzburg. She grew up a Bloch-Bauer, which, from how it sounds, was like growing up a Rothschild or a Rockefeller.

As we continued down the sidewalk, I asked her about her Aunt Adele, who is the woman featured in Gustav Klimt's famous painting, *The Gold Portrait.* I remember Tom telling me Maria was involved in a Supreme Court case to get the painting back. Now I'm hearing about it from the horse's mouth. You can Google Maria to read about it, but honestly the details I'm hearing about today can't all be in public domain.

She went into depth about her escape in 1938, her move to California in 1942, and her post-war life in Los Angeles as a dressmaker. We even took a few moments to rest on a park bench. I've always loved art and learning about the lives of the great painters in history, and it appears I've stumbled upon someone who may even be able to tell me she knew some of them.

*I'm caring, by the way, for someone who grew up before World War One ended, before women had the right to vote, before the NFL was created, before band aids, stainless steel, the electric fridge and the modern zipper were invented. Yep. I'm kind of a big deal. I may even have to change my phone number.*

We made our way back to the house at eleven, and Rex—Maria's kids' high school English teacher—was due to come for lunch in an hour. I made tuna salad, even though my cooking skills leave something to be desired.

I'm what you'd call an "extreme bachelor." I live in a tiny studio apartment in East Hollywood. I own one plate, one bowl, one spoon, one knife, and two forks—I decided to splurge on forks. I throw away fans when they get too dusty, and I throw away George Foreman grills when they get too dirty. My bathroom sink is my only sink, in other words I often find myself brushing my teeth over a dirty bowl of cereal. And I wish I was lying about this one: There isn't food in my freezer, only documents, bills, statements I'm too lazy to file or can't find any other space in my apartment to file them. Once in a while I like to feel them to see if paper freezes. It definitely doesn't. If my bank were to call me and tell me they were freezing my funds, I could legitimately tell them, "You and me both."

Maria's housekeeper, Elisa, was here today. She's a very sweet Mexican lady who has been with Maria for fifteen years, and comes once a week on Thursdays. Occasionally Maria will call her into her room to help her find an article of clothing, and Maria thanks her genuinely for the littlest of things. I speak Spanish with Elisa, and she's impressed with my accent, which I've been told is unusually native sounding for a gringo.

As I placed the bread on the tuna sandwiches, Maria watched me with intense interest, and I was fascinated to see a woman so fascinated with what I was doing. I had a fan today, a fan I didn't have to dust or throw away. I gave her a spoonful of the tuna, and as she swallowed, she made a face.

"You're going to become a chef, and then leave me for a restaurant."

I told her to stop it, and she blushed. I asked her if she's looking forward to seeing Rex, and she answered, "I am, but I'm afraid he's going to eat you, not the sandwiches."

Apparently Rex was in love with all her sons, especially Peter.

"All the gay men liked Peter for some reason."

In Rex's defense, from the pictures I've seen, Maria's sons were all studs. Turns out Rex didn't eat me. He's 82, and looks great. Between Rex and Maria, age might just be a number. Rex brought his significant other, who Maria referred to as "The adorable little Japanese gentleman."

After Maria's nap, I learned two new things: she loves a good friend of mine named Scrabble, and she enjoys the occasional bourbon and soda. She's actually very good at the game. Okay, she won. I'm not going to say I went easy on her, because I didn't. I love watching her in her thick reading glasses as she squints curiously at her letters, then the board, then back at her letters, then back at the board... all the while with an engaging smirk just waiting to erupt into a golden guffaw.

During the game I pointed to a picture on the wall with an older man standing in the snow next to a black Schnauzer who looks like Hannibal Lector.

"That's my father and our dog, Satan—that's what his name was when we got him at the pound. It was the law at that time that all dogs had to wear muzzles in public."

The little guy used to walk Maria two miles to school every day.

"He would wait at all the crosswalks, follow all the rules of traffic, and when we got there I would say, 'Go home, Satan!' And he'd scurry on back to the house."

Then she suddenly turned into a whimsical five-year-old. "My father never had it in him to be nasty. He couldn't stand Satan, you see. So he would nuzzle his nose in Satan's face and say sarcastically, 'Oh, you ugly little thing, you! You're so ugly! Yes! So ugly!' But he would say it so sweetly that the dog would wag his tail and nuzzle his nose right back. To Satan, my father was his biggest fan!"

Tom strolled in around six. I don't cook, as you know, but the combination of a nice kitchen and this exquisite company has somehow brought to life my dormant domestic instincts. I made some chicken breast, broccoli and yellow rice, and served a nice bottle of California Chardonnay in crystal wine glasses. Look, Mom, I'm a homemaker! I can't remember the last home-cooked meal I made that involved other people.

## February 16, 2008

(Eleven-year-old Maria holding Luise's train at Luise's wedding in 1927)

*"You deserve far better things than seeing
a 90-year-old bag in a bra."*

What a life this woman has had! I can't wait to tell you more about it, including her escape from the Nazis, and how she made it to America. And her court case—that just happened a couple years ago—that made her famous. The only reason I'm not unloading it all here is because I have to take some time to put together all the amazing details. It's a movie.

I feel like I'm already the Hunter S. Thompson of caregivers—the *Gonzo Caregiver.* Instead of standing on the sidelines merely "reporting the facts" of the story, I can't resist committing the cardinal sin—*entering* it. Less than a month as her caregiver and it's already impossible not to throw myself into my job. I can't cook and I know nothing about medicine, but that doesn't seem to be hampering anything.

———◆———

Today was my first big responsibility as Maria's caregiver—to take her to Doctor Taw, her cardiologist, for a routine checkup. When we parked I asked her about her older sister, Luise, because Chuck said to me earlier in his booming voice, "Ask my mother about her sister." She died about ten years ago.

"Once, Luise needed to rent a car in Vancouver, so she went to a car rental place and looked around the lot and pointed to the only one she liked and said, 'I want that one.' The employee told her that was the only one she *couldn't* have, because it was *his* personal car. Well she continued to insist that she have that car. So the guy ended up renting his own car to her!"

Luise Story Number Two: "We were driving down Beverwill over by that Ralph's, and we stopped at a traffic light, and a man rolled down his window and started anxiously pointing to our roof. Luise rolled down her window and yelled, 'Nice way to talk to an old lady, you little bastard!' Turns out she had left her purse on the top of the car."

So this was Luise.

We arrived at Dr. Taw's office. He's one of the most respected cardiologists in town. He's very stern, about six foot six, and has these deep, narrow shark-eyes a la Will Ferrell, which he seems to revel in using to stare into your soul. He's an avid fisherman, evidenced by the dozens of pictures of fish around the office. Maria said to me as we waited in the waiting room for what seemed like an eternity, "If I were a fish, he would get to me a lot sooner!"

She loves to make me laugh. She's very good at it.

When we made it to the room, the nurse told Maria to take off her blouse, and Maria turned to me and said, "You may leave now." I told her I wasn't leaving—Peter insisted Tom and I stay with her through the entire process at the doctor, and update the family later via email. She sat there blushing and stammering that I wouldn't budge. I tried to relieve the tension.

"Now you must know it's been a life-long dream of mine to see you in a bra, Maria," to which she replied with a smirk, "I feel sorry you have nightmares."

Maria stared at the nurse and I, who were staring right back at her waiting for her to lose her blouse.

"Why do you both stand there like a question mark?" Maria asked, before giving in and disrobing. Dr. Taw dropped in for a quick visit, and Maria "The Master Disarmer" Altmann turned his droopy mouth upside down by knowing exactly what would do the trick: asking him about his latest fishing trip.

"You deserve far better things than seeing a 90-year-old bag in a bra," Maria playfully lamented to me on our way back to the house. I decided not to remind her she was 91.

I love being in Maria's home! For one, her full kitchen, which in comparison to the "closet" they call a kitchen in my apartment, is like comparing a whole ham to a slice of ham. Speaking of, I made a feast tonight as if I'd been a chef my entire life: Steak, asparagus, yellow potatoes, and a nice lemon dill sauce for the tilapia. And guess where the lemon came from? Maria's backyard lemon tree. Apparently, if you give me some counter-space, a dishwasher, and an engaging lady, I turn into renowned chef Joachim Splichal, who by the way is my boss at the Music Center.

I'm fascinated with Luise. I mentioned her again tonight, and was rewarded with Story Number Three.

"I had a clothing client at my house and my sister was there, so I let her tend to them while I took a few phone calls. The client tried on a blue dress she ordered, and said, 'This doesn't fit.

I don't want to buy it.' Luise shrugged her shoulders and said, 'Well... you said blue.' As if that was that, and she was stuck with it! I could have killed her! You don't say that to a client!"

The way Maria speaks about her sister, it sounds like the *opposites attract* rule applies to their relationship.

Over rum raisin ice cream Maria smiled at me like I was four years old and asked, "When is your birthday?" I told her August 22. "You're kidding! Twenty-two was my mother's lucky number. She would go to Monte Carlo and would always win when she bet on the number 22. No wonder we get along!"

Maria's magnanimous masseuse of nearly a decade, Rebecca, came over at eight, as Maria and I clinked our spoons on the bottom of our ice cream bowls. I helped Rebecca carry in her massage table and unfold it in the middle of Maria's room. Chris, the night caregiver, who's in his early sixties and a total goofball, strode in a few minutes later, and I enjoyed telling him that it didn't even sound like a massage was going on, and that all you could hear the whole hour were two friends at a coffee shop having a pleasant chat behind a closed door.

Maria is a bundle of charm snuggled under a blanket of love nestled inside a basket of sweetness.

*February 18, 2008*

*"Was there a large Russian man in my room?"*

"Was there a large Russian man in my room?" Maria asked me with her usual buttery genuineness, as I held up a mysterious thick black trench coat we found hanging in her closet. I threw it over her shoulders, and, as we both stood staring in the mirror, she frowned.

"I look like a chestnut roaster. You try it on."

So I did. "It's all yours," she said, proudly giving me the thumbs up.

Maria made her world-debut on this very day in 1916. We're going to her youngest son Jim's tonight, to celebrate her ninety-second birthday. Maria tends to be comfortable lounging around the house in her robe, but this morning she jumped out of bed and right into the shower. One of the catalysts that forced Peter to hire Tom and I was one morning a year or so ago, he heard a scream coming from her bathroom while he was in the kitchen. He ran to find she had fallen in the shower. He vowed from that day forth to get a caregiver if for no other purpose than to sit in her bedroom desk chair ready to run in at a moment's notice.

As Maria walked toward the bathroom to take her shower I reminded her I'd be sitting in her little chair if she needed me. She suddenly got really bashful and tried to come up with something funny to say. She is still not used to this "caregiver" thing let alone having a strange young man in her room while she's in her *literal* birthday suit. Wearing her adorable little blue "assembly line" shower cap, she stopped short of the tub and turned around to see that I was still secure in my little chair, and laughed giddily again at the whole concept of having me monitor her shower. I don't think she remembers she fell. She needs to be reminded of things like this sometimes.

I had trouble keeping a job when I was a teenager. I was lazy and irresponsible, and never took pride in anything I did. This is one of the first times in my life I actually take pride in a job, and find it invigorating to be at my best. There is nothing like feeling what truly loving a job feels like.

So there I sat while she showered, reading one of the special, large-print *Reader's Digest* magazines resting on her desk. I love sitting here because my fingers start pulling open drawers and discovering cool things like her old mahogany address book that looks like it's from the 60s. After her shower, still dripping wet with her bathrobe on, we sat down and thumbed through it together, stopping at certain names I was curious about. Like a guy named Erich Zeisl (who I later found out, thanks to Wikipedia, is an Austrian composer). She told me, "I was always pregnant, so Erich used to tell me, 'You're worse than our cat!'"

You would not believe who this woman knows, and who her family knew. We're talking about some pretty big names in the world of European art and music. Stay tuned.

Once Maria was dressed in a pair of white slacks, a pink cashmere sweater, and one of her many spiffy silk scarves, I walked with her to the front door in my jeans and a grey blazer. She let go of my arm and stopped to look me up and down, trying not to make it blatantly obvious she was checking me out.

"You look just fabulous in a morning jacket." Then she lifted her right hand, made the "OK" sign with her index finger and her thumb, and winked at me.

She explained "morning jacket" is what people used to call blazers in Vienna. I told her everyone was going to laugh at me because I was wearing a morning jacket at night, and she belted out a laugh that had more sex appeal than a lot of women my age. To me, Maria is my age.

I met her at the front door to give her a turkey sandwich I'd made to hold her hunger until we got to Jim's. I helped her fasten a button on her blouse and connected her necklace that she so cutely held in her hand for me to place around her neck. It all felt so natural, so perfect, like a couple ready to go out on a date. We were off to Jim's in the Klimt.

———— ♦ ————

Jim, 54, lives in Agoura Hills, near Malibu, and has a girlfriend named Jesell as sweet as baklava. Donna—who's as chipper as a chipmunk—was there with Chuck, who's as chipper as an old ox. Peter, as gentle as a cool ocean breeze, flew in solo from Tacoma. Margie, Maria's only daughter, is in her early sixties, leggy and sporty, beautiful and charming. I wonder where she got all *that* from.

In saying hello, Margie rubbed her face against her mother's, giving her butterfly kisses and whispering sweet nothings into her ear as if they were an item. Myron, Margie's husband, is a compact man of superior intelligence and culture, and an excellent question-asker. I never had a chance to ask him one question because he was so busy asking them to me. They've been married for over 30 years and still treat each other like newlyweds.

Maria's great-grandchildren Colin and Avrick were there. I like other people's kids and other people's pets. I can enjoy them without taking them home. I don't think I have a stronger driving need in life than seeking, and possessing, innocence. Since I've chosen a life that may not involve having any kids, at least the traditional way, I like to enjoy them when I can.

Avrick strutted right up to Maria all night strumming his rockin' Fisher Price guitar like a miniature Elvis Presley, and Maria sat there in complete bliss. At one point she turned to me and said spiritedly, "Look at those gyrating hips... and that swagger!"

Maria is always game for fun. I love that in a woman.

Jim's children were there. The youngest, James, is sixteen and a top-ranked water polo player at his high school, and Alana, eighteen and as stunning as a young Margie, is ready to go to college. Gregory, 21, just graduated college and will be going to Stuttgart, Germany to intern with Mercedes. It's funny to see Jim act more like his shoe size than his age, and at times his own kids seem more adult than him.

In my limited experience with elders at family gatherings, they're clenching their cane in a chair in the corner, for the most part ignored by the family. Life is pretty much done for them. Maria, however, is the center of attention, the *Queen Bee*, The *Godfather*, sitting in her graceful power, entertaining little visits with family members who don't take her the slightest bit for granted. And then there's me, next to her in my favorite pink shirt, soaking it all in. I sat there all night drinking red wine, eating Jim's delicious prime rib and watching Avrick and his gyrating hips, and I was having, excuse my French, a shitload of fun.

I've embraced "alone" my entire life. But tonight I have a family; a family I can touch. Being able to pay my bills is awesome, really, but this woman and her family are already giving me more than any amount that can be written on a check. Life really doesn't suck when you're surrounded by love.

## March 1, 2008

*"She's not a bad person..."*

According to the *Los Angeles Times* this morning a caregiver was arrested for torturing elders in a retirement home in Long Beach. I showed Maria the article, and after she read it she said, "They probably drove him nuts."

Later, Maria described a former friend of hers from Vienna: "She's not a bad person. Not *evil*. Just disgusting."

She was on fire all day. Lisa the next-door neighbor, who is a professional flautist and occasionally plays at the Music Center, came over with homemade split-pea soup. Lisa is a real doll. And Maria always says just the right things to people, like she said to Lisa as she stepped through the front door: "You look like your own daughter."

Lisa asked Maria later, "You were the youngest of five children, right?"

Maria responded, "I *was* the youngest, but now I'm the oldest." Laughs abound.

Later in our Split-Pea Soirée, I asked Maria about her middle name. "'V' is for Victoria, right?" At this Maria nodded, and said, "My father gave me that name."

Then Lisa asked, "Because he thought you'd win the war, right? *Victorious!*"

Maria smiled wryly and took her time sipping her water, and then said, "Well unfortunately I didn't win."

Lisa told me about her first encounter with Maria. She and her husband, John, had just moved next door. One evening they were standing on their front porch just as Maria was pulling out of her driveway and into the street. When Maria saw her new neighbors standing there waving to her, she stopped the car in the middle of the street, threw it in park and jumped out, stood there with her arms spread out like she wanted to hug them, and said, "Will you look at this??"

It was the first time Maria had seen them.

Lisa said proudly: "After that we called her 'The Eagle.'"

When Lisa left, I walked Maria to her room to take a nap, and she said: "Don't worry, I won't croak."

I was left with time to prowl around my new home. My tour began and ended with the den. I was transported to a Viennese library of the 1920s. Most of the books were written in German, and I dusted them off as if they'd been buried in a cave for centuries. There was a photo album entitled, *The Altmann Cashmere Company*, and the pages literally crackled alive. Bernhard, Maria's brother-in-law, was heavily featured. He's credited with introducing argyle and cashmere to the States in the mid-1940s. The album was filled with newspaper articles, advertisements and media on his contributions to the fashion industry. Bernhard also played a significant part in Maria and her husband's escape from Vienna, which you'll be reading very soon. It will have its own entry, and be told from beginning to end.

There's an entire shelf dedicated to Plácido Domingo, with dozens of VHS tapes and DVDs of his greatest performances, photographs of him as a strapping young stud, and a picture Maria took with him at a special dinner a couple years ago at the Music Center. I noticed a framed piece of knitted cloth on the wall. I lifted it off the hook and turned it over, only to discover that Fritz's mother made it in school in 1877, when she was fourteen. Fritz, in case I haven't mentioned, was Maria's husband, who died in 1994. He spent a few weeks in a concentration camp in Vienna in 1938.

I opened a pink, flower-covered photo album, and the first page began with the oldest photos the Bloch-Bauers have on record. Each subsequent page went up in years. Under the first photo on the first page was written: *Gustav's mother*. She looked to be in her thirties, maybe forties. To put this in perspective, Maria's father, Gustav, was born in 1862, while *Abraham Lincoln was still alive*. So that photograph of Gustav's mother—Maria's grandmother—must have been taken around the 1850s. The world I'm in right now!

There were photos of Maria's Aunt Adele (the woman in Klimt's *Gold Portrait*) in plain clothes, and her husband Ferdinand, hanging out with their German Shepherds on the grounds of their estate around the early 1900s. Ferdinand enjoyed his hunting, as shown by a photograph of him standing heroically with one foot on the ground and one foot on top of a large buck he had just shot.

There were a few pictures of Maria's "devilishly handsome" brother Leopold (who enjoyed hunting as well), a bunch of Luise (also a hunter—in fact I think Maria might be the only Bloch-Bauer who doesn't hunt), and some black and white photos of Maria as a child. She looked like a little Italian girl with dark skin and big adorable brown eyes. And there's an impossibly tender photo of her at a stable looking down so sweetly at a portly pig.

As I looked at these young pictures of her in 1935—there's one in particular of her sitting in the lobby at an opera house with a shiny white satin dress on—her gaze so knowing and provocative as she looked at the camera, that I couldn't help but imagine myself as the young camera guy taking the pictures, and her looking at me with a glint in her eye thinking, "He looks familiar." But as the camera guy *I* know exactly who *she* is. I know that in a few decades it will be clear why I look familiar. And all evening she would continue to study me trying to figure out how she knows me but too coy to say anything about it. It would fester inside her all night. She would be unconsciously seeing into our future. She would be looking at now.

I can't say that I know many people who wake up from a nap with a smile, but the moment I touched Maria to wake her up after I was finished in the den, she was smiling. Her first instinct was to smile. It's all you really need to know about this woman.

She lit up like a street lamp as we talked for the rest of the afternoon and evening about everything from her father to her beloved governess, to her (don't tell her I used this word even though it's so true) *obsession* with the Great Plácido Domingo.

March 3, 2008

*(Maria and 33-year-old Randy Schoenberg in 2000)*

The woman for whom I'm caring was a Holocaust refugee from Austria. At the age of 82 she waged what was universally perceived as a hopeless legal campaign against her native country to recover five paintings by artist Gustav Klimt, all looted from her Uncle Ferdinand's home in 1938 by the Nazis. Hitler subsequently had the works hung at the Belvedere Museum in Vienna, where they were considered national treasures for nearly 70 years.

Maria and her lawyer, Randol E. Shoenberg, launched the lawsuit in 1998 in the civil courts of California, where it would remain for six years. In early 2004, what had been thought to be impossible suddenly became reality—they stood in front of nine Supreme Court judges awaiting word if they had the legal grounds to sue Austria for the paintings.

"After a great day at the Supreme Court where everything seemed to go our way," Randy said in an interview in a documentary I was watching called *Art of the Heist: The Lady in Gold*, "I read an article the next morning that said something like 'Supreme Court Likely to Reverse Altmann Case.' So I called the reporter and said, 'What do you mean it's going to be reversed? I thought it went well, the judges seemed receptive,' and the reporter said, 'Trust me, I've been reporting for 30 years. I could tell by their body language. You lost.'"

The judges returned a few days later with a ruling in favor of Maria. The Supreme Court verdict was beyond merely unheard of—it was *historic*. It was the first time an individual was given the right to sue a sovereign nation over Nazi-looted art. Austria, not to mention the rest of the world and anyone who loved or appreciated art, was stunned. The reporter who had predicted a certain loss called Randy to congratulate him.

When news spread of the court's decision, Maria's case was no longer just being whispered about in small intellectual circles or in high government. Average, everyday people around the world started to talk; the international media turned on their cameras. With so much momentum swirling around their win, Maria and Randy appeared in front of a panel of three Austrian judges on January 16, 2006, where it was essentially a done deal. The art had to be returned.

On November 6, 2006, in what would be the most successful auction of all time, four out of the five Klimts sold in a record seven and a half minutes at Christie's Auction in New York City, and the fifth—*The Gold Portrait*, featuring Maria's Aunt Adele Bloch-Bauer in a dazzling glittery gold gown—was sold in a private sale to billionaire businessman Ronald Lauder for $135 million, at that time the highest price ever paid for a work of art. When it was all said and done the five paintings garnered more than $325 million. It was bar none the most significant event to happen in the art market since World War Two.

Today, because of Maria, hundreds of families who suffered from the loss of artistic treasures during the Holocaust have filed claims or had art returned. Without her, none of them would have had a chance.

But it was far from just *what* she did that led her to victory. If she were the bitter old Holocaust survivor out to embarrass a country and collect her millions—as everyone assumed she was—her case would have likely died in the civil courts, and her Uncle Ferdinand's paintings would probably still be hanging at the Belvedere. Instead she was a Granddame of the highest pedigree, sashaying up to press conferences sporting cashmere sweaters and silk scarves, firing off the truth in style. She was like the Viennese Mrs. Doubtfire, with her sparkling intellect and effortless wit, fortified with a genuine warmth and grace that made everyone feel good about themselves. In a spectacle that spawned bitterness and hatred throughout Austria and Europe, Maria was just too lovable to hate. She wooed the judges and the media with her Old-World elegance and charm—a deadly one-two punch that disarmed even the most aloof in the Austrian government.

It was every bit a modern-day version of David and Goliath—Austria donning its shield and armor, and Maria wielding her staff and sling. And that it all centered around arguably the most recognized portrait of the twentieth century— the iconic painting of Adele—turned it into cinematic proportions.

Is a month too soon to be in love with someone?

*March 7, 2008*

(Walter Slezak)

**"I told her I didn't think I'd be in a joking kind of mood
around Hitler."**

I had an audition yesterday for a cable TV show called *Sons of Anarchy*. Tom agreed to fill the morning half of my shift. I gave my read. Afterwards the casting director said to me, "If the director wants you to come in again later today, can you be available?"

Words started shooting out of my mouth, and they weren't the ones I approved of when I heard them. Some other person named Gregor was telling the director he couldn't because he had to get to a day job that had become "extremely important" to him.

She looked at me, rightfully confused. It was unheard of, what I'd said. Actors never—and I mean never—say no to directors. *What the hell am I doing?*

But the moment I arrived at the house to relieve Tom, all was forgotten. I showed up wearing my T-shirt that said "Old Navy."

Maria looked at it and said, "But, Darling, you're too young to be in the Old Navy."

Breakfast was playful. When I asked Maria if she'd like some OJ, she responded, "The juice or the murderer?"

As we sat in the kitchen reading the paper and sipping our Earl Grey tea—something I never did before I met Maria—I showed her a book dated 1902 I'd found during my "Viennese library" visit last week in the den. Her face came alive as she fingered through it. She wondered where I found it, as if she'd been looking for it for years. It contained German songs she sang as a child at school in Vienna, and she hummed a few euphorically as if she were in class 85 years earlier.

I asked Maria if she knew any of her grandparents. "Her name was Jeanette," she said, "and she was my mother's mother. I was about five when I met her. She was known for her wit. Her husband was the head of the railroad, you see, and one day she stepped on the tracks, and someone said, 'You shouldn't do that,' to which she replied, "Sure I should... my husband owns it!'"

She told me a funny story about her husband and her mother. "Warm in German is slang for homosexual, you see. So my mother always used to say to Fritz—'What I like about you, is that you're warm.' After Fritz heard this a few times, he finally said to her, 'Stop saying that, it means I'm gay!' Well she was so embarrassed, from that moment on she didn't so much as say it was warm outside!"

Still seated in the kitchen with nowhere to go and nothing to do but enjoy one another's company, a popular actor from Austria named Walter Slezak came up in conversation. He was one of Maria's good friends, who died about 25 years ago. She offered an amusing anecdote. Back in Vienna in the 1930s, when Maria was a teenager, Walter's sister was friends with a powerful politician on a meteoric rise to fame. She constantly badgered Maria to meet him.

"She would say to me, 'Maria, you simply *must* come with me, he just *loves* to laugh. He's *so* funny, and would *love* your sense of humor! You just *have* to meet him, can I please introduce you?' Well I told her I didn't think I'd be in a joking kind of mood around Hitler."

I like to think that if Maria had met Hitler, the course of modern human history would have changed.

I love hearing Maria's voice. It's so much a part of her charm. No wonder she wooed all those Supreme Court judges. She was an English major in Vienna, and is very proud of this. She's polished and educated in her speech. Like a good little student she'll never end a sentence with a preposition.

"On what did you set the oven?" she'll ask. Or, "In which cupboard did you find that mug?"

She also goes out of her way to say "one" instead of "you." For example, if we walk by an open door she'll say, "One can close that." Or if we walk by an empty wrapper in the kitchen: "One can throw that away." And the thank-yous for every little thing come like a swarm of bees.

## March 12, 2008

(Maria sitting on her mother's lap in 1919)

*"He was too decent to be a Nazi."*

When I get around to telling it, you'll notice that throughout Maria's thrilling escape from the Nazis there was a light that accompanied and protected her, a light that never flickered during her entire life. And of all the extraordinary things about Maria, what may be the most extraordinary and why I'm convinced she was some kind of angel, is that the light that has been with her since birth—which guided her through one of the most remarkable lives I've ever known and through one of the most critical times in modern world history—was not generated by the universe, or by God, or by some otherworldly force. It was generated by her. Maria was the source of her own force.

Maria's lawyer, Randy, arose in conversation again this afternoon over my famous egg salad sandwiches, which, by the way, have impressed even her most finicky houseguests.

In 1998, when Maria first shopped her case around to various law firms, she met with two lawyers and told them about her wonderful plan to get her uncle's Klimts back. A few days later she received a letter saying that she was a very nice lady but if she thought they were going to get the U.S. Marshal to go into Vienna and take those paintings that had been a part of its culture for seven decades, she was, with all due respect, nuts. Everyone thought she was nuts. But she didn't give up. She spoke to Randy, a young, inexperienced employee at the same firm.

Because Randy was well aware that Austria had just passed a law designed to return looted artwork, he decided they had a shot, quit the firm, took a corner office in an old office building in Santa Monica, and worked pro bono for nearly eight seemingly hopeless years, before their stunning victory.

I asked Chuck to clear up how Randy was able to sue a foreign country in the first place, which from what I've researched, is virtually impossible.

"Well, first of all, after Randy sued Austria they countersued saying he couldn't do that. But from what I understand—and this was one of the many factors—the only way it was possible to sue Austria on American soil was to prove that the Austrians do business in America using *The Gold Portrait*. So Randy argued that there were public advertisements all over America where the painting was shown, saying things like, 'Come Visit Austria.' Austria was basically using it to sell themselves to

Americans, in a sense. The judges bought it. Apparently this sort of tactic had never been used in a case of this magnitude before."

Maria went on: "After Randy walked up to the podium and gave his opening remarks at the Supreme Court, one of the judges responded with this long, drawn-out question that no one in their right mind would have understood or have been able to follow. When the judge was finished with his question, Randy said, 'I'm sorry, Your Honor, I didn't understand the question, can you repeat it?' The whole courtroom went silent. I was sitting there in the front row with Peter and Jim and we were bracing ourselves for the response. Then the other judges began to snicker with each other. We found out later that apparently this one judge always asks a confusing question on purpose, to test the lawyer, sort of like an inside joke. I think the judges respected Randy after that. Most lawyers would have just started talking without understanding the question."

She added, "Clarence Thomas fell asleep during the hearing. I was told this is business as usual."

———◆———

Maria was scheduled to have dinner tonight with family in town from Vancouver. We hopped in the Klimt and headed for one of her favorite places to bring guests, an Italian restaurant in Beverly Hills called Il Cielo.

Maria's dinner guests were her great niece, Lisa, Lisa's extremely obedient teenage kids Ben and Tosh, and her husband Terry Turner, a filmmaker who just finished a documentary about Adele, called *Adele's Wish*.

We all sat down and Terry ordered us a bottle of Pinot Noir. When it arrived, he turned to Maria and asked, "Will you be having any?"

Maria responded, "You go ahead, Sweetheart," and looked around the table for her napkin, which I noticed fell to the floor.

Terry raised his glass: "Then I'll drink in your honor."

Maria continued her napkin search, muttering in response to Terry, "What's left of it."

I picked up the napkin under her chair and showed it to her, and her face turned into the bright, burning sun. I placed it on her lap, and noticed that the entire table was amused at our wordless napkin exchange. We're getting good at sharing looks with no words.

After dinner tonight was the first time Maria saw me cut someone off in traffic. Look. We're in the Turtle Capital of the World: Beverly Hills. If you were to do the math, I'd say 60-70 percent of these sloths are driving, on average, ten miles an hour less than the speed limit.

Maria called this particular slow driver a "swine," and then said, "Probably a woman." As we passed the car, we both saw that it was indeed a woman. Maria flipped her off over my shoulder, and looked at me and brightened when she saw that I was thoroughly entertained. Then she reveled in lifting her middle finger again in front of my face in case I missed it the first time, and, gesturing toward her finger, she said with a sparkle in her eyes, "*This* is a wonderful thing."

Once we got home, Maria barely made it through the front door. She tends to get really tired really suddenly. I think back to when I first met her—only two months ago—and how we easily circled her block twice on walks. Now it's only once if we're lucky, and sometimes we get 50 feet into it before she has to sit down and catch her breath. But then I fix her hair or adjust her scarf, and we have at least enough energy to get back to the house. It's amazing to see how quickly the body wears down in its 90's.

I helped her into her room, retrieved her nightgown from the closet, and laid it at the foot of her bed. When she finished in the bathroom and stepped into her nightgown, I reentered, and she perked up as she got into bed and pulled up her comforter. I sat next to her, and after she was finished making sure I had enough to eat at Il Cielo, she offered an anecdote about Hans Albers, considered the most popular movie star in Germany in the thirties and forties.

"I met him at a party at my parent's house when I was eighteen. He was sex incorporated. Boy, was he a sexpot. He was like a male Marlene Dietrich. You only find that sexiness in a German. And his voice—my Uncle Ferry would laugh whenever I tried to copy it. And he had these beautiful blue eyes that would light up a street at night! I don't think he was a Nazi. He was too decent to be a Nazi."

I left her alone to read her *Opera Magazine*. When it was time for me to go for the night, I entered to find her lying with her eyes closed, her magazine and reading glasses resting on her bosom. Her eyes fluttered open. She looked like a sleepy little child, and her voice was as soft and soothing as a silk pillow. She patted the bed sheets for me to sit next to her.

"Did you get enough to eat, my love?" she asked me.

I suddenly shouted histrionically, "Hinreisend!" (*Adorable* in German).

Her eyes widened with pleasure. "I'm going to teach you a new German word every day."

Maria already sees me as perfect. There are things about me, though, that she'll never know. She'll never know that when I leave her house I really and truly want to jam my thumbs into the thyroids of every single driver in front of me; she'll never know how deep my "women issues" seem to run and how bleak that whole world seems; she'll never know how frustrating and hopeless Hollywood is at times; and she'll never know that I, too, see her as perfect. But what may lurk beneath our hearts won't ever hurt us and won't ever matter. We can both safely exist in our chosen fantasies about each other without any judgments or a need to explain.

The Sleeping Beauty in the Nightgown is the light of my life right now. *The* light. I've been with her a short time, I know, but when you have something special, you just know. When I see her face when she sees me, I know. I'm not claiming to be a savior, or a saint, or even a caregiver, but I know that I will never leave this woman. Whatever I have to do away from her I will do, but as long as I live, as long as she lives, I will always come back. That is a promise.

*March 20, 2008*

*"Anything that rebuffs an idiot is okay in my book."*

In 2000 I stuffed everything I owned into my green Geo Storm, and with the $500 I got for graduation sitting in my glove box and not knowing a single soul other than the guy I was interviewing with for a production assistant job for a TV show called *Blind Date*, I sped down Route 40 West toward the rest of my life. It took four days to reach The Rest of My Life: a city in California called Los Angeles. A week later the trusty Storm took its last breath. It died at the CarMax on La Cienega near LAX, as I held it in my arms. The ungrateful bastards gave me $90 for it. With that money I took a cab home, and had just enough left to buy a steak at Outback. I will always remember how good that steak tasted.

How far I've come. Where I once only cared about myself I now find myself answering my phone every time the caller ID indicates it's Tom, no matter what time it is or where, because the call probably has something to do with a certain woman I've grown to care about deeply, apparently even more than I've cared about anything else. It's bittersweet seeing Tom's name, though, because it makes me nervous something bad has happened to Maria. Like he called me the other night around eleven, and I winced as I answered it, and it turns out all he wanted to know was if I'd seen her purple scarf. Relieved, I told him it was on the top right shelf of her left closet.

I'm falling out of shape, another indication I'm not focused on myself. First of all, how come you never fall *into* shape? This is a big deal for me, to be in shape, and anyone who knows me knows I stay fit. The only drawback to this job is that it involves a lot of sitting, albeit some pretty entertaining sitting. The problem is, I have no self-control if there's anything resembling a piece of bread with sugar on it in my own house, and there seems to be a new pie or pastry on Maria's counter every week.

Maria and I continue to bond in playful ways and we often communicate without words. First of all, she likes my hands, and I don't know why. They're nothing special, and no one has ever gone out of their way to compliment me on them. Another thing is, when I decline bread for a sandwich, she smiles and raises her pinky finger to me, to indicate that her finger represents my body, to say that my not eating bread will make me as skinny as her pinky. "Don't you dare lose another pound," she always warns. Maria loves bread and would eat it every meal—she's not unlike a duck in this respect. Since I consider it part of my job to keep her fit and on this earth as long as possible, sometimes I'll tell her we're out of bread even though we aren't, and I'll offer her a cracker instead, and then we'll take a walk.

We're also getting pretty funny when it comes to her pills.

"Poison, right?" She loves to say to me as she picks them out of my hand and puts them in her mouth. I used to tell her emphatically, "No!" but realized saying "Yes" gets a chuckle. This morning I amended it further to, "Arsenic," which got a giant laugh. "You are just lovely," she said to me as she gathered the "arsenic" from my hand.

It's a relief when I've accomplished the morning duties. Then I can give her the paper and relax in the den with the TV. I like for us to enjoy sufficient time apart, to enjoy the time more when we're together. Peter was right: she loves reading the paper. It's her portal to the outside world. She could spend two hours reading it front to back, without being bored. To her, every little story is fascinating.

Today as I watched the likeable yet frustrating CNN Anchor Rick Sanchez on the big-screen TV, she sat contentedly in the kitchen reading the paper. I heard her read aloud the headline: *Supreme Court Rebuffs Bush.* I muted Rick and ran into the kitchen. She lowered the paper, removed her glasses, and looked me square in the eyes. "Anything that rebuffs an idiot is okay in my book."

She awaited my reaction and put her glasses back on, raised the paper once more, and continued reading. A few minutes passed and, suddenly agitated again, she lowered the paper again and re-removed her glasses.

"Will you look at that dumb face?" She turned the paper around to show me George Bush's "dumb" face. And then she got caught up in my face, and said, "Now *that's* a face."

The Altmanns are liberals, and this is refreshing to see from a family that's rolling in the dough. Chuck and I have a crush on Michelle Obama, Barack Obama's wife. Smart women do it for me more and more these days. I like the kind of girls who have no idea they're hot. The long, straight auburn-haired ones usually do it for me, and the bookish ones, who are a little left of normal. I like minimal make-up, I like them understated but spunky, and I like an imperfect face and a pronounced nose. They have to be open-minded, they have to have an unforced masculine side, and they have to love salads but also love protein. And be loyal. And have a very sexy personality. I might throw some black-rimmed glasses on her, and I might not mind if she's Gothic. But the thing I consider most important is a warm smile and heart. These have eluded me most in Los Angeles. Until Maria.

An email I wrote to the family tonight. Occasionally I'll be including these.

Dear All;

The woman of the house (no, not Chuck) got up today from her kitchen chair with absolutely zero help from me. In fact, I didn't even get up to act as if I was thinking about helping! Tom informed me that recently he noticed this happening as well. It should also be noted that Maria, Chuck and I went out to lunch today and she got up from the fairly low toilet seat without any help. I have also been a real stickler for her posture when she walks with the walker. She is actually very proud to walk erect. I tell her to use her legs and hips, not her arms and wrists. I'm guilty of cowering over her at times ready to assist her, and I think this is an excuse for her to take the easy way out. There's a fine line between being attentive and letting her do the work. If she's struggling to get up, just tell her to sit back, do a couple wind-ups, and catapult up using her legs. Legs are key. I also tell her "nose over toes."

We finally watched the stage production of *Otello*. She's seen it maybe ten times, and was absolutely mesmerized as if it were the first. I looked over at her when her boyfriend (Domingo) would walk on stage, and her mouth hung open like a little kid watching Shrek. I actually saw tears in her eyes when it was all done. She had to take a few moments alone. In her defense, Plácido is quite a force.

G

P.S. Maria lives two doors down from Ray Bradbury! Did anyone know this? I guess I'll know where to point the fire engines if I smell smoke.

March 31, 2008

*"Let's start an affair."*

If there's one thing that can get challenging it's Maria's clock milking. She's an expert milker of the clock, in fact if a clock could actually be milked then she would definitely make a great farmhand. I, on the other hand, am a fierce embracer of time, always have been, and I am terminally confused by people who aren't. So I need to tell her it's twenty minutes later than it actually is, and plan that after I tell her we need to get ready for the doctors, or wherever we're going, she'll say her token "Okay, Mein Galibtes"—one of her many ways of saying My Beloved One—and continue sitting there sipping her tea as if we have all the time in the world, poised to tell me another anecdote about Poldi, or remind me that my nose and teeth are "exquisite." I'm on to her tactics. I've set every clock in the house twenty minutes late, and informed the family that "Maria Time" and "Real Time" are two entirely different entities.

I dropped Maria off at Analiese's house for lunch. Analiese is an old clothing client of Maria's, originally from Germany, who came to California in 1938 (weeks before the Anschluss—Hitler's annexation of Austria), as a 24-year-old woman. "I'm a teenager compared to her," Maria told me this morning.

Later that afternoon after we had gone home for Maria's nap, Analiese called Maria to tell her how happy she was about their reunion. Before hanging up, Maria said, "We should start an affair before we get too old."

Maria called me "elegant" before I returned to my George-Foreman-grill apartment. As I stood there bidding my prolonged goodbye as if I would never see her again, she said, "You are such an elegant man." I've never been called elegant, and hearing it makes me look at myself in a whole new perspective. Good night, Dear Reader.

*April 4, 2008*

*"If I were 50 years younger, Mr. Domingo..."*

Maria and Fritz bought season tickets to the Music Center Opera when it opened in the 60s. One evening as they were sitting in their front row seats, a woman approached them and introduced herself as Plácido Domingo's assistant. There began Maria's lifelong love affair with the man from Mexico.

I asked Maria why she thinks Plácido is the best living opera singer and arguably of all time. "He has a wider range than anyone I can think of, and he has something no other singer has to the degree he has: the ability to act, and really sell it."

Then I asked why she thought so many of history's greatest musical virtuosos came from Austria and Germany. As baffled as I was, she said, "Perhaps it's in the lilac blossoms."

On one clear level it was fitting I met Maria. As I've mentioned, my "day" job is catering (mainly on the weekends now that I'm with Maria during the week), for large gatherings surrounding the opera, at the aforementioned Music Center in downtown Los Angeles. I occasionally see the merry maestro bouncing down the hallways in that permanent good mood of his, exploding with soaring salutations to anyone he passes, including us caterers. I'm amazed at how easily accessible he is.

Once, to save time during a huge post-opera gala, I took a little-known shortcut down a quiet back hallway carrying a stack of dirty dishes to the kitchen. I rounded a corner at breakneck speed and I nearly steamrolled over a man standing in the shadows humming cheerily to himself.

"You scared the hell out of me," I grumbled, and barely got through the sentence before I realized who it was. My heart bounced in embarrassment. He apologized to me as if it was his fault for being there, and asked how the party was. I can see how Maria and Plácido go together. They both seem to have this unquenchable *joie de vivre*.

"Plácido's first job was at nineteen, as a piano player for a Mexican ballet company," Maria told me. What she really meant by "ballet company" was Bordello. According to her, his payment came in the form of women. There must have been some truth to it.

When Plácido wasn't working, according to Maria, he was working on a girl, who he would serenade at night. The way Maria explained it seemed right out of a silent movie from the twenties: The neighbors would be awakened at night by Plácido standing on the front lawn singing his dramatically acted-out falsettos to the girl as she sat at her bedroom window. They would all shove their windows open and raise their fists in protest, screaming, "Shut the hell up!" and, "Do you have any idea what time it is?" The girl in the window, Marta, would later become Mrs. Domingo.

"I was at the opera," Maria went on, "and I happened to be seated next to this young boy who sat there watching it so attentively. I had never seen such a poised and well-behaved young boy. During intermission I leaned over and told the older gentleman who was with him how impressed I was. The man smiled, pointed to the stage, and said, 'Plácido. Grandpa.'"

"Pavarotti had a beautiful voice," Maria continued, "but Plácido's has something his didn't—a kind of warmth, and cheer. Plácido was born with gold in his throat, and Pavarotti had to be taught."

"Mozart would have killed to have someone like Plácido. Back then they didn't have singers like that."

Maria loves the YouTube clip I found for her from the late 70s of Domingo being interviewed on 60 Minutes. The interviewer asks him, "Are you faithful to your wife?" His response: "I am faithful in my soul... and that's all I am going to say about that." He could have refused to answer it, or he could have lied. But he told the truth.

It's one thing for me, a man, to appreciate the truth in the response—that a man can be wayward and still love his spouse (not to condone being wayward)—but Maria seems to get it too. It takes one courageous and special woman with an amazing sense of the big picture to understand that the little human speed bumps along the way don't matter; what matters in the only life we're given, is, in the end, love. What a brilliant and brave woman it takes to understand and admit that.

A couple of years ago, on the heels of her Supreme Court case win, Maria donated a big chunk of change to the Music Center opera. She was subsequently invited to a special dinner with Plácido. As fate would have it, she was seated right next to him.

Knowing who she was from reading the papers, Plácido turned to her and sang the West Side Story song, "I Just Met a Girl Named Maria!"

Later in the evening, Maria said to him, "If I were 50 years younger, Mr. Domingo, we may have gotten into some trouble."

He replied, "Maria... a woman is aaaaalways a woman."

You should see how red her face gets as she tells this!

I told Margie her mother had been schooling me on Plácido lately, and she told me, "What my mother failed to tell you is that, after the Klimt auction, she announced on TV that 'Aside from my children I want my money to go to Plácido Domingo.'"

*April 13, 2008*

(Maria Reitler)

*"You're getting old, I understand."*

I've set my alarm for an ungodly hour this morning, yes, an hour of which God would not have approved. My desire is to keep some semblance of what my body still looks like, and continue to resemble something of a leading man, and not a leading fat man. After all, I'm still an actor, at least at heart, no matter how many Holocaust refugees I fall for.

But Maria likes me just as I am.

"How *are* you??"

She asked me this over a soft-boiled egg and Omega 3 English muffin, and the italics and extra question mark should give you an idea of how this woman greets people. I told her I was good, after which she said, "You should be a little bad."

I explained I was in an acting showcase over the weekend.

Her eyes suddenly shot open like window blinds. "Did you play the prince?"

She stared at me as if she were staring at an actual prince. I stared back at her like I was staring at an actual princess, which, come to think of it, she is. The exchange ended as we transitioned out of our respective imaginations.

We bounced around to different topics this morning. I brought up my friend Archie. "Aaahchie?" she asked curiously with her adorable accent, and then she suddenly melted thinking about her husband.

"There was this lovely poem Fritz used to sing called *Archibald Douglas*. I'm sure it's in the den. Let's look for it later."

I told her Archie has jet-black hair, and has a younger brother named James who has fire engine red hair. She wondered if they had a milkman, and this reminded her of a touching little story that has stuck with me all day.

"My best friend Maria Reitler and I were in England at the same time after leaving Austria, and we shared this lovely young boy, Christofer, who delivered the milk. He was nineteen or twenty, and such a decent, delightful young man, who always went out of his way to be polite and friendly. One day he had told Maria he was going off to fight in the war. He loved his country so much, and was so proud to be a soldier in the British Army. Well... he ended up being one of the first ones killed. Maria never cried over anything, but she cried about that poor milkman."

With all the negativity and death and destruction Maria Altmann has seen in her life, she's still a rose-colored romantic who can't get enough of the "only-in-the-movies" fantasies. I've learned of two she loves: *Pretty Woman*, and *My Fair Lady*. "Richard Gere is the perfect combination of strength and sensitivity. He's wonderful. And Julia Roberts is just so charming. My favorite in *My Fair Lady* is the man who plays Audrey Hepburn's father."

Then we proceeded to sing his song together, "With a little bit 'a luck, with a little bit 'a bloo-min' luck!" Maria is a 92-year-old 16-year-old: Everything is viewed through the lenses of princes and castles and mountains and flowers. I am sure God has been taking careful note of this.

———— ♦ ————

Four male ducks crash-landed into the pool after breakfast. Maria enjoyed pointing out that they were all male. "They must have flown in from San Francisco," she quipped.

Ever since 2006, ducks seem to hold unlikely significance inside these walls. A few days before the Klimt verdict was announced, Maria was at home and thought she heard some sort of a strange noise coming from the front of the house. She opened the front door, and there were two ducks quacking away on her welcome mat. "The only thing they didn't do was ring the bell."

A day or two after the ducks left she got a voicemail message from Randy, who had supposedly just returned home after a poor night of poker with friends. It was to inform her that they had won the case. "I think those ducks were telling me we won."

Maria seems to accept, even appreciate in a way, male homosexuality. She doesn't understand it on the female end. "I don't understand lesbians. Men, I can live with... but women? Disgusting."

I can see where her attitude comes from. The most influential people in her life have been men: her father, her brother-in-law Bernhard, her best friend Peter Koller, Plácido, and the list goes on. Her governess Emma seems to be the rare exception. The first man she ever got to know in life was her father, who was a saint in her eyes. Further hitting her point home that men are "better" than women, she reveled in saying that male ducks—and male animals in general—"are always more striking than females."

Maria got to talking about her best male friend Peter Koller, who died a couple years ago. He had called Maria from his home in Palm Springs one Sunday evening around 11pm, and said, "Drive to Palm Springs. I must see you tonight."

"I told him I couldn't come, but would be there first thing in the morning. And those were our final words."

Unaware of Peter's dire situation, she drove to Palm Springs the next morning. When she got there she knocked on the door and instead of Peter answering it was a nurse who led Maria to his room, where he laid unconscious in his bed. Maria sat in a chair next to his bed in silence, and watched her best friend, who she couldn't speak to, take his last breath. It wasn't until after his death that the nurse learned Maria was his best friend. Maria told me, "Had the nurse known this beforehand, she told me that she wouldn't have given him so much morphine, so he would have been able to hold a final conversation."

When it comes to women, I've only ever bragged about my mother. But now I have two women to brag about. I don't believe I will ever in my life meet another woman who measures up to Maria. The bar has been set. I really understand her incredible qualities. For example, her traditional views, and how she believes the primary job of a woman is to please the man. This, coming from a strong and independent woman who commandeered her escape from the Nazis, who built her own business with her own hands, and who served as the matriarch to her family. She was always home in time to make dinner, listen to her kids talk about their day at school, and give her husband the affection he needed. She found a way to do it all, and love it all. Now *that's* the definition of a well-rounded woman.

The stories had to stop because we had to get ready for the doctors. I got lost getting her to the correct suite of her endocrinologist. By the time I realized I took the wrong elevator, which threw us to the wrong side of the building, Maria was out of breath. I dashed through a door and stole a chair from a waiting room.

As she sat and caught her breath in the middle of the hallway, I raced up and down like a madman, poking my head through doorways and elevators, trying to make sense of the confusing numbers and arrows lining the walls.

Maria had never seen me this flustered and frantic. She took advantage of my vulnerable state and said with a calm smile, "You're getting old, I understand."

I slowed to appreciate her comment, and took a deep breath. Right on cue, a nice woman walked out of a door, fetched us a wheelchair, and pointed us in the right direction.

After the appointment we decided to go to a German deli Maria has been going to for decades, called The Sausage Kitchen. She told me the afternoon after she won her Supreme Court case, she walked in to buy some schnitzel for dinner to celebrate. The owner walked out of the back kitchen with a devious grin and a newspaper, and said, "May I be the first to offer my hand in marriage?" Ever since then they've enjoyed a playful relationship.

He's quite a character, this owner—a paunchy, pugnacious man in his seventies with unruly white hair, leathery skin and a raspy voice, who won't let you leave with your sausage until he gives you his advice on life. Before you give your order he intensely studies your eyes to see if you're even worthy of his advice, and if he decides you are, he proceeds. Today his guidance was, "Do you know what zee secret to life ees? Lot of sex and lot of money."

Of course Maria laughed the hardest.

So we bought some delicious veal hotdogs called wurstel. As I stood over the stove twenty minutes later, Maria told me how to cook them: "You don't boil them, you boil the water, then turn the burner off and cook them with just the steam." Since I was now officially a Wurstel Cook, I served us our wieners with baked beans, potato salad, and two Corona Lights. We clinked bottles before diving in.

It's all worthy of a book and a movie: the Klimts, the court case, Maria's formative years as a member of one of Europe's most elite families. But in my story these are turning out to be the mere ambience. At least in my mind and in my world, to label Maria Altmann a Supreme Court Case Winner would be like labeling Abraham Lincoln a Rail-Splitter, Daniel Day Louis a

Cobbler, or Winston Churchill a Painter. One hundred percent true, but only ten percent right.

## May 1, 2008

*"I thought that was so gross!"*

I don't know many daughters who rave about their fathers as if they were a ride at Disneyland. Maria raves this way about Gustav. Gustav could do no wrong in her eyes, and she could do no wrong in his. I can do no wrong in Maria's eyes, and she can do no wrong in mine. It's a perfect world, we three live in. I wish I could see myself how she sees me. At any rate, I'm sure Gustav would be happy to know his dearly beloved is still walking this earth. I wonder if he knows, sitting up there. Are there even chairs in heaven?

———— ◆ ————

A letter came from Austria last week—some sort of pension Maria was entitled to. In order to get the money she had to prove she was still alive. So we went to a notary, and this trip turned into the first time Maria saw how angry I get.

We drove to a mom-and-pop mail store. I walked through the door holding the hand of what surely appeared to be my sweet grandmother. We showed the tiny Thai man behind the counter our note from Austria. It was written in German, and had a little statement in English explaining everything. But this official English paragraph wasn't enough for him. It wasn't enough for this polite, polished old lady who had been on this earth far too long to be lying about her identity to tell him in perfect English (better than his, frankly) that he was talking to Maria Altmann. No amount of Altmann charm was going to get this guy to notarize our piece of paper.

I became tormented over his insistence on not only denying our request, but doing it in an arrogant way. He had made up his mind we were trying to deceive him, treating us as if we were notary vigilantes on the run. He didn't even want our money. I lost it.

I yelled and cursed at him like a pit bull would if it could. We didn't have time to find another notary. The guy didn't care.

During my tirade Maria watched me like she was watching an opera. The more I yelled, the more her eyes sparkled. She thanked the man politely and we left.

"It's okay, *My La-Zona*. Tom and I will do it this weekend."

I'm no stranger to Mr. Temper. When I was in my early teens I used to play doubles with my family at the local tennis club in Northern Virginia, and if the ball wasn't cooperating or if I wasn't happy with how Christian was looking at me, I'd storm off the court and lock myself in our Volvo until they were ready to go home. Which wasn't long, since doubles doesn't work so well with three people.

Once in junior high I got in a fight with my mom in the kitchen after dinner. I don't remember what it was about, but I remember pulling a knife out of a drawer and waving it at her.

A week before heading off to college at Ohio Wesleyan, my friend Will and I were in the process of pulling out a stop sign near my house, when a police car pulled up. I was so angry that such a productive evening was ruined, I said to the cop, "Of all the times to come around the corner, why the fuck did you have to come now?"

It was then that he slapped handcuffs on my wrists. We spent the night in jail.

As I've matured I've channeled this explosiveness into an overall lust for life, which has mostly helped me get to where I am today. I don't lock myself in cars anymore, at least intentionally, and I don't wave knives at people or pull out street signs. I'm a productive member of society. And now I have Maria to remind me that the world isn't worth fighting.

The Sicilian/Irish/Leo part of me was still buzzing, though, when we walked through the front door of Maria's house. Maria made her way to her room to change into her bathrobe, and I decided to log onto Chuck's old IBM computer to calm down and check my email.

A few minutes later she showed up at the door. I guided her into the office and into her seat. Now that I had her there, it occurred to me to type "Maria Altmann" into Wikipedia, and tell her to start reading. I got up to leave and secretly watched her from the doorway.

She was drawn in like a cat to a ball of string. When she came across a portion that read: ...*living in the Netherlands before moving to Hollywood, California*, she called me back in. As if I had written it, she said heatedly, "I never lived in the Netherlands, I was only there for a day!"

I left her alone to read more about what someone else had to say about her life.

————◆————

We had a last minute hair appointment today. Maria still goes about twice a month, and sees the same friendly French Hairstylist, Maite, she's had for twenty years.

"Have you ever been drunk?" Maria asked me as she sat there getting her head warmed by that helmet-warming thing.

I told her the last time I'd been drunk was in college during "Big Brother" night at my fraternity. When I woke up the next morning still in my suit, I was sprawled out on the floor under my bunk bed with two bottles of empty Mad Dog 20/20 lying next to me.

She jumped to a woman named Liz Lesser, who used to sit next to her at the salon for years.

"About ten years ago she died on the morning of her one-hundredth birthday. Up until then she still drove, still wore high heels, still stood straight up like a Ziegfeld Girl—she was a lady up until the very end. And as a little girl she was on one of those lifeboats that rescued the *Titanic*."

The nail lady was eating French fries, and this reminded Maria that in Europe, French fries used to be only served at dinner, never at lunch. Beside herself, she said, "Now, you can eat them at every meal!"

The topic of Maria's childhood arose, and she told me at holiday dinners their butler would put a carp in the bathtub to swim around before cooking it for the first course.

"I thought that was so gross! I took baths in there! I don't even want to think about it." Then she scrunched her nose and said, "Yucky."

As Maria pulled out her purse to pay Maite, a large man in his 70's approached me to inform me I was blocking him in. "So you're Maria's caregiver, huh?" the man asked me as he tottered ahead of me toward our cars in the back parking lot. "I may need one soon. I mean, you're probably busy and all, but I tell ya, it's just getting harder to do certain things that I used to be able to do."

It occurred to me for the first time that what I was doing for Maria was attracting others in need. But I declined. I gave him Tom's number.

I left the man in the parking lot with my compassion, and returned to hear Maria and Maite having their regular argument about whose accent is more charming. Maite thinks it's Maria's, and Maria thinks it's Maite's, and as always they agreed to call it a draw.

Yo Tom —

Definitely don't mean to sound ungrateful, cuz you know how grateful I am for you, but please ALWAYS get Maria a filet. I thought I wrote that on the notepad on the fridge, and I could have sworn you said you got New Yorks, but they were Rib Eyes... and just assume, come hell or high water, to get her a filet. She just can't bite through any other cut of meat. You're the best, I mean it. See you tomorrow morning.

P.S. Did Maria tell you that Bryn Terfil story? That chubby Welsh opera star? When she randomly ran into him at a restaurant in Vienna and they hung out together the rest of the night? Ask her about it. Hugely entertaining.

**May 10, 2008**

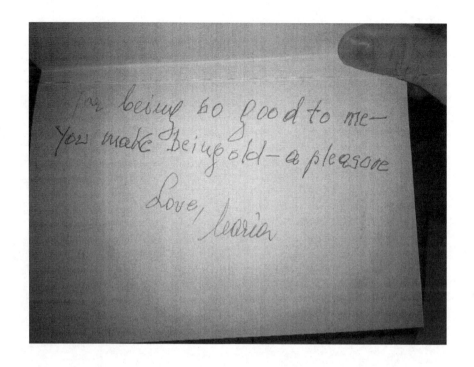

*"Most of the time you want a woman to get <u>un</u>dressed."*

I didn't shave over the weekend, and I wore a baseball cap today. When I greeted Maria in the hallway she stopped to squint her eyes, and didn't recognize me until I kissed her on the cheek.

"Oh! I thought you were a painter!" I told her I was here to paint the house today, and she giggled, a giggle that always has me looking forward to Mondays.

As we walked to the kitchen, she said, "You know, you wear that hat all the time. You should let your hair breathe once in a while."

By the end of today she'd reminded me about the hair-breathing thing at least four times. It got to the point that I had to take it off and put it in my car. Today was the first time I'd ever worn a cap at the house. It reminded me of her age. I didn't like it.

Set to take a walk, I got Maria to her room fairly quickly after breakfast, and left her there to get dressed. When I returned, all I could see was a tuft of hair peeking out from underneath her comforter. Sensing someone was in the room she pulled the cover down from her face and opened her eyes to see me standing there with my chin nearly to the floor, showing my melodramatic disapproval.

"Get dressed!" I yelled like a playful drill sergeant.

"Most of the time you want a woman to get undressed... but I'll get dressed, darling."

———— ◆ ————

"You know, Hitler changed everything," she said to me on our walk through Cheviot Hills Park. "It never used to be, 'He's Catholic,' or 'She's Jewish,' or 'He's Christian.' It didn't matter who or what you were. Many people didn't even know they had Jewish roots until Hitler came. Now, it's a big deal."

She mentioned that as a youth, Hitler saw a public viewing of Klimt's work for the first time, and "He lost interest because the subjects were all Jewish."

Later in the walk I said, "You were so beautiful that if you had stayed in Vienna the Nazis surely wouldn't have hurt you."

She paused and looked up at me like a professor to a student: "The same monsters who would toss live babies into the air and then let them fall onto their bayonets? No, my love. They didn't care about beauty. They were cold-blooded."

The walk fell mostly silent after that. We returned to the house, settled in the kitchen, and I began warming up some potato leek soup Lisa brought over yesterday.

Chuck walked through and caught a glimpse of his mother's hand on my knee as we were enjoying the squirrels in the backyard performing Matrix-like moves to sneak little drinks out of the hummingbird feeder.

"Get your hand off his knee!" he declared with his usual joking dissatisfaction.

"I happen to like him," she said defensively.

"I noticed," Chuck said before disappearing into his office. As his door closed we looked at each other and smiled, she lifted her hand from my knee, and I rose to get our scalding soup.

Again, Maria's affinity toward men began with her father. Gustav Bloch-Bauer would support her unconditionally.

"My mother would come home from my school and say to me, 'Professor Natansky said you disrupted class again, and you do nothing but joke around all the time.' My father would immediately come to my defense. He would say to me (referring to the teacher), 'What injustice did the old swine do you this time?' He was always on my side no matter what!"

————◆————

When Maria got up from her nap this afternoon, I noticed her at her desk concentrating on writing. I left her alone and waited in the living room. As she wheeled around the corner a few minutes later she was carrying a little card, finding it difficult to hold onto while grasping her walker. She stopped and handed it to me, and said, "I found this by the doorway," before proceeding into the kitchen. I opened it.

Dear Gregor;

Thank you for being so good to me. You make being old a pleasure.

Love,

Maria

I had a few moments in the hallway alone to get emotional. It was the first thing she ever wrote to me.

When I met her in the kitchen she kissed my hand, then suddenly shook her head in faux disgust. "If my mother would have seen me kiss your hand, she would have killed me. The man kisses the woman's hand. But your hand, I'll kiss any day."

Altmanns!

Today there was a nice little package by the door with something Maria has been telling me about since I started working here. A CASHMERE SWEATER! I'm not a sweater-wearer, but I tell you, this piece of clothing is very special. It's a China Blue cashmere, and it fits like a glove. It feels GREAT on my bare skin, which is the problem I have with wearing other sweaters. Maria's look of pride and admiration as I modeled it for her was a sight to behold. Surely it made her think of her beloved Bernhard.

G

*May 18, 2008*

(Petra)

*"Time to make up a true story."*

Never in my life have I obsessed about a woman I was able to touch, other than perhaps my mother during infancy, which must have been more her breasts than anything else. Like many men, I've taken the easy way out and obsessed a whole bunch about women in magazines, in movies, or walking down the street. Today I find myself professing, sometimes to complete strangers, how I've met the most amazing woman on earth. But loving Maria is almost cheating, because it's so easy. I should try loving someone like Kim Jong Il, or Ann Coulter—now that would be the mark of a great human being.

Maria sort of reminds me of Catherine the Great, whom I've become fascinated with recently. Like Maria, Catherine was powerful and tenacious in her business life, and charming and playful in her personal life. Like Maria with Austria, Catherine dominated a country to seize power, and ultimately became the greatest Russian ruler of all time. She ruled with an iron fist but a fair fist, and believed in the goodness of people. Catherine the Great. Maria the Magnificent.

This morning an open window carried an angelic medley from Lisa, Maria's neighbor, who was practicing her flute on her back porch. Unfortunately Maria can't hear it. Her hearing seems to get worse every week.

I handed Maria an apple with breakfast, and before I handed it to her I cautioned her. "This may be a little old."

She bit into it and said, "Old? It's a schoolmate of mine!"

I tossed it in the trash and made her a bowl of cereal with fresh raspberries.

"You did not get any uglier over the weekend," she said. "And I only tell you that because I know it doesn't go to your head."

I have two new habits now: I lay out Maria's clothes, and I open her mail. She gets very flustered that her closet is a mess. She's consistently convinced some outfits hanging there aren't hers, and someone else is using her closet to hang clothing (remember the black Russian trench coat?). It's sad to see that she needs me to make things like this clear. We spend so much time being each other's muse and making each other laugh, that it pains me whenever I have to be what I was hired to be.

As far as her mail, I know exactly what she'll want, and what she'll throw away. Any bill she gets goes right into her friend/accountant Petra's box on the upper right corner of her desk, and anything relating to opera I open myself, knowing that if it doesn't involve Plácido speaking or performing she's probably not going to want to go. The opera invitations list an RSVP number, so she always insists on leaving a sweet message that she can't attend. *Real women have manners.*

She still gets all the L.L. Bean catalogues and the out-of-date fashion magazines. She offered to buy me a "Powder Blue" cashmere sweater, and I reminded her she already bought me one, and that the color is now called "China Blue." She insisted I was incorrect until I showed her in the magazine.

"Well I'll be darned," she said. How times change.

It's interesting watching age. I've never seen it so intimately. I don't think she spends any time thinking about her aging, but of course I do very deeply. I want to be here for her, to point things out, to correct her in the most humble of ways, and to help her navigate her way through something we will all need to face at some point in our lives.

———◆———

"Time to make up a true story," Maria said after breakfast. She picked up the phone to dial Lily. She didn't want to do dinner at Lily's house tonight because she had it in her head she and I should enjoy a roasted chicken from Vons.

"Lily's not going anywhere."

Lily's 97.

So we went to the grocery store to get this "delicious" roasted chicken worthy of cancelling a dinner with Lily.

What an unforgettable experience our first shopping trip was! Maria was fascinated with every little item, like Dorothy was when she arrived at Oz. She would stop at the TV dinner freezer, pull open the sealed door to greet the whoosh of cold steam, and examine the items as if they were rare stones. She'd pick one out and show it to me. "What is *this*, my love?"

"That's some fried chicken thing, we don't need it." Then she'd pick up the next item, an oversized bag of Tater Tots, carefully pressing on portions of the bag to feel each mystical tot. All this question-asking was tiring her out, so I found her a chair near the manager's desk. Even as she sat there catching her breath she still said hello to everyone who passed us.

When we returned to shopping, I was the mother snatching items away from her daughter.

"No, we don't need an MCI Calling Card, Maria," and, "Maria, I don't think we need glaze for peaches," and, "I'm pretty sure we are good on stopwatches."

Waiting in the checkout line at the end of our trip I watched her struggle to find her wallet in her purse. I thought of her years ago walking these same shiny floors picking up dinner for the family, knowing exactly where that credit card was and handing it crisply and confidently to the checker. Now I'm with her in her 90's, helping her do it, which four months ago would have sounded crazy. The passage of time really is something. It's the ultimate, unavoidable tragedy. But here this woman is, still dancing along, living and loving as if she has decades to go.

And look at me, suddenly in a position to enjoy every moment of it.

*May 31, 2008*

*"I want to look out the window and see twelve virgins
swimming nude around you."*

Life is writing my book right now, and that life just happens to include a 92-year-old woman who says things to me like, "I'm going to take a nap, and when I awake, I want to look out the window and see twelve virgins swimming nude around you."

For some reason the topic of virgins has been coming up at an escalated rate. Maria admitted, "I was what they called an Iron Virgin. I had no idea all my friends had already 'done it.' I thought they were all innocent like me."

Today she asked me if I like virgins. I sat there staring at her with a smirk on my face, refusing to answer. Then she said, "You would prefer a pro. I can tell by the look on your face."

Maria and I share an insatiable need to connect with others, and an endless curiosity about everything. Maria asked on our walk today around the block, "Have you ever tried pot?"

I told her I did it once, but it wasn't my thing. She asked if she could get me a joint for my birthday, and I joked, "Only if you smoke it with me."

Maria stopped walking, looked up at me and said, "Want to?"

Later in the walk we passed an Asian woman. Maria smiled at her and we continued. A couple minutes later she turned to me and asked, "Have you ever done it with an Oriental?"

After I finished laughing, I shook my head and pulled her arm in to continue our walk. But she would not be distracted.

"Well?" she insisted.

I obliged. "I think I might have done it somewhere along the way." Satisfied, we continued our walk. This definitely beats auditioning.

We were back at the house in time to see the new stove arrive. The former was the original that came with the house over 30 years ago, and at this point it was about as useful as a screen door in a submarine.

"I don't need a new stove, it's ridiculous," Maria kept saying all week. Today she showed more peace with the change: "Let's have a drink so I can tolerate it more easily." Then she laughed at the whole thing. "They might mistake me for the stove, since we're both so old."

We sat in the kitchen and watched the movers rip the old stove out of the wall and haul it away. I did what I do best, and that was study Maria's face like I was watching a Terrence Malick film. I could tell by watching her that deep down she was nervous, saying goodbye to her stove. Maybe there's an old wound there. Maybe it dates back to the Holocaust and how she spent years searching for a home where everything would always stay the same. She's found her home. No more change.

Chuck grew weary of hearing his mother moan about her loss. He told her to "Get over it already."

An argument ensued. Usually they make up before parting, but after this she retreated to her room a haggard old woman, and he to his office a haggard old man.

I kissed her on her cheek before she sat on her bed, and she looked up at me and said, "I needed that."

Chris was due to be at the house to take the reins in an hour. I sat on Maria's bed and asked her, "What was the best time in your life?"

She thought for a moment as she looked out her sliding glass door into the backyard, then suddenly grinned from ear to ear. "December, 1937. Fritz and I had just gotten married and his older brother, Bernhard, let us have his apartment in Paris for a weekend. We walked through the door, and there were white spring flowers everywhere, even going up the stairs! Spring flowers in December, can you believe it?" She laughed and shook her head. "That was a pretty good time."

Her smile faded. She ran her finger along the surface of a pillow and pursed her lips. "Then Hitler came."

———— ♦ ————

*In the ensuing, one-hundred-percent true account, any line or paragraph written in italics is a quote from Maria's present-day reflections.*

## Thursday, March 10, 1938
## Vienna, Austria

It was three months and eleven days into 1938, and 22-year-old
Maria had three things going her way: one, she was born a Bloch-
Bauer, which meant she was guaranteed a life of good fortune.
Two, there wasn't a more flourishing city in the world to be living
a life of good fortune than Vienna, Austria. And three, just 90
days prior, her Uncle Ferdinand had thrown her a lavish wedding,
during which she married her first love, Fritz Altmann. Having
just returned home from their honeymoon in Saint Moritz, Fritz
was set to pursue his dream of becoming an opera singer. Maria,
three months pregnant with their first child, was preparing for
motherhood.

> *We had a party at our house in 1936 and Fritz came. I had
> already met him a couple of times. He was charming and
> handsome, but I didn't think twice about him until he asked
> the piano player to play a Schubert song. And then he
> started to sing, and I heard what a beautiful voice he had.
> That's when I knew I wanted to spend the rest of my life
> with him."*

## Friday, March 11, 1938

The next day began like any other. The grandfather clock in the
Bloch-Bauer home struck two o'clock in the afternoon. The
evening always meant Maria's father, Gustav—with his beloved
Stradivarius Cello leaning against his knee—was playing live
chamber music in the living room with his usual group of friends
and colleagues. Fritz was in the kitchen helping Maria and her
mother, Therese, begin the early preparations for a big dinner.

At around 2:15, Gustav's gang heard a ruckus in the
kitchen, and left their instruments behind to join Therese, Maria,
and Fritz, who were all huddled around the radio. Kurt von
Schuschnigg, Chancellor of the First Republic of Austria, spoke
urgently to the citizens of Vienna:

"The Germans have just crossed the border... we do not want any bloodshed... we shall offer no resistance... God bless Austria."

*I happened to have flunked my car exam that morning. I should've known Hitler was coming.*

It was Schuschnigg's final speech before he was thrown into a concentration camp and the last time Gustav—whose deepest passion in life was music—was able to play his Stradivarius Cello. The good old days were gone in an instant.

The Bloch-Bauers peered out their window at all the sudden activity.

*Church bells were ringing, the people were running through the streets, celebrating and throwing flowers and gifts at Hitler's feet. It was one big party. I remember thinking, how in the world can they be celebrating all this?*

Hitler appeared on the radio first thing Saturday morning to reassure all citizens that he was proud to be back in his hometown, and had no plans of leaving again.

After discussing Maria's pregnancy with Fritz, they decided on an abortion.

*We didn't want to take any chances with the baby, so I went to a Jewish doctor at the top floor of an elementary school. Fritz told me to dress like a schoolgirl to blend in.*

On Monday morning three men in casual clothing visited the Bloch-Bauer residence.

*They dressed like that so they could surprise you when you least expected it.*

The Nazis knew exactly where all the valuables in Vienna were located, and held particular interest in a number of possessions the Bloch-Bauers were widely known to have. These possessions were, in order of importance to Hitler:

1. The jewelry of Maria's Aunt Adele.

(Adele Bloch-Bauer in 1910)

2. Maria's Uncle Ferdinand's 400-piece porcelain collection that no museum in the world could match, along with his extensive sculpture and art collection, including five original paintings by Gustav Klimt.

(Maria and Ferdinand at his castle in Prague in 1932)

*Hitler's main loves were china, jewelry, and art. They were more into the "old master" paintings. Since Klimt was contemporary and considered avant-garde, they weren't into him and didn't consider him to be worth any significant sum of money.*

3. Gustav's Stradivarius Cello.

*That cello was given to my father by the Rothschild brothers, both of whom he sat next to weekly at church. He would call it his "sixth child." When the Gestapo came to the house and hauled it away, he didn't seem to care. And that's the moment when I knew the end was near for him. He had lost all will to live.*

The last item Hitler's secret police came for that morning was Maria's husband. Besides the fact that Fritz was Jewish, the enemy race, they wanted him as collateral for the knit-ware business of his older brother Bernhard, a well-known textile manufacturer in Vienna. The police said that if Bernhard signed his business over to them, Fritz would remain a free man. To be even more certain the transaction would happen, Maria voluntarily told them there were more jewels in a safe at a bank across town, and arranged for them to be picked up that day.

> *They would never have known about that additional jewelry, but I told them because I was sure it would keep Fritz out of a camp.*

When they got their hands on Maria's bonus jewelry—stealing her engagement ring right off her finger while they were at it—they arrested Fritz anyway.

> *You know, I stood to inherit a lot of Adele's jewelry, including a large diamond necklace that they just took out of a red velvet box and slipped into their pocket. But all those physical things meant absolutely nothing to me. It was my husband I cared about.*

Fritz was arrested, put on a plane, and then a train. On the train to Dachau—Austria's first transport to a concentration camp—he sat next to the grandsons of the former emperor Franz Joseph, the current head of the Vienna opera, and a Jewish Comedian named Fritz Grunbaum.

> *I remember reading a few years ago how dreadfully Grunbaum perished at Dachau. He would do these stand-up routines about life in the camps, and would keep the prisoners laughing day and night. Fritz had so many wonderful stories about him. And one morning they took him off to the gas chamber.*

**March 15, 1938**
**Vienna**

Before any deals were made with the Nazis to free Fritz, Bernhard abandoned his factory and fled Vienna in the middle of the night. He made it across the border to Hungry, and then to France, where he wrote to all his customers to send to Paris any money they owed him. Maria's sister Luise, her eight-year-old daughter Nelly, four year-old son Francis, and her husband Victor, left abruptly for Yugoslavia.

And Maria's Uncle Ferdinand, who just hours earlier was the owner of Austria's largest sugar refinery, was now just another frightened Jew running for his life. He grabbed his butler and just enough food and clothes to last them until they made it to his castle in Czechoslovakia—a sprawling countryside estate where Maria and her family spent time every summer. When they arrived there were unexpected houseguests. One of them was SS Commander Reinhard Heydrich, nicknamed "The Butcher of Prague." He banished Ferdinand from his own home.

> *My oldest brother Robert was in charge of signing over Ferdinand's things to Heydrich. I remember Heydrich's wife would write Robert letters saying things like, "It's him, not me," and that she's sorry about the whole thing. I believe her. These were ruthless men.*

Ferdinand would eventually make it to Zurich, Switzerland, where he would die nearly penniless, in 1945. Unfortunately he would learn about the fate of his two favorite nieces, Paula and Elisa, before he died—they were both murdered in concentration camps.

> *I can still hear Uncle Ferry's voice in my head—he would look out the window and say, 'Look! The weather just changed! It's raining HARDER!' He always had such a great sense of humor.*

### Early July, 1938

While Jewish families, political dissidents, homosexuals, and any "deviants" of any kind were being uprooted around Central Europe by Hitler's ambitious army, Maria and her family tried desperately to remain hopeful that the deal Bernhard and the police had on the table would lead to Fritz's release. Maria sent regular care packages and post cards to Fritz at Dachau.

> *I remember Fritz wrote me in a letter that counter to what one might think, the Viennese were the nastiest, and he would thank his lucky stars when he dealt with a German.*

As if her husband's being in a concentration camp wasn't enough to worry about, Maria's father's health was declining. Within the week Gustav died at age 75, in what was to be the most profound tragedy of Maria's life.

> *My father was 54 when he had me, so he was really more like a grandfather. But I never felt like I had an old father. We had an unusual relationship. It wasn't normal, actually. We did everything together. We went to social functions and balls, everything.*

*He was so sad when I got married because it meant I was
leaving him. Looking back on it now he died at just the right
time, before he fully understood who the Nazis really were.
And if he had lived, I would have stayed behind with him
and faced the consequences.*

The next morning at Dachau a friend of Fritz brought him the
day's newspaper, showing him the obituary section accompanied
by Gustav's picture.

"Aren't you married to his daughter?" Fritz knew how
much Maria loved her father, and that he couldn't be there to
comfort her made being at Dachau even harder.

### July–September, 1938

Hitler was tightening his grip. Jews were now prohibited to buy
or trade goods and services, to practice law or medicine, and if
you were over fifteen you had to apply for an identity card to be
shown on demand to any police officer. Maria, her brother Poldi,
and their mother Therese, all Jewish of course, remained safe in
Vienna for the time being. But no one had heard a peep from
Bernhard. Was he still in France? Was he even still alive?

*You see, it was much easier to carry on during these times if
you were young. If you were old, it was basically a death
sentence. Elders had lived their entire lives in Vienna, and
most had no money outside Austria or Germany. If they
were still able to work, they were forced to retire, only to be
thrown into camps for the remainder of their lives. There
was very little hope. Elder suicides and suicides in general
were happening all over the place.*

Maria's 62-year-old pediatrician died by his own hands.

Therese's good friend took both her own and her ten year-
old son's life, for fear of being arrested.

A neighbor's daughter, who had just had a baby, strangled
it to death because she knew the Nazis would have soon done it
themselves.

A professor was seen at a window in a school, yelling down below, "Move! I don't want to hurt anyone!" And when the coast was clear, he jumped.

A well-to-do Austrian couple in their late fifties escaped Vienna and made it all the way to South America, where shortly thereafter they committed suicide together.

Gustav's sister, Agnes, who was 86 and legally blind, fled to Prague, and the last anyone heard of her was that she was picked up by the Nazis somewhere along the way.

The father of Maria's best friend Crystal, who married a Jewish woman in the twenties, just now realized the implications of having a Jewish child. The revelation was so powerful that he shot himself in the head.

(Crystal and Maria in 1932)

And Herr Neumann, the 76-year-old friend of Maria's late father, shot himself with a small pistol, leaving behind a suicide note: "An old Austrian who can't cope with the times."

### *Early September*
### *Dachau*

Finally. Bernhard signed all the papers, turning over the ownership of his textile business to the Nazis.

(Bernhard and his wife Wilma, in Vienna in 1949)

An immediate release of his brother was authorized. A frail Fritz with a freshly shaven head walked through the gate at Dachau and greeted Maria at the police station. It was their honeymoon all over again.

### House Arrest
### Vienna

But it was a brief second honeymoon. Maria and Fritz were forced under house arrest in a small Vienna apartment. They were permitted to leave during the day provided they returned home at specific times to check in with a parole officer. They became model prisoners by meeting curfew, always being polite, and never putting up a fuss about anything. Since Fritz spent nearly eight weeks in a camp and had little desire to be social with the people who put him there, Maria stepped up as the kind and innocent girl who always did and said just the right thing.

> *They trusted us. In their minds we weren't capable of fleeing.*

Maria used this trust to her advantage. She had begun to notice that when she left the apartment on an errand, no one monitored her as she walked around the city.

> *I thought, how could this be, that there was no one following me?*

She decided to put it to the test. After visiting the market five subsequent mornings in a row, she was sure she had not once been followed. She told Fritz. They decided to make a break for it in the morning.

> *We didn't tell my mother we were escaping because we didn't want her to have to lie. They were certain to be questioning her.*

But later that night, Maria got word her governess, Frau Lynn Emma Raschke, who had worked for the Bloch-Bauers for 35 years and whom Maria considered her second love behind her father, was diagnosed with intestinal cancer, and given six months to live. Visiting her took priority.

(Maria and Emma in 1933)

*I remember it vividly. Emma was standing in the doorway, and I said to her, "We're leaving tomorrow. Come with me. Stay with me wherever I go. I will share with you my last penny." And she responded, 'I can't. I'm too sick.'*

As hard as it was for Maria to leave Emma, at least she didn't have to worry anymore about her father. But if they were ever to make it out of Austria alive, it was now or never.

*Late September*
*The morning of the escape*

The big day arrived. Maria told a parole officer her husband had a cavity and was in urgent need of a dentist. The officer allowed them to go so long as they were home by curfew. With just the coats on their backs, one passport between them, and a pair of Adele's earrings stuffed into Maria's brassiere, they left their apartment and headed for a train destined for a plane bound for Cologne, Germany. There they were to meet a Dutch peasant Bernhard had paid to drive them to the border station at Kolshied, where they would hop the fence and reconvene with Bernhard in Holland.

> *At that point I felt like the Nazis could take over Austria, they could imprison my husband, they could steal all the physical things they wanted from us—but they could never, ever take away those moments Fritz and I shared in the mountains of Salzburg.*

Maria and Fritz boarded the old propeller plane, and as the motors rumbled alive they sat there dreaming of freedom a flight away. But suddenly the motors cut out, and there was a deafening silence. Wheels creaked toward the cockpit.

*We were sure they were coming for Fritz.*

The creaking wheels suddenly stopped. More silence. The plane door swung open. Four men stepped aboard—two police officials, and two men in maintenance uniforms. The two maintenance men disappeared into the cockpit, and the two officials skulked up and down the aisle leering at passengers. Maria and Fritz stared forward knowing full well how high-profile a couple they were.

The pacing lasted twenty tense minutes. Then the pilot came on the speaker and announced the reason for the delay: bad weather in Munich. The four men exited, and within minutes they lifted into the air. As Vienna grew smaller and smaller, Maria and Fritz had no way of knowing whether they'd see Austria or their family again.

*We were extremely fortunate to get out then. Six weeks later—after "Kristallnacht" and all the horrible death and destruction that ended up causing—we would have been dead. This is really when the Holocaust began.*

———————◆———————

Just hours after Maria and Fritz boarded the plane to Cologne, Poldi was awakened in the middle of the night by a high-ranking Gestapo claiming to be Hitler's nephew.

*They did that. They would visit you at an ungodly hour, because they knew that when you woke up you were not as alert, and the truth tended to just flow out.*

The Gestapo had apparently been reviewing a list of names that morning, and the name Leopold Bloch-Bauer looked familiar to him. This prompted him to drive to Poldi's house and knock on the door. When Poldi opened it the Gestapo knew right away that Poldi was the right guy. He began grilling him.

"Where were you three years ago, New Year's Eve?" he asked Poldi for some reason.

"I was at a tavern with my friend at the foot of the Alps."

"And what happened at midnight?"

Poldi recalled earnestly. "A couple of hikers were stuck on the summit in inclement weather. We climbed up and helped them down the mountain."

"And what would have happened to those men if you hadn't done anything?"

"They would not have made it down alive, Sir."

He paused and said, "I was one of those men you rescued. You have three days to leave town. After that, I cannot protect you."

The Gestapo got up and left.

With little time to appreciate his good fortune, Poldi quickly gathered everything he could carry and headed for Vancouver, having no idea if the rest of his family had made it out of Austria alive.

(Maria and Poldi in Salzburg in 1935)

## Cologne, Germany

Maria and Fritz landed safely in Cologne, and hailed a taxi at the airport to find the house of the peasant Bernhard had hired to help them cross the border. After driving around in circles for nearly an hour, the frustrated driver pulled to the side of the road to flag a border policeman to point him in the right direction.

> *As soon as I heard him say the words, 'Border Police,' I said, 'Oh, I just remembered where it was!' I told him to drop us right there in the street. We were left there, with no clue how to get to this peasant's apartment. Suddenly standing before us was this giant priest. He looked like an apparition. We asked him if he had heard of the peasant we were supposed to meet, and, if you can believe it, he had! He'd been sending a lot of Catholics to him—it wasn't just Jews who were escaping, you see. And he even walked us to where he lived! He was so charming and handsome, I'll never forget him. But Fritz had nothing to worry about, he was a priest for Heaven's sake.*

Maria and Fritz knocked on the apartment door. The peasant answered it, and led them to his car and drove them to the border, where stood a twelve-foot high fence they had a ten-minute window to scale during the changing of the guard. The guards always changed at midnight. The peasant fled to help others.

Maria and Fritz waited 40 minutes until it was midnight. When the guards changed they hopped a small brook and made a break for the barbed wire fence.

> *As we got closer and closer, Fritz suddenly screamed, "Hopsa!"—the German word for "Leap!"—but amidst the commotion for some reason I heard "SR!"—the acronym for Hitler's Storm Troopers. I had so much adrenaline pumping through my body thinking they were right behind me that I made one last leap over the fence. I tore my knee on the barbed wire, and I actually kept those ripped nylons for years!*

Bernhard stood waiting at the Border Station.

> *Fairly recently I was at a Dutch gathering in Los Angeles and I met someone who knew that peasant who helped us. They told me he was eventually caught and questioned for suspicion of aiding dozens of refugees others across the border. And then they murdered his son. But they reassured me it had nothing to with our escape. I guess we'll never know.*

Bernhard walked Maria and Fritz about a hundred yards from the station, where they convened with a young Dutch couple, whereupon the four swapped husbands and wives until they felt safe Maria and Fritz weren't being followed. They hailed two taxis. Fritz and the Dutch woman took one, and Maria, the Dutch man, and Bernhard took the other.

They drove to a hotel and met the concierge whom Bernhard had paid to tell anyone who walked through the door they were all booked up for the evening. Bernhard paid the Dutch couple for their help, and stayed the night with Maria and Fritz. The morning arrived with no sign of trouble. Before Bernhard saw them off, he gave them enough money to fly to England and find a place to stay.

### October 1938
### Liverpool, England

The first thing Maria did when they arrived in England was call her mother and tell her where they were and that they were safe. Therese bore bad news:

> *She told me my Roman mythology teacher had been killed by the Nazis. He was my favorite teacher. He was such a good man. I still remember him so fondly.*

The newlyweds found a small apartment in the heart of Liverpool, and began building their new home.

(Therese reading in her living room in 1932)

## Vienna

A few days after she learned her daughter and her husband were safe in England, Therese—all 5 feet, 100 pounds of her—answered a knock she knew could come at any moment. Two SS Men stood at the front door. Before they could speak, though, Therese glared at them.

"Remove your hats when you speak to a lady."

*And do you know what? They actually took their hats off! My mother was one fresh chicken! I could never have done that!*

Holding his hat by his side, one officer said, "We know your daughter is with her sister in Yugoslavia, and we will find her and bring her back to Vienna."

Therese replied with conviction. "You are incorrect. She is in England with her husband, and you will never get to them there!"

There was little else they could do then. But something was done eight years later, in 1946, on Maria's thirtieth birthday, that may or may not have been payback for the humiliation the two officers endured at Therese's house.

## February 18, 1946 (eight years later)
## Yugoslavia

Poldi, who had been in Vancouver since the bedroom interrogation nearly eight years earlier, sent a letter to Luise, Victor and the children, who were still in Yugoslavia, warning that he had a hunch they were in grave danger. He urged they leave the country immediately. They stayed. A week after receiving Poldi's letter, Victor was arrested and executed.

They accused Victor of mistreating his employees, which if it matters was a blatant lie. Luise flew to Belgrade to beg Prime Minister Tito for a last-minute pardon. He told her he'd try and do something, but nothing was ever done. Nelly frantically collected signatures from every employee at her father's company saying he was a decent man who was good to his workers. It was true. But it was too late.

On the day before his execution, Victor wrote a letter telling his family and friends how much he loved them, and expressed no ill will toward anyone. Luise and Nelly paid him a final visit at the prison. At one point Victor looked at his wife and daughter with an eerie certainty, and said, "Don't cry. Everybody has to die sometime. So I die a little earlier."

(Nelly, Luise, and Francis in 1946, shortly after Victor's execution)

The next morning Victor put on his navy blue jacket and they took him into the woods, forcing him a few feet ahead. He walked ten minutes before two shots rang out.

Later that day a prison guard donning a blue jacket marched proudly past Luise. She noticed two bullet holes in the back of the jacket, one in the center, and one near the left shoulder. There was no mistaking it was her husband's jacket.

(Victor)

*They say it was the communists who killed Victor. From what I was told the Nazis had nothing to do with it.*

In their attempt to flee Yugoslavia, Luise, Nelly, and Francis were arrested at the border. The Chief of Police forced Luise to be his mistress for six weeks, then permitted their exit out of the country. They flew to Vancouver to join Poldi.

### Back to Maria in England
### November 1938
### Liverpool

A nearly broke Bernhard flew to Liverpool to join Maria and Fritz. With what little money he had left he opened a factory in the middle of town. Lucky for him the impending war in England brought great demand for his textile manufacturing. He hired Fritz for $30 a week. Life for the three was the best it had been in months.

*In Liverpool we lived in an attic in a small apartment for $5
a month. My friend came down the stairs one day, sobbing
at what 'became of me' and that it was such a departure
from all the wealth back in Vienna. But I was at my happiest
living in that little attic.*

Maria took a liking to a neighbor named Maria Reitler. It was
soon discovered they had been schoolmates in Vienna. Years later
they would inadvertently end up living down the street from each
other in the same neighborhood in Beverly Hills, and would
remain best friends until Reitler's death in 2006.

Life in Liverpool was so tolerable that Maria became
pregnant, and began to teach her husband English.

*To be honest I had a much easier time dealing with the
Nazis. For some reason Fritz couldn't nail down the word,
'snow.' "Say 'snow,'" I would say. He got so frustrated... "If
'now' is pronounced, 'now', then why the hell is 'snow'
pronounced 'snow'"? So one evening Fritz's English was put
to the test. He was invited to sing Baritone—all in English—
at a church, in a production of "The Creation" by Joseph
Haydn. I was recovering from a miscarriage and wasn't
feeling well so I gave my concert ticket to Ms. Mason, our
Charlady. The next day I was eager to learn how the concert
went, so I asked her, 'Did you enjoy Fritz's singing?' To
which Ms. Mason—who spoke perfect English—replied, 'How
could I enjoy it? It was foreign!'*

### December 1939

Within a year, the Altmanns had to leave England.

*We were really loving it, the people, the country, everything,
and we would have lived there for a long time, but you see
we were in danger of being labeled "enemy aliens" and being
"interned" on The Isle of Man. We had to move almost
immediately. And that's when the whole Blitz happened.*

Before leaving England, Maria and Fritz celebrated their one-year wedding anniversary in the quiet of the home they were about to abandon.

Sobering numbers were coming from Vienna—of the five thousand priests sent to Dachau since Fritz's release, three thousand had been brutally murdered, and Lord knows how many other innocent people were perishing by the hour. One thousand six hundred and sixty eight synagogues in Austria had been ransacked or destroyed.

> *One of them was the Turnertempel—the synagogue where Fritz and I were married.*

It was clear they had escaped in the nick of time.

### *Fall River, Massachusetts*

Bernhard, now also an enemy alien in England, was forced to desert his flourishing factory. He turned his attention to the States, and with the money he made from his short-lived success in Liverpool, he opened a new factory in Fall River, Massachusetts. He offered Fritz another job, which Fritz took. Fritz and Maria embarked on a ship called the *Britannic*, "The Sister Ship of the *Titanic*." They reached America safely. On the ship's return to the UK, it was attacked and sunk by a German U-boat.

In Fall River, while Fritz worked at his brother's factory, Maria conceived her first child. She named him Charles Gustav Altmann.

> *I always said Chuck was like a cashmere sweater: made in England, and imported to America. We raised him on English. German was the enemy language.*

## Fall River
## August 9, 1940

As Maria lay in a hospital bed in Fall River holding baby Charles, a nurse walked in with a letter dated two months prior:

> My Precious Maria. I am sure by now you have had a beautiful baby boy.
>
> Love, Emma.

> *It was one of the last things Emma wrote before she died. We would always talk about my having a baby boy for my first child. We both just had a feeling. I arranged for a pine tree to be planted at her grave in Vienna. She always wanted her very own Christmas tree.*

## Summer, 1942
## Los Angeles

Maria, Fritz, and two-year-old Chuck decided to leave Bernhard behind in Fall River and board a Los Angeles-bound train filled with American soldiers ready for war. Little did the Altmanns know as they headed west that they would spend the remainder of their lives in the City of Angels.

> *I heard this joke when we first moved to Los Angeles: "One friend says to the other... 'They are still just as anti-Semitic here as they were in Vienna.' To give you an idea, I was in the grocery store the other day, and I asked the worker, "Do you have oranges for juice (Jews)?" The worker said, 'Sure, the small ones, right over there.'*

When they arrived they found a modest one-bedroom house on Horn Avenue above Sunset Boulevard. Rent was $40 a month, with a backyard full of chickens, and a porch overlooking a Victory Garden.

*I remember Fritz and I looked out the window above Sunset Boulevard one morning, and all of Hollywood was covered in snow. It made the city look just magical. It hasn't happened since.*

The house across the street belonged to Humphrey Bogart and Lauren Bacall.

*It was awful. They used to keep us up in the middle of the night, drunk, screaming and yelling at each other. Quite a healthy relationship, don't you think?*

Thankfully Maria's mother had been able to fly out of Vienna two years earlier to live with Poldi in Vancouver. She flew to Los Angeles to visit.

*My mother loved picking up the eggs in our garden! You see, there were always people that did that sort of thing back in Vienna, so to her it was new, and great fun.*

Maria became pregnant for a third time, but she decided to have her second abortion.

*It wouldn't have made sense. We didn't have enough money.*

Fritz landed a job with Lockheed Aircraft. He began taking the bus to work.

*I couldn't bear to see Fritz take that bus every morning, so I sold my engagement ring—the one he had bought to replace the one the Gestapo took—for $6,000, and got him a Chevy. He was so proud to be in America, and to own an American car.*

At Lockheed, it didn't take long for Fritz to organize an opera group. He and a few colleagues met at his house twice a week. While they practiced in the living room Maria made dinner, and afterwards they'd all pile into the kitchen for a special taste of

Vienna: Wiener Schnitzel, potatoes blended with four types of vinegar, a dill cucumber salad, and homemade Strudel for dessert.

Now that Fritz had a car and a steady job, and Chuck was old enough to start school, Maria was at home with little to do.

### New York, 1942

Bernhard's factory in Fall River had failed. He had been living in New York for the previous few months, settling for a lowly job at a yarn manufacturer in Manhattan earning about $50 a week. In his spare time he focused on what had been his passion during his heyday in Vienna: cashmere, and a pattern called "argyle." Both were well known and distributed throughout England and most of Europe, but the states hadn't seen either product, at least on a mass scale. He saw a golden opportunity.

> *Bernhard sent me a package, and inside there was a note that said, 'See what you can do with these in California,' and he included a cashmere sweater and a pair of argyle socks.*

### Fall, 1944

One morning a tall, striking woman wearing argyle socks and a beige cashmere sweater—not knowing the first thing about sales—strode through the front door of Kerr's, a posh sporting goods store in Beverly Hills, and asked the lady at the front desk if she could speak to the buyer.

> *He said five words any salesman would dream of hearing—'How many may we buy?'*

Bernhard had delivered the goods, and Maria had delivered the charm. The first sale later led to the building of her dressmaking business in and around Beverly Hills, catering specifically to middle-aged women. What Maria loved more than anything was dealing one-on-one with her customers. Spencer Tracy's mother was on a long list of her many satisfied ones. Maria would travel as far as Italy or France to find that perfect outfit for her "women." She would eventually run her boutique business out of her own home until she retired in 2006, at age 90.

*Jimmy used to love to joke around. An ugly, high-pitched voice would call on the phone, saying, 'I am five feet tall, I weigh 250 pounds, and I'm a size 18—can you find a dress for me?' The voices he could do! He'd fool me every time!*

Bernhard eventually built his biggest factory to date in Texas. By the 1950s, Altmann Cashmere Sweaters became a multi-million dollar empire. At the height of Bernhard's success it was estimated that one in every three cashmere sweaters made in America came directly from his Texas mill.

**1944—1998**
**Los Angeles**

Over the next five decades, Maria ran her dressmaking business and Fritz worked as a sales representative for Altmann Cashmere Sweaters. They became parents of three sons and one daughter—Chuck, Peter, Margie and Jim, and became grandparents of five grandsons and one granddaughter—Philip and Ken from Chuck, and Greg, James, Garrett, and Alana from Jim.

On their thirtieth wedding anniversary in 1967, Fritz gave Maria a gift—her original engagement ring. Somehow he had gotten it back from the Gestapo who stole it nearly 30 years earlier. It was a reminder of the storms they endured together, and the love they would share forever. Fritz died in 1994. Maria would become a great-grandparent alone.

**Fall, 1998**
**Los Angeles**

At 82 years old, after nearly three decades staring at the same framed *Gold Portrait* poster of her Aunt Adele hanging on her living room wall in Cheviot Hills knowing full well that the original in Vienna belonged to her family and not to Austria, Maria decided that if she was ever going to do it in her lifetime, she'd better do it now. So she did.

  "The Altmann verdict was earth-shattering," says Ori Soltes, Chairman of the Holocaust Art Restitution Project in Washington. "Not only because of the fame of the Klimts and the value of the works, but because it completely revamps Austria's position in this whole issue, pushing them toward the head of the class of trying to right wrongs."

Before launching the lawsuit Maria sent numerous letters to the Austrian government in an attempt to make a deal out of court. They were all ignored.

Chuck spoke passionately about this. "My mother, being the reasonable woman she was, didn't want to have to sue Austria. All she really wanted was to get an apology—some sort of acknowledgement that they took the paintings. But they were so arrogant and so nasty to her, that they basically dared her to sue them. This really got her angry. It brought out her toughness, and boy, my mother could be tough when she wanted to. They really messed with the wrong woman. From that moment on she made it her life's work to win."

Once Maria's gloves were off her strength and charisma opened the eyes and hearts of everyone who heard her speak. Early on an Austrian consulate reportedly watched an interview with her talking about her aunt, and he told a colleague there was no way they'd win if a woman this dynamic was at the helm.

"They weren't so much scared of Randy," Chuck went on, "they were scared of my mother, and how charming she was. They saw her as a threat."

"Maria was the star," said Steven Thomas, the lawyer who negotiated the sale of the paintings. Maria and Steven had spent nearly every day together for a year going over all the financial possibilities for the Klimts. "There were a lot of people who had a hand in her case, but it was *The Maria Altmann Show* from the beginning."

While Randy was clearly the brilliance behind the curtain, Maria was the actor on center stage. As the lead actor she was provocative when she needed to be, and tenacious when she had to be. She told the *Los Angeles Times* in 2001: "They will delay, delay, delay, hoping I will die, but I will do them the pleasure of staying alive." And she told a reporter post-verdict: "They asked me, 'Would you loan them to us again?' and I said, 'We loaned them to you for 68 years. Enough loans.'"

It was never about the money. The marriage of Ferdinand Bloch to Adele Bauer on December 19, 1899, not only merged one of the most cultured and connected families in Western Europe at the turn of the century, it gave us, on February 18, 1916, a child who in all practicality should have grown up out of touch with the world. It should have given us someone who didn't understand the value of money.

Aside from paying out her lawyers and the other three heirs in Canada, her portion of the purse was distributed to her family, organizations like the Los Angeles opera and the UCLA Medical Center, and to various charities around the world. She never spent a dime of that Klimt money on herself. For one, in the thick of her newfound fame and fortune she continued to call home her modest, one-story redwood bungalow with all the original wallpaper and carpets and dishware. And she lived entirely off her pension from her dressmaking business. This, from someone whose parents and Aunt Adele would host cocktail parties and salons where the likes of composer Gustav Mahler and opera star Leo Slezak could be seen milling about.

Maria was never comfortable in this world of ostentation, raised not to need the normal accoutrements of wealth. Her mother helped shape her daughter's humble views, teaching her children that money and status didn't come with a license to show it off.

"My mother came from a wealthy family, and when she was an adult she went from having five servants, to having to do everything herself. As a child all my friends were given big allowances, but she made a point to give us all very little pocket money—only about 50 cents a week. And I always had the ugliest clothes!"

This early understanding of the value of a dollar helped Maria adopt an attitude of gratitude, and enabled her to truly live her life in the moment. At 92 the world is still her oyster; everything is a miracle, every day she's a child playing in a playground, that flower growing determinedly through the crack in the sidewalk. Postal workers, waiters, or the Gestapo—she treats everyone with the same respect she gives her family, exploiting the beauty and splendor in everyone, under every circumstance.

On April 4, 2006, during the press conference and official unveiling at the LACMA Museum in Los Angeles, a reporter asked, "Mrs. Altmann, did you know Klimt?"

Maria casually lifted her microphone and responded: "I am old... but not that old."

The room erupted in laughter. It was clear the press wouldn't be dealing with your average 90-year-old woman. And it's clear I'm not either.

*June 6, 2008*

(Maria and Francis off the Coast of Dalmatia in 1937)

*"She put her head in an oven."*

I had arrived at the house early and was reading the paper in the kitchen, when Chuck—as naked as the day he was born—walked leisurely out of his room and weighed himself on the scale outside of his door. I froze, quietly lifting the paper above my head to avoid any early morning gasps. He never noticed me, thank goodness. He disappeared into his room and meandered out moments later wearing his usual plaid L.L. Bean nightshirt from the 80s. He sat down with a bowl of cereal and I grilled him about his father. Here was what I found most worthy of immortalizing:

"When I was 21, my friend Dick and I were arrested for petty theft, and had to appear in court in front of a judge, where we were given a fine. Somehow Dick's fine was $100, and mine was only $50. So since we were 'in it together' Dick demanded that I split the fine evenly with him—$75 each. Well I didn't want to give it to him, and I was torn about how to handle it. So I asked my father for his advice. He told me, 'You can't buy a friend with 50 bucks, but you can certainly lose a friend with 50.'"

We moved to Mom.

"God, my mother put so much energy into that case. I mean, she was close to 90, and she was travelling, she was fielding nonstop interviews, she was just beyond amazing. You should have seen her! There were four, maybe five interviewers in her living room at once, and she would turn to one and speak French, she'd turn to the other and speak Italian, turn to the other and speak German. When the paintings came in, it was one big celebration. Then all of a sudden it's like she aged twenty years. She started to really look and feel like an old woman for the first time in her life. It's almost like she had done her job, and was ready to step back and just... die. But then we found Tom, and then you, and she's really found her old self. You more than anyone else make her young. She has a reason to live."

Chuck kept telling me I should have met her when she was younger. I told him I've come to realize I already have.

He went into his office and I went to wake Maria to get ready for a routine check-up with Dr. Fox, her dermatologist. "She's far more excited than one should be about skin," Maria said lethargically as she struggled out of bed. Dr. Fox and Maria sat chatting away like old girlfriends for ten minutes before the exam even began. Maria has this friendly rapport with all her doctors.

Sometimes it seems like she just sits in a room for ten minutes socializing with them and then goes home, like with Rebecca. Her foot doctor, Dr. Alongi, came over for dinner last year, and she's always inviting Susan, Dr. Taw's assistant, over for dinner. Everyone Maria meets seems to be invited to the house for a home-cooked Viennese meal. And I'm always the one who ends up cooking it!

We decided to eat a late breakfast at Norms, on Pico. I ordered the Sausage Lover's plate, and Maria ordered a giant waffle with fresh strawberries and whipped cream. Between bites she shared a story about her nephew Francis.

"In 1938, when Hitler came to Vienna, the governess who looked after Francis was forced to leave her job. This was a new law that Hitler mandated, that it was now illegal for Germans to care for Jews. She loved him so much and was so distraught that she couldn't care for him anymore, she put her head in an oven. Francis walked in and found her bent over like that."

When she was finished with her waffle, she looked at me, convinced I'd find what she was about to say amusing.

"What would you like to have when I croak?" I acted like I was looking for the bathroom and got up before I had to answer.

————◆————

Johannes Czernin—the brother of Hubertus, the Viennese Journalist who first published articles about the suspicious ownership of the Klimts—and his wife, Gertraud, were headed to the house. Knowing they were coming to take her to dinner, Maria described Johannes' reaction to Hubertus's sudden death in 2006.

"When Hubertus died, Johannes called me, sobbing like a little boy. You know, when a man cries, I melt. I go to pieces. There's so much power in it. When a woman cries? I don't feel a thing."

I don't like Maria to leave the house twice in one day, but the Czernins were taking her back to their home in the Pacific Palisades.

When I let her go I stood at the front door like a father seeing his daughter off on prom night.

"Make sure to stay close to her when you walk her!" I yelled as they walked down the driveway. "And try and cut up the meat for her in small pieces, so she doesn't choke!" I stood there watching and waving as the car disappeared over the hill. I did everything short of yell, "And use protection!"

Dear God, look who I've become.

June 11, 2008

*"Look, she wants to fuck."*

I realized this morning as I got ready to leave for Cheviot Hills, that I haven't been on a date since I met Maria. This hasn't been intentional, it's just the way the cookie has crumbled. And what's sort of weird is that after thinking about this in the car the whole way, Maria greeted me at the house with a first ever peck on the lips. It was an intimacy only she and I shared, a moment only she and I understood.

This morning over breakfast Maria had much more to tell about her insanely handsome brother, Poldi. When he was 22 he suffered a tragedy he would never get over his entire life. His best friend's wife had fallen in love with him—and he was in love with her too—but he couldn't act on it because he could never betray his best friend. So Poldi was forced to shun the woman he loved and could never have, every chance he got. One day she was found hanging by her bathrobe tie. If she couldn't have Poldi, she didn't want to live. She left behind a four year-old son named Frederic.

"I remember that day like it was yesterday," Maria said. "I was twelve years old, and I walked into Poldi's room. He was slumped over on his bed looking at pictures of her, roses strewn all over the floor, his hands buried in his face, sobbing like a little boy. He never got over her."

Maria offered an ending to the story that seemed right out of a movie. About 45 years after the suicide, around the early 70s, Poldi, then living in Vancouver with Therese, answered a knock at the door. It was a well-dressed man who looked to be in his 60's, who introduced himself as Frederic de Hoffman. "Are you Leopold Bloch-Bauer?" the man asked. Poldi confirmed he was. Then Mr. Hoffman asked the question he had travelled halfway around the world to ask. "Are you my father?" After a few back-and-forths it was learned that this man standing before Poldi was the son of the woman he loved who'd killed herself. Mr. Hoffman had known about Poldi and his mother's love for each other, and had found Poldi in a phonebook. Poldi took Frederic to lunch, and reassured him he wasn't his father. It turns out Mr. Hoffman was the current President of the Salk Institute, one of the premier institutions in America for scientific research. He had made quite a life for himself despite his childhood tragedy.

Maria says beautiful women threw themselves at Poldi, and he just "brushed them aside as if they were nothing."

After the suicide he married a woman whom he stayed with for the rest of his life. Maria said of this new woman, "she could have been a nun. She was devoid of any charm or sex. I think he married her to feel better. He could never truly love another woman."

I asked her what sorts of things made Poldi happy, and she said, "Hockey. Poldi loved hockey."

I feel a certain kinship with Poldi, maybe because I, too, tend to brush women aside for no reason, save the one sitting next to me. I hope you deem me worthy of your little sister, Herr Bloch-Bauer.

———————◆———————

It was an afternoon rife with stories, and Maria was tired from talking. She went down for a nap. I woke her up an hour later to remind her that Tina, her physical trainer, was coming for a workout. When she was dressed in her purple velvet jumpsuit, she plopped back down on her bed out of breath.

"I don't want to work out today but I know you want me to so I will do it." She forced herself into a standing position.

As she extended her arms and twisted her hips during the workout, she said, "I feel like an old wind mill." Then she said, "I feel like the Christians in Rome," and later, "like the horses in Vienna."

At one point, Tina, who is like a spry little spider-monkey with the most unbelievable legs I have ever seen on a woman, yelled, "C'mon! Stick that butt out!"

Maria, smirking, stopped to glare at her. "How elegant."

She told her she was sadistic, and that she felt sorry for her boyfriend, who is a Santa Monica cop. Maria loves to say to her, "I want your boyfriend to come here and arrest me."

Tina attempted her escape after the workout, but Maria was too quick for her, of course not letting her leave without edible parting gifts.

Tina said what I always say: "I don't think any one person has ever offered me more food in my life than you, Maria!"

I asked Maria about the Christians and horse references. "The Romans used to make the Christians do funny tricks and then laugh at them," she said. "The horses in Vienna used to slip on the ice in the winter and lay on the ground like a pretzel. It was so sad. I wanted to help them."

The ducks are back, only now it's a heterosexual couple. We sat observing them in silence sitting at the edge of the pool. Suddenly the female sprang up and started ruffling her feathers and jumping around. Maria, with her eyes locked on the scene, said, "Look, she wants to fuck."

Hey, All;

Mutzi wheeled her way into the kitchen this morning with pep in her step. Her voice was crisp and clear, in fact she started telling me about how Tom was to go on an important audition today, and asked me how catering at the Walt Disney Hall was last night. I've rarely seen her more acute and on the ball. Tina came for a visit, and she of course rose to the occasion despite threatening to cancel her.

We ended up postponing Alongi, instead we went to the hair salon. I dropped her off and took a walk around the block. When I returned, my worst fear seemed realized. I couldn't find her! I paced around the entire salon. The customers were beginning to wonder if I was nuts. I started thinking she may have wandered off down the street. I was growing frantic. Then I was beside myself. How in the hell could these people let a 92-year-old woman just wander off?? Are they that into themselves?? Does the world really just revolve around them??

I finally implored the nail lady to tell me where she went. Her answer: "She's sitting right in front of you." I looked down and there Maria was in all her splendor, looking up at me. Exhale.

I suggested Scrabble later in the afternoon since we hadn't played in a whole week. She was sharp as a tack. Virtually no time in between turns to think. I beat her (not physically), but only because I got lucky with a "Z" on a triple letter score, which bled into a double word score. Don't want to brag, but 72 points in one turn, thank you very much. She was in such a peppy mood today that she even accused me of cheating.

It's within the next two hours that we had one of the most pleasant conversations we've ever had. It was just me, Mutzi, two Coronas, and a German candy that tasted like "soap." We shared jokes, and we talked about girls and rabbits and opera.

I know one day she's like a million bucks, one day she's like 900,000, and I don't mean to overlook the times she's not on top of the world, but I tell you, I feel lucky to cherish the good ones while she's here with us.

-Gregor

*June 21, 2008*

*"What has four legs and chases cats?"*

Chuck walked in this morning in a playful mood. Maria, of course, immediately put down the paper to give her son her full attention. They went back and forth with inside jokes.

Maria asked, "What has four legs and chases cats?"

Chuck answered, "Mrs. Katz and her attorney."

They both rolled with laughter.

"So after everyone goes to sleep," Chuck went on with a sardonic smile, "three mice raid the fridge. They all sit around eating cheese and drinking wine. One really drunk mouse stands up and says, 'All right! I'm gonna go fuck the cat!'"

Margie and Myron, who live in Hawaii, arrived at the house, in town to see an opera at the Music Center. I let Margie dote on her mother for a few hours while I did a few errands. Then Peter showed up from Tacoma, snuck in the front door, and asked where Mom was. I pointed to the kitchen and he pulled out his cell phone, dialed the home line, and waited in the wings for her to answer.

Maria picked up the phone on the wall. "Hello?"

"Hello, Mother, it's your son, Peter."

"Hello, Pootzle!"

"I'm just here in Tacoma."

"Well good, honey, what can I do for you?"

Peter took this as his cue to round the corner and enter the kitchen. Maria, still with the phone glued to her ear, looked up and saw her son suddenly materialize in front of her. Stunned into submission, she kept the phone to her ear. He put his phone in his pocket and went to hug her. She still clung to hers as they hugged and yelled: "Wait! Don't hang up! My Peter's on the phone!"

When Peter has to go you can see the pain in her eyes: "I'm very sad. But it's a sadness that will pass."

Every moment she spends with Peter and Margie is cherished, what with them living so far away.

Maria treats death in a lighthearted manner. "When I croak..." she says often. Margie says her mother used to fear it a lot when she was younger.

I don't think anyone will ever know what it feels like to be at peace with death until death is knocking, and they feel a peace. I look at retirement homes differently now. Elderly people living in them seem to have little else to do other than sit in foldup chairs outside, staring at the pigeons or the people walking by. Every so often they have visitors, who leave as quickly as they come. It's a lonely end to a life, an end Maria is lucky to be avoiding because she has the money to pay people. Young men. Young men who have youth and innocence. She can see and touch them every day. What a lucky woman who deserves every ounce of it.

I constantly see firsthand how I'm adding years to this woman's life. I'm so grateful. Which is strange. I'm feeling gratitude at what I'm giving to someone else. I've always just felt gratitude only for what I was given.

*July 2, 2008*

(Gustav Klimt and his cat Katze, circa 1912)

*"How dare you ask such a question!*
*It was an intellectual friendship!"*

I popped my head into Maria's room to see if she was still asleep this morning, and she caught a glimpse of my shadow.

"Hello? Who is that?"

When she saw me she slapped the bed sheets like a seal. "C'mere! C'mere!" I sat down next to her. "How was your weekend? Did you find some fun ones to be naughty with?" I raised an eyebrow, and, suddenly losing her energy, she warned, "Don't be too naughty, or it might fall off."

Knowing Maria and Fritz were neighbors to television and film actor Danny Thomas, I told her I was at Canter's yesterday—an old Jewish deli on Fairfax—and noticed there was a hot salami sandwich on the menu called "The Danny Thomas." Maria still remembered one of his famous routines, called "The Golden Jack Story."

I cut and pasted the original version from the internet. It hearkens back to a time when comedy was told with clean, clever stories.

> "There was this traveling salesman who got stuck one night on a lonely country road with a flat tire and no jack. So he starts walking toward a service station about a mile away, and as he walks, he talks to himself... 'How much can he charge me for renting a jack? One dollar, maybe two? But it's the middle of the night, so maybe there's an after-hours fee. Probably another five dollars. If he's anything like my brother-in-law, he'll figure I got no place else to go for the jack, so he's cornered the market and has me at his mercy. Ten dollars more!' He goes on walking and thinking, and the price and the anger keeps rising. Finally, he gets to the service station and is greeted cheerfully by the owner: 'What can I do for you, Sir?' But the salesman will have none of it. 'You got the nerve to talk to me, you robber," he says. "You can take your stinkin' jack and...!"

Chuck ambled in to contribute to the conversation about a man for whom he had the utmost respect. "Danny was a real class act. He never swore. He was the only clean act in Vegas." He went on. "Once Danny was turning part of his front yard into a circular driveway—this was popular at the time—and my dad noticed and yelled across the street, 'What's going on over there?' And Danny yelled back, 'I lost a quarter!'" Chuck also mentioned Danny handed out full-sized candy bars every Halloween. "Needless to say he was a favorite of all the kids in the neighborhood."

"One day Fritz was playing the piano and practicing his singing," Maria went on. "It was a hot summer day and we had the windows open. Suddenly the phone rang. 'Hello?' I said. A voice on the other end yelled, 'Tell your husband the talent is on *this* side of the street!'"

Fritz never made it as an opera singer. "There were so little opportunities, maybe two operas in the entire country—New York and San Francisco. He had a good voice, just not a great voice. Today, there are dozens of operas. He would have worked as a singer in today's world." Fritz also wanted to be an actor. "He was featured as a German U-Boat Captain in a movie once," Maria continued, "and he invited everyone he knew to see a showing of it. About halfway through he turned to me and whispered, 'Look, my part is coming up!' Well it never came. It had been cut it out. He was absolutely devastated."

Because she went through it with Fritz, Maria understands the artistic struggle. She pines away when I talk about how difficult it is to make it as an actor. I try not to talk about it because I know how much she loves me and how much it hurts her to hear it, not to mention how it hurts me. She's convinced every director who sees me act should want me in their film.

This afternoon I invited my acting counselor, Jeffrey Marcus, over for lunch. I told him a few weeks ago I was caregiving for a woman named Maria from Vienna. He asked what her last name was, and when I told him, he couldn't believe I was caregiving for the same woman about whom he had written a screenplay. He came to the house this afternoon with an orchid, Maria's favorite flower.

We sat in the living room sipping tea and California chardonnay and eating Brie and wheat crackers. At one point Jeffrey asked, "Did Adele and Klimt... you know...?"

Maria put down her tea and smiled wisely. "The number one question people ask me is, 'Did Adele and Klimt have an affair?' When I was little I would ask my mother, 'Did Adele have an affair with Klimt?' And she would say, 'How dare you ask such a question! It was an intellectual friendship!' There was a pause, and Jeffrey and I were on the edge of our seats awaiting her final response: "So... I'm sure they did."

Jeffrey left, and Maria called him her favorite word: "Fabulous." We sat in the living room in comfortable silence, until we found ourselves talking about Jim.

A few years ago, he and his mother were staying in a hotel in Vienna. Jim told her there was a brothel across the street, and he asked, "Mom, can I borrow $100?"

His mother replied reluctantly: "I'll give it to you only because your father would have given it to you."

Jim returned later and wanted her to meet the Madame. "Then he started going on and on about the décor, how ornate it was. He said the couches had this yellow satin cloth that I just had to see. He was nuts if he thought I was going to walk into a brothel!" Later, she met the madam to appease her son. "She was actually very nice."

Maria and Jimmy are best buddies. He begs her to stay at his house every weekend. "If he had his way, we'd be roommates," she says, jokingly rolling her eyes. He calls the house constantly asking if his mother can "come out and play." And she'll never say no to him because she doesn't ever want to let him down. He's got a big heart, so big he doesn't know what to do with it. I think Maria's passing is going to hurt him the most. She's concerned he won't be able to handle it, and has told me on a number of occasions.

Jeffrey just sent an email to me tonight. "Maria is one of my heroes. Thank you."

Hey Y'all;

Chris said Mutzi fell last night. She was making soup and tumbled backwards near the fridge. We're EXTREMELY lucky she's okay, but let's all take heed of this. I'm a fan of letting her do things herself, because I think she appreciates having some of her independence, but we have to stand right behind her when she's doing it, without seeming overbearing. This is a heads up for Peter too, when he visits again in a couple weeks.

-Gee

*July 14, 2008*

*"Who was that handsome man in that truck earlier?"*

We were nearly up the steep slope of the driveway after a stroll around the block, and suddenly Maria lost strength in her legs and down she went. I caught her, luckily, before her limp body slammed against the pavement. I lowered her as best I could to the ground, and sat her there on the concrete like a teddy bear I'd won at a carnival. I tried to pick her up under her arms, but couldn't, because she didn't have enough strength to help me. She was confused and dizzy, and we could do nothing but sit there and wonder what to do next. I thought about calling Tom, but what could he do all the way in the valley? I looked around for a Cheviot Hills angel, and one happened to be driving a Sparkett's Water truck. I flagged it down, and it stopped in the middle of the street and spit out a driver who ran to help me pick up Maria. We each lifted an underarm, and carried her into the house and dumped her onto the bed like a sack of potatoes. She regained enough consciousness to tell me to get her purse and give him twenty dollars.

This is the second fall in two weeks. She's been getting dizzy on a moment's notice more often. Tom says it's called orthostatic hypotension, which is caused by suddenly plummeting blood pressure.

An hour or so after the Sparklett's man had left it suddenly occurred to her to ask, "Who was that handsome man in that truck earlier?"

Then I took her blood pressure and she said, "All you have to do is walk into a room, and my blood pressure skyrockets."

While I dabbed a little extra make-up off her nose with a Kleenex, she said playfully, "Listen, I'm not a carpet. You can't just go dabbing me like a carpet."

The topic of women always arises at a moment's notice. She loves to ask, "Have you met any young ones?" On one hand she wishes I had a woman, and on the other she's secretly glad I'm all hers.

When she was up from her nap it was as if the fall never happened. We played our daily Scrabble game. At one point she placed the word "NA" on the board. I told her it wasn't a word. "Sure it is," she said. "My mother used to say, 'Na! Na!' When she wanted me to stop doing something." Later I spelled "Meth." She asked what it was, and I told her it was a drug.

"What kind of a drug?" she asked.

"This nasty drug that ages you prematurely."

"Obviously not my kind of drug."

So many games we play. We invented a drinking game. Since I've built up somewhat of a reputation as a chef here at Cafe Altmann, she's always excited to know what I'm making for dinner. "What does the chef have prepared for the night?"

So I said this afternoon, "What we're having tonight starts with a $p$, an $r$, and an $a$. Each time you guess incorrectly, you have to drink."

She was game, no pun intended. "Poultry!" she said, sure she was right.

"Drink!" I demanded. "The r is obviously rice," she said confidently.

"Drink!" I said again. She couldn't believe she had to drink again, but she did. Seeing that she was taking direction so easily, I was convinced she would have eventually drunk to inebriation in the interest of ensuring I was having a good time. So I spared her.

"For protein, think pig." Her eyes widened... "Pork Chops!"

Prepared for another "no," she got a "Yes!" The $r$ and the $a$? Red potatoes and asparagus.

I've never been able to play this way with a woman I was attracted to before. Boy. One chance meeting has turned into a thousand one-night stands.

*July 20, 2008*

(Peter, Margie, Chuck, Jim)

*"It's not that I'm trying to molest you..."*

Agent: "You have an audition tomorrow at 1:45 in Santa Monica."

Me: "I don't think I can make it. I have to take Maria to the doctor, I just—"

Silence.

Me: "Maybe I can try to... no, I'm just going to have to skip it. I'm sorry."

Agent: "You have to do what you have to do."

Seeing auditions more as nuisances these days would have scared me even a few weeks ago, but now I know where I am, why I'm here, and where I'm going. I really don't care about them to be honest. Unless the auditions are really big and important and doable, I miss at least one every two weeks, and my agent is clearly chagrinned about this. I used to get Tom to fill in for every single audition that arose, even ones for those cheesy Scientology videos (every struggling actor out here has auditioned for them at least once), but now these days I can't find a reason any of them are more important than Maria.

I'm having more fun at the house anyway. I've discovered how to inject more zest into administering Maria's eye drops in the morning. As kids, Peter and Chuck were into baby turtles. According to Maria everyone just had to have baby turtles in the fifties. One day she heard a scream from Peter's room. She ran in to find Peter and Chuck jockeying for position over the turtle cage. Peter complained that Chuck's turtle was sitting on his turtle, and was suffocating it to death. "Do something Mom, do something! He's gonna die!" Maria asked, "How do you know which one is yours?" Peter responded, "Mine goes like this," and he impersonated his turtle by blinking his eyes for dramatic effect. So, after I drop the drops in her eye, as she sits there in displeasure, all I need to say is, "Okay, now blink like Peter's turtle." She laughs every time. Maria impersonating Peter impersonating his turtle is worth any ticket price.

Maria was always solving problems. When Peter was eight or nine, he had a parakeet named Jacquo, which he named after his father's parakeet. One day, Jacquo was out of his cage exploring Peter's room, and Margie inadvertently swung open the door and smashed him against the wall, killing him. Peter, thank goodness, wasn't home.

Maria learned of the accident, took the dead bird to a pet shop, slapped it onto the counter and said, "Match this bird." They gave her one that looked the same and she took it home and put it back in Peter's room before he returned home.

Later Peter looked at his bird strangely. "Mom, why does Jacquo have bug-eyes?" Maria couldn't keep the lie going. She came clean, and took the blame for Margie.

———————◆———————

Today on the way to her general physician, Doctor Hartenbower, I wanted to turn right on red, and there was a Nimrod ahead of me with his right blinker on refusing to turn right despite the lack of a "No Turn On Red" sign or any cars in sight. I honked and inched closer to his bumper to make my point, but he was so lost in his own world that I was dead to him. I never intended to hit him, I just wanted to get really close to scare him into moving along, but I was in the Klimt and its front end is longer than my tiny Toyota's front end, so I misjudged it and accidentally tapped his back bumper. Maria felt the tap and immediately came to my defense, as if it were the driver's fault he was in my way.

"That old goose," she said dismissively. "You didn't do anything wrong, darling."

I waved to the guy, who only now realized I wasn't dead, and he waved back, and was on his way.

Dr. H strolled into our little white waiting room with his familiar cunning smirk. He's her oldest doctor. They've known each other for 30 years. He operated on Fritz in the 80s, and after the successful procedure he called Maria and said, "We like your husband so much, we've decided to keep him." Today he felt around Maria's head and neck, and she turned to me with a shrewd grin and said, "Are you watching this? I may need you as a witness."

As Dr. H stepped out of the room she leaned in close to my ear and said in a loud whisper, "He dyes his hair," as if it were some big secret only she knew. I was sure he heard her through the door. I offered my silent disdain, then shushed her and showed her I was serious by staring at her and rolling my eyes. She quieted, folded her hands, bowed her head, and sank into her chair.

As I helped her into the car, she grabbed my arm for stability, warning, "It's not that I'm trying to molest you—I'm very wobbly." It was funny enough. But when we got home, she needed my arm for stability again, and this time, warned, "It's not that I'm wobbly—I'm trying to molest you." I texted this one to Margie. She roared with laughter.

On the way home we picked up some wurstel for lunch and brought it home. Bernhard and his cashmere arose.

Apparently the only place in the world cashmere goats can be bred is in the Himalayas, an area that has the perfect temperature, perfect surroundings, perfect everything. Like champagne in France. The Swiss thought they'd attempt to "outsmart" this system, figuring if they had similar weather and the same general surroundings as the Himalayas, they would be able to breed a cashmere goat.

"You can't fool a cashmere goat," Maria said. "The Swiss goats turned into regular goats."

She explained how the cashmere goats rub their backs against the thorny bushes, and how the farmers pick the fur off the bushes to be made into clothing. "There's a portion down the middle of the goat's back dubbed the cashmere portion of the goat," she said as she lightly ran her finger down the middle of mine to illustrate.

Bernhard wrote the book on cashmere. Literally. It's sitting in her old desk in the living room, dated 1947, the year of its introduction to America. Bernhard also made sweaters and coats out of a llama-like animal called a vicuña, said to yield the finest wool on earth.

Chuck and Donna walked in.

"We have a terrific marriage, Mother," Chuck declared.

Donna chimed in. "Yeah, as long as we stay away from each other."

Then Chuck announced, "Donna wants me to get jeans to fit my ass better."

Donna modeled his backside for Maria, who said, "But you don't have an ass, Sweetheart."

Later, Chuck admitted to me he'd resisted Donna for years. Early in their relationship he went to a shrink. "There's something about her that really bothers me, and it's holding me back from really liking her," Chuck told the shrink. "And I'll never forget this. He said, 'Well do you think there's something about *you* that bothers *her?*' From that moment forth I fully embraced Donna."

Dear You People!

We have an interesting problem here at the house—Maria keeps giving away umbrellas. As you know by now, she's a sucker for a charming guest, and for some reason she is obsessed with offering, of all things, umbrellas to these people. Not cookies. Not candy. Umbrellas. And apparently she's got a lifetime's supply of them. Perhaps it's because she has so many of them, or that it pains her to think of people getting wet. Where did she get all these? Anyway, I've written Tom a note to pick up some more at Costco, and we'll find a good hiding spot to keep them away from The Umbrella Thief.

## *July 28, 2008*

*"He took his shotgun, walked into his backyard..."*

I told Maria we had a free day today and asked her what she wanted to do, and she said, "Go to bed with you."

When she saw I had no witty comeback she started laughing, and exclaimed, "I just wanted to see the fear in your face!"

After breakfast on the way to her room, she told me about a rash she was battling over the weekend. I asked her where it was, and she responded: "You would have enjoyed the area when I was sixteen."

When I woke Maria from her nap in the early afternoon, I said, "Let's swim!" She lost her smile, and called me what she calls Tina on some occasions: "Sadistic."

I laid the bathing suit on her bed, and told her I'd be back in five minutes. When I returned, she was back under the covers, fast asleep. I rubbed her shoulder and she opened her eyes with a guilty smirk.

"Okay, my love, I will get dressed, I promise."

I returned ten minutes later, and she was in the suit... only she was passed out again. At least she was in it.

Maria is quite the swimmer. Her limited mobility on land is almost entirely freed up in water. I like to go in with her, and we tread water together in the deep end and she tells me stories, like today, about when she was a child and how she used to swim in the cold lakes of Vienna. Then we moved to her husband.

"Fritz was driving his new Chevy down Sunset, and there was a rather revealing billboard of Jayne Mansfield, and he looked up at it a little too long, and crashed right into the post that was holding it up. I can't say that it taught him any lessons."

This segued into Jayne Mansfield, who was allegedly decapitated in a car crash on Sunset Boulevard in 1967. Maria said, "If Jayne Mansfield was really decapitated in that car crash, she certainly would have had plenty left!"

I asked her who her idols were. "Sofia Loren! Oh, she's my idol! If I could walk like her for ten seconds! I think she was the only woman who was able to snap Cary Grant out of his homosexuality."

On the topic of old Hollywood, I asked her who her favorite actors were, and one of them was Fred Astaire. "I'll never forget how he got into a car! So elegant! It's like he flew into it!"

———◆———

Walter Slezak—the popular actor from Vienna who worked in a few big American movies, and played The Clock King in the *Batman* series—arose again today as we sat in the kitchen eating cantaloupe. Walter's father, Leo—the premier opera star in Europe during his time—was a friend of Maria's father.

"Walter was always trying to get me in bed. I used to say hello to him and touch his arm or whatever in a completely harmless way, and he would say: 'A little further down and to the left, please.'"

Here now, according to Maria, who said she spoke to Walter's wife on the phone after the incident, was how Mr. Slezak's final week on earth went:

"Walter was around 80 at the time, and wasn't nearly what he used to be. He was in a lot of physical pain. Well he was in a mall somewhere in New York, sort of standing off to the side, and a beautiful young woman approached him, and said: 'Pardon me, are you Walter Slezak?' Flattered, he replied, 'Yes, I'm Walter Slezak.' Well it turns out the young woman just wanted to offer him a chair, nothing else. Later that evening he sat down and wrote a letter to his wife that said something to the effect of, 'When all a pretty young woman wants from me is to offer me a chair, my life is over. There's no point in continuing.' You see, his whole life he had women falling all over him. Later in the week Walter took a shotgun, walked into his backyard, and shot himself in the head."

Suicides have been a big part of Maria's life. Aside from those she saw first-hand during the Holocaust, two of her neighbors' children committed suicide within the last few years, her hairstylist (not Maitie) of many years in Beverly Hills recently committed suicide, her dear friend Bill Tandler's sister and mother committed suicide, and Lily's sister Gerta's only child committed suicide in her twenties. I can't imagine anyone having seen more suicides in their lifetime. My troubles seem shamefully insignificant.

Hey guys;

Within a week, Mutzi seems to have declined regarding her sharpness. For some reason she has really been into Scrabble lately, which I don't have a problem with, but here's the part I'm talking about: it's been taking her about 10 to 15 minutes, average, per turn, and she gets very confused about rules that she's known for years. I've had to swivel my chair around to help her, whereas even as short as a week ago, I never had to do that. This isn't a call for alarm, I just wanted to keep everyone updated on her status. I guess we need to remember she is in her 90's, and age is something that happens to everyone, even Maria Altmann.

Gregor

*August 3, 2008*

*"I DO <u>NOT</u> NEED A LIVE-IN MAID!"*

An enemy lurks inside the walls of the Altmann household, only it can never be found, it can never be contained, and it can never be killed. It survives only because it has a host, and it has a host only because the host was born. The Golden Lady has been chosen to be forced to battle the dark side of having a brain, which means being subjected to the early stages of dementia. The symptoms began about a year ago, a few weeks before me.

Part of enduring these stages is losing short term memory. Maria doesn't intend to cause friction when I tell her she has a dentist appointment, and she insists she was just there last week, when in reality she hasn't been in six months. Why get frustrated with someone who, because of a depressing inevitability of nature, believes what she's saying is true?

When she obsesses about something that isn't true, I excuse myself and go and sit in Fritz's green chair in the den to take a deep breath and put it all into perspective. Then I reappear in the kitchen, sit down and look at her and smile, and she smiles back. What's most often the case is that she's forgotten about the incident entirely. Often the only upside is to know that when someone is going through this memory loss they have no idea they're going through it.

The "d" word is for the weak-minded, though, and Maria's strength of character forces it into submission. She surprised me today with her memory.

I told her a while back I wrote a screenplay about a cicada named Simon who wakes up early from his seventeen-year sleep cycle to find he must end a brewing animal war before it's too late. One of Simon's lines I told her is, "Are you going to take a nappy?"

Now, weeks and weeks later, she said to me before she headed to her room to take her nap, "Are you going to take a nappy?" I don't think she remembered where it came from, it was just kind of hanging out somewhere in her subconscious and decided to make its way out of her mouth.

Tom recently attended a seminar on dementia. The panel of medical experts all agreed on its most effective treatment, and it had nothing to do with medicine: consistent stimulation of the mind.

———— ♦ ————

I'd like to share with you the following exchange Chuck had with his mother this morning.

Chuck: "You look great."

Maria: "Huh?"

Chuck: "I SAID YOU LOOK GREAT!"

Maria: "Not bad for an old bag."

Chuck: "Huh?"

Maria: "I SAID NOT BAD FOR AN OLD BAG!"

Chuck: "Did you work out with Tina today?"

Maria: "Beg pardon?"

Chuck: "MOTHER, YOU NEED A HEARING AID!!"

Maria: "I DO NOT NEED A LIVE-IN MAID!"

Chuck: "THAT'S NOT WHAT I SAID!"

Maria: "I can hear you, you just mumble."

Chuck: "I don't mumble, YOU JUST CAN'T HEAR!"

Maria: "Now that I know you mumble, I'll wear my hearing aid."

Chuck extends his hand across the table, and Maria clasps it.

Maria: "I still like you."

Chuck: "You have poor taste."

———— ♦ ————

The way in which Hitler's alleged successor, Hermann Göring, committed suicide in his jail cell on October 15, 1946—which from what I've researched is all conjecture—became a lot clearer today thanks to Maria. Like many of the Nazis, Göring used cyanide to kill himself, but there's great dispute as to how he was able to sneak a cyanide capsule inside his cell, what with every nook and cranny of it being searched and vetted daily. Maria is friendly with a guard ("I'm pretty sure he's still alive," she said) who worked in close proximity to Göring during his stay in prison, and here is what Maria remembers him telling her.

"Göring was visited frequently by his wife. As his execution date neared, she would make sure to give him a kiss, and inside her mouth were cyanide pills, and she would transfer them to him through the kiss."

*August 10, 2008*

*"Don't you dare lay a finger on me."*

We were driving down Doheny today after our bimonthly hair salon visit, and a rare silence befell the Klimt-mobile. Suddenly it was shattered by the girl sitting to my right.

"I'm going to miss you," she said with utter ease, as if she'd told me to take a right at the next light. But my heart took a sucker punch. I felt the tears coming, and when they came I turned my head and cried at all the poplar trees out the window.

I drove the rest of the way home looking out that left window secretly crying, not at the sadness of her leaving but the beauty of her sitting next to me. It was so clear to me in that moment, that before I met Maria—at a time when I had all the love to give to a girl and not a worthy one in sight—she was the one to whom I was meant to give it.

When we arrived home it was as if it had never happened. I eased the front-end of the Klimt into the garage until it lightly tapped the hanging tennis ball. I threw it in park and got out, quickly wiped the remaining wet from my eyes, and shimmied around to arrive at her window.

She was already smiling. "You know, pretty soon I'm going to be too old for you," she said as I opened her door and handed her her cane. We both laughed, only mine was pronounced enough to cause her to look up at me with playful petulance. "You shouldn't laugh so hard at that."

I'm the luckiest guy in the world.

———◆———

Tonight I dropped Maria off at Lily's for dinner. Before we left I offered to help her get ready, but someone kneeling down to help Maria Altmann tie her shoe, at this stage in her life, is like punching her in the face.

"Don't you dare lay a finger on me, I'll feel like a cripple."

I let her struggle to put them on, but then she had trouble buttoning her pants, and using the excuse that we were late I went to help her with her zipper and she threw up her arms in frustration.

"You want younger ones to open it, not older ones to close it," she said, letting out a defeated whimper.

I looked up at her trying to catch her breath, and I thought about the time when she could zip up a pair of tight pants herself, even as little as a year ago. Days come, and then they go... and then they're gone forever.

We arrived at Lily's.

"Lily no here yet," said her maid. "Market." She invited us in.

"I'm sure Lily is driving whomever is driving her to the market crazy," Maria smiled and said to the maid, who bowed and smiled back, not understanding a word. The maid disappeared into the kitchen to make us tea. Maria always goes out of her way to be nice to her, because she has it in her head that Lily doesn't pay her very well.

Lily finally showed up at the front door on her walker, alongside her grandson, Mark. She insisted I stay for dinner. Maria never wants me to stay for dinner because she thinks Lily will bore me to tears, but I accepted. As we sat there on the couch listening to Lily tell what Maria perceived as a boring story, I caught Maria rolling her eyes at me and gesturing toward Lily, as if we were classmates making fun of the schoolteacher.

Dinner consisted of delicious stuffed green peppers and this unbelievable German potato/apricot dessert called Marillenknoedel. Afterward, Lily, who struggles to stand these days, insisted on standing with no help, and shuffled over to her friend of 80 years.

"Come here, Maria, I want to give you a kiss before you leave." Maria met her halfway, the two embraced, and despite always bickering at each other, it was a moment rife with genuine respect and love.

Maria can't fool me.

*August 16, 2008*

*"I wish I knew you 70 years ago."*

Maria donated $30,000 to the USC Thornton School of Music this year, which will be utilized for what they've dubbed "The Fritz Altmann Endowed Scholarship for Voice."

The donation made it possible for a group of students to fly to Venice to perform in a special concert last year. In gratitude for the donation, USC sent four opera students to the house to give Maria her very own personal opera show in her backyard.

I wasn't able to be there for the set-up, so Tom made up a nice table of hors d'oeuvres and drinks. I arrived just as the last student was finishing their performance. The porch was teeming with people. Jim and his daughter Alana were there, along with Chuck and Donna, and all the USC staff along for the ride. Maria was seated in a chair front and center. Each student introduced him or herself, thanked her for the money, explained how it's affected them personally, and indicated his or her voice type. To Maria's delight they were all tenors.

When they sang they sang to Maria as if they were the only two people on earth. It could not have been a more exquisite afternoon. Even though all this surely sounds cliché—the birds chirping, the scent of freshly mown grass wafting through the air, the cloudless sky, and the occasional curious neighbor peeking over the bushes to see what all the hubbub was about—it was actually true!

I waved to her through the blinds as I snuck through the kitchen and into the backyard. Her expression when she saw me was of relief, as if she'd been wondering if I was ever going to show up. A few USC people saw this exchange and wondered who I was, which for a fleeting moment made me feel like Fritz, and that I had just managed to escape work to catch the tail end of a special event for my wife.

After the performances it was time for a nap. On the way to bed she passed some pears on the kitchen counter, studied and fingered one for a few moments, then put it down and said, "I'm going to die before these are ripe."

She disappeared into her room.

When she awoke she was in a rare gloomy mood. "I'm allowed to feel my full 93 years sometimes."

I tried to boost her energy with a shoe-in joke: "What do you call a light Italian rain?" A bigamist. I went out of my way to act it out using a thick Italian accent and over-the-top gestures, but it didn't penetrate as deeply as usual. I brought her the book she'd been reading, *The Private Lives of the Three Tenors*. Plácido Domingo couldn't even cheer her up.

Her sorrow brought her to say stupid things that only made it worse.

"I wish I knew you 70 years ago."

She's said this kind of thing before, but always laced with levity. Today, for the first time, it was rife with regret.

My own regret hurts plenty, I don't need hers on top of that. Why do I have to be reminded that a perfect situation isn't perfect, and never will be? Men spend their entire lives searching for their dream girl. Most never even find her. I'm one of the lucky few who has. Here mine is sitting right in front of me... but we can never be together. What cruel trick has God played on us?

I don't know. I hate this. I've never felt more frustrated at the impossibility of rewinding time, more lost and confused that someone so perfect, so beautiful, so available... can never, ever be everything to me.

I can't stand love. I really can't. How can anyone ever embrace something that only leads to heartbreak?

*August 18, 2008*

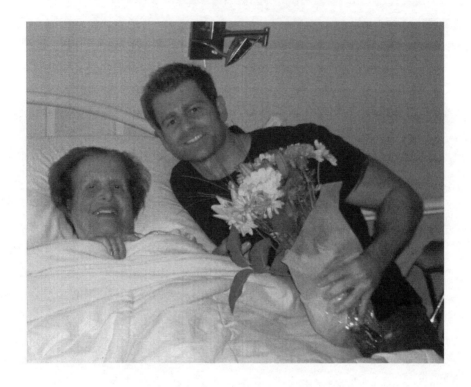

*"Hide it under your handkerchiefs!"*

During my day off today Tom called to tell me Maria checked into the UCLA Medical with chest pains.

Since I wasn't at the house when it happened, Tom later relayed to me the story. Suspecting a stroke, he had called the paramedics. Ten minutes later, four tall strapping studs in blue uniforms ran through the door, and at the sight of this a nearly unconscious Maria suddenly sat straight up in her bed and decided the pains in her chest should take a back seat to these hunks. Maria's physical agony quickly turned to nervous laughs, and soon she was a giddy little schoolgirl, their looks serving as defibrillators that sparked her heart back to a normal rhythm. If I were to explain much of what you need to know about Maria Altmann in one paragraph, it would be the one you just read. All problems—even dramatic flirtation with death—disappear when there's a beautiful male mug in front of her.

I picked up some flowers and sped to the hospital. Tom's tired face said he was ready to go home. You'd think the nurse staff at the hospital would be sufficient to give Tom and I a few hours off, but the problem is, Maria forgets where the button is to call someone to get help to use the bathroom, so Nurses Tom and Gregor are ready and willing hospital employees.

I gave Maria the flowers, and told her I don't bring flowers to many women. "You say that to all the women," she said in good spirits, and immediately became concerned that I hadn't eaten all day. Chuck ambled in with a book, went over and kissed his mother, and made friends with the couch. His back is really bothering him these days. It's sad that his own 93-year-old mother can stand for longer periods than he can.

Maria's attention remained on Tom and I. "Both of you take money out of my purse, and go get yourselves a sandwich." Tom told her the hospital doesn't allow food from the outside. At this, she looked at us both like we were utter morons.

"Hide it under your handkerchiefs!"

She stared at us expecting a light bulb to have gone off in our heads that we should be hiding "outside food" under our handkerchiefs, but no bulbs went off, and she dropped it. Tom was ready to keel over from fatigue, so despite it being my day off I told him to go home and rest and I'd take the reins until he returned.

Maria turned to Chuck and asked how he was doing, and he responded, "Beautiful. Fucking beautiful." This reminded her of a joke, which she told the whole room, including a nurse who happened to be passing through. "A teacher asked his class to use beautiful in a sentence. The first student stood up and said, 'Today is a beautiful day.' 'Good,' the teacher said. The second one stood up and said, 'You look beautiful in that dress.' 'Good.' The third one stood up and said, 'Beautiful. Fucking beautiful.' Appalled, the teacher asked, 'Where did you learn that?' The little girl replied, "My Daddy, when he found out my sister was pregnant again.'"

At midnight the mighty Tom returned rested and ready for a sleepless night on a couch that was too small for him. Before I left we stepped into the spit-shined hallway of the hospital. I told him I felt good because she looked like she was on a road to recovery. But he had spoken to the doctor. Maria has developed an irregular heartbeat that will never beat the same again. Her blood will never again be distributed around her body normally. A pacemaker is out of the question because she's too old. She'll have to live with this until she no longer has to live with it. But I didn't want to think about that.

*August 22, 2008*

*"It's very strange to see the people you grew up with*
*become a part of history."*

"I've been under the weather the last few days," Maria said on the phone to Lisa this morning, comfortably sprawled out in her own bed again.

Lisa asked what was wrong, and Maria responded, "I'm 92... that alone is a sickness."

Maria had a bladder infection. Tom tells me this is common in the elderly. His grandparents used to get them at least once a year.

Still in bed, Maria fielded another phone call, this one from her oldest grandson, Philip—an entertainment lawyer—who informed her there was a pending actor's strike. "As long as there isn't a grandson strike, I'm happy," she said, and ended the call.

We Scrabbled later in the afternoon, and an anomaly—a Scrabbomaly—occurred: I had six I's. Six! I showed Maria, who quickly said, "If you go home there will be six virgins waiting for you... one for each 'I.'" I didn't go. I'll never know if she was right.

"Did you know Howard Hughes?" I asked her later in the game. No, but...

"In the forties I guess it was, I had just pulled into our driveway, and I saw black smoke billowing out of a house down the street. I saw in the paper that Howard Hughes had crashed his plane into it."

———◆———

My friend Janet called me the other night to tell me she happened to rent a movie recently that featured Gustav Klimt as a character, called *Bride of the Wind*. I borrowed it for the night. From now on if someone asks me what Maria's formative years in Vienna were like, along with *The Sound of Music* I will suggest this film. *Bride* features Maria's Aunt Adele, and many prominent people Maria was exposed to in her youth.

The plot centers on Alma Mahler, who, along with Adele, was considered one of the leading socialites in turn-of-the-century Vienna. Maria's mother knew Alma well, and Alma was at the house often during her later years drinking tea with Therese in the living room. Alma's daughter, Menon (whom Alma mothered with German architect Walter Gropius), and young Maria would go off and play with Maria's porcelain dollhouse collection—a gift from her Uncle Ferdinand. (By the way, it turns out Ferdinand was good friends with Expressionist painter Oskar Kokoschka, and Kokoschka painted a picture of him in the woods behind his mansion, holding a hunting rifle. It still hangs at the Kunsthaus Museum in Zurich).

While watching the film, every five minutes Maria would swivel her head toward me to say things like, "I remember that square," or, "I knew him," or, "Fritz and I used to go there."

There's a line from a lady talking to another lady at a café: "Klimt has been linked to every woman in Vienna."

Maria and I looked at each other and shared a knowing snicker.

As the credits rolled, Maria said: "It's very strange to see the people you grew up with become a part of history."

I reminded her that *she* was a part of history.

When the screen went black we sat in silence. I looked over at her, and she continued to stare at the TV as she said, "I think you are going to be sad when I die."

*September 3, 2008*

(Arthur Schnitzler)

*"When I croak, I'll be watching over you—I think that exists, you know, that people can watch over certain people they love when they're in Heaven."*

A basketball player can't tell you he doesn't play basketball. An accountant, "I don't account." But I'm an actor telling you I don't act. I became an actor—and come to think of it, a caregiver—to give all I've acquired as an owner of a heart, and a liver of a life. If my acting is acting, I have failed. Acting, to me, is not pretending. I cannot pretend.

The deeper I look within myself to find the truth the more I'm reminded of why I became an actor, and I would not have become an actor if I was going to be an actor. I have led a life of no fear, of passion, of lust, of love, angst and honesty, and I have lived these emotions unabashedly to the extreme, and these feelings are palpable and waiting inside a bubbling cauldron of controlled chaos. I cannot separate my life from my art.

I believe everyone is human. I believe a mass murderer is as human as a priest, just as prone to saying profound things, showing love, showing humor. That is life. That is truth. We actors must show the flaws. There is beauty in showing the flaws. A real man—a real actor—displays his flaws like a medal of honor. I am not an actor.

Before I leave you for the night I just want to say that I'd like to thank the guy who invented the idea of reincarnation. It's one of the all-time greatest concepts man has ever come up with, and has no doubt caused rampant pleasure among humans, putting people in bad moods who were sitting there happening to think about life and the ultimate drear of it, suddenly in an enterprising mood. I have questions about the inventor, though, like, who was it? Was it a guy? A girl? And did they actually experience it firsthand, somehow, or did they just want us to believe it to be true to make life more tolerable? It really doesn't matter. The mere thought of it being true makes life worth living.

Hey kids;

Over the weekend I was reading about an un-produced Stanley Kubrick script called *Napoleon*. In an interview Kubrick said Napoleon's sex life rivaled only that of Arthur Schnitzler's. I looked Arthur up and he was a renowned Viennese author and dramatist. I mentioned this to Maria, and she said, "Arthur had

a crush on me, but I never let him do what he wanted to do."
She had a few more amusing stories about him and how he
used to come with them during their summer drives to
Ferdinand's country home.

Also, one thing I learned that I'm ashamed I didn't know, is that
Kubrick's film *Eyes Wide Shut*, was based on the Schnitzler
novella, *Traumnovelle*.

-The Caregiver

*September 14, 2008*

(David)

*"I had a dentist in Vienna as a teenager, and to this day I can't bear to think of him..."*

We had an appointment with Dr. Mead today, her dentist. According to Maria, Chuck said to him one day: "My mother only goes to you because you're good looking." Maria shouted to me sarcastically: "I could have killed Chuckie for saying that!"

Then she said: "Even if it might be true, he shouldn't have said it."

"I had a dentist in Vienna as a teenager, and to this day I can't bear to think of it. He had this ugly red beard, and when he leaned over to work on my teeth it would scratch my face. It was awful. When I came to America I made a point to find a clean-shaven dentist."

Sheila—the mother of Chuck's kids—stopped by the house today, and what a delight she is. She was at the dentist all week, and had missed visiting Maria in the hospital. "I had a root-canal appointment, and it was either the root-canal, or visit you in the hospital."

"You made the right choice with the root-canal," Maria said.

We replaced Chris, Maria's night caregiver. He was too busy. His replacement is my friend David Branin (who directed *Night Before the Wedding*, and just started hosting the radio show *Film Courage* with his fiancée, Karen Worden). We all went out to the steak house, Ruth's Chris, in Beverly Hills. Maria is fond of him already. "David is a jewel."

Here I am, just a penniless actor lounging in an establishment that charges $48 for a porterhouse and $22 for a glass of Pinot Noir, gesturing to the waiter to fetch us more sparkling Pellegrino, and you know what? None of it goes to my head. I don't understand how anything could go to anyone's head in this one life we are given.

David—gentler than a man should ever be, in fact I'm convinced he's some sort of modern-day Jesus—had his satellite radio already tuned to an all-opera channel when he pulled up to the valet area to take Maria back to the house. He's been well trained. On the way home they played the "Opera Game," where he would play an opera and she would guess which one it was. According to him she was near perfect.

Despite my trust in David, I'm very nervous tonight, and imagine I will be the whole week. Will he remember her pills?

Will that old horrible foldout bed he has to sleep on in the den be comfortable enough? Will he hear Maria if she needs him during the night? I don't do too well with things out of my control. My phone is next to my ear. This is not a way to live and love, but I'm living it, and I'm loving it.

*October 3, 2008*

(Paul Henreid)

*"Late in his life he could hardly walk,
but boy did he still want sex!"*

A mere month after he was let go, it appears Chris has been erased from Maria's memory. Here is a man whose presence was always felt, who quite literally pranced through the door every evening donning his motorcycle helmet and his smile, and sat and regaled Maria with his stories about being a commander in the Navy and about all the women he's courted. "Who's Chris?" she asked me after I'd brought his name up. I mentioned the motorcycle and the women. Nothing. Out of sight out of mind.

Will she forget *me* one day?

All I know is that what is love, is real. And this family is love. Donna met Chuck before the Supreme Court case was even in the picture, and upon thinking about it, every current woman belonging to Maria's three sons have either come aboard before the Klimts, or knew nothing about them when they met. And there were no family disputes when it came time to distribute the money. With $50 million of tax-free money floating around Cheviot Hills (Randy, Luise's daughter Nelly, and Poldi's son Peter Bentley, split the other $275 million), you'd think there would have been tension about who got what. "There were no egos whatsoever. It all went perfectly smoothly," Chuck said. That says all you need to know about this family.

I'm surrounded by love. But giving love to Maria doesn't mean I'm a good person. I could be more patient with people outside my inner circle of family and friends—like bad drivers, or stupid or boring or lazy people. And I could be nicer to women in general. I could be as good to all people as Maria is.

———— ◆ ————

We sat down in the den to watch a movie after dinner. While I perused the shelves for something to watch, Maria filled me in on a poodle they owned named Frizzy. "Late in his life he could hardly walk, but boy did he still want sex!"

Then she said, "He was so charged up one day that he ran over to the neighbor's yard and knocked up their little dog. Since Frizzy didn't have papers the woman decided to get an abortion. A doggie abortion, can you believe it?" After Maria got through being appalled, she said, "Only in Beverly Hills would you find such a woman."

We decided on *Casablanca*. Maria was a good friend of Bogart's co-star, Paul Henreid, who lived down the street from them in Beverly Hills for years. As the credits rolled, Maria, so intensely lost in another world, stared dreamily at the television. "It gets me here every time. And Bogart—with just the twitch of an eye he communicated so much."

When she finished, we sipped and we basked in what I've come to know as the most comfortable silence I've ever felt with another human being. "You know, people today just say 'I love you' like we used to say, 'hello,'" she said after a few moments. "How can people say it so quickly and casually after a sentence? It holds no meaning anymore."

At this, Maria raised her glass, and, almost as if suddenly occurring to her, she said, "I love you." My heart paused. It was the first time she ever said it to me directly.

*October 12, 2008*

*"I should tell those movie directors how old I am..."*

MY VOICE HAS BEEN RAISED PERMANENTLY. It became clear
this weekend having dinner with friends at a bar in Hollywood
called Cat n' the Fiddle.

"Dude, lower your voice, you're yelling."

This was news to me. I'd bragged to Tom recently that I
couldn't believe, after months and months of having to speak at a
heightened tone at the house, that I didn't yell everywhere I went.
Now here I am, the guy I was convinced I'd never become. I blame
it on Maria and Chuck, and I'm fine with that. One of the few
times I can legitimately place blame on someone else.

SO ANYWAY, THIS MORNING... sorry, I'm yelling again.
This morning Maria peered out the kitchen window and implored
to the universe: "If the Germans were so artistic and cultured and
civilized, how could they have let the Holocaust happen?" Her
eyes scanned the backyard then she looked to me as if I had the
answer. I'd known her to speak somberly about the Holocaust,
but I'd never seen her this emotional and vexed about it. She went
off on a lengthy diatribe about how awful the Nazis were, the
damage they caused and the lives and families they ruined. "It's
still so unthinkable to me," she lamented.

"At least they loved and preserved art," was all I could
come up with as a response. After a long, ponderous silence she
shook her head and said cheerily, "Shall we have some toast, my
love?"

Maria likes my nose. Have I mentioned this? I honestly
don't know if I have, but she tells me at least once a week. Her
best friend Peter Koller had an "equally beautiful nose." He also
read *The New Yorker*. When I brought in the latest issue this
morning, she smiled and said: "Both men I'm attracted to read *The
New Yorker*."

I told her "Great noses think alike."

She laughed for at least 30 seconds. Then she said, "I
should tell those movie directors how old I am and that I've never
seen a better nose."

If Maria were my nose agent, I would clearly be an
olfactory star by now. And of course be surrounded by an
unlimited supply of olfactory virgins.

David arrived on time as usual. I had to run to a screening
of a friend's film, so I left dinner for him to construct. No one

would ever accuse David of being a chef. But he makes up for it with the great thing he has going with Maria. He brings his brand new iMac desktop, and after dinner he sets it up on the kitchen table. When she sees him she knows this means he's unveiling his "magical" machine, going to the "magical" website called YouTube, and then "magically" making her Plácido appear. On the first occasion Maria was dumbfounded at David's seemingly magical fingers. She couldn't figure out how he was able to bring her Plácido at the click of a button. I'm sleeping better these days.

*October 19, 2008*

(Hubertus Czernin)

*"I'm not regretful about not being young anymore, but the one thing that saddens me is that I'm too old to take you to Vienna with me."*

How I wish I could go to Vienna with you, Maria. We could have, even if we had met only a year earlier. But as you well know, the doctors have spoken against it. I'm sorry. Timing is always the opposite of nothing.

For Maria to have any luck knowing what day it is now, she needs to look at the day's newspaper. "Oh, it's Wednesday. I thought it was Sunday." For some reason she always thinks it's Sunday, and endures a moment of confusion when I tell her it isn't.

"Why is Tina coming on a Sunday? Sunday is for relaxing." Or when we go to the doctors—"Why do they want me in on a Sunday?"

At breakfast, I decided to bring up Hubertus Czernin—the Viennese investigative journalist who in the mid-1990s (before Maria began her case) wrote a series of articles exposing Austria's anti-Semitic past, one of them about the Belvedere's "suspicious ownership of the Klimts."

Hubertus had visited the Vienna archives in order to find proof to support his claims about the suspicious ownership. He found two pieces of evidence that would indicate to Randy he had enough to build a case and begin the lawsuit. The first find was various documents stating Austrian museums had hundreds if not thousands of works of art stolen by the Nazis, as well as numerous correspondences between Austrian gallery officials admitting that the Belvedere had no proof of its right to the Klimts.

The second and most damaging: the wills of Adele and Ferdinand. In Adele's will, it was clear she *requested* that the Klimts be donated to the Belvedere Museum, and that her husband Ferdinand do so upon his death. She died in 1925 of meningitis. When the Nazis took over Austria, Ferdinand fled, and the Klimts were confiscated. He died in exile in 1945. In his will, it was found that he *declared* the paintings be given to his nephews and nieces, which included Maria. And he specifically stated: "I declare all earlier wills null and void." But the Belvedere tossed aside Ferdinand's will. For nearly seven decades they clung to the claim that Adele donated the paintings.

It was clear that not only had Adele's will only *suggested* to her husband the Klimts be donated to the museum, she didn't even own them. Ferdinand did. He commissioned Klimt. Randy argued that since Ferdinand owned the paintings, he had the right to empower his heirs as the inheritors of his estate, not his wife. Clearly the Belvedere had no legal right to the paintings.

Hubertus's articles and investigations eventually led to the passage of Austria's Art Restitution Law in 1998, which would return art that Jews were forced to donate to museums in exchange for export permits. Randy stated that Ferdinand had no choice but to donate the Klimts to the Belvedere to be allowed out of the country.

Even with all this firepower, it would still take eight years to get the paintings back.

Because of Mr. Czernin, the Vienna archives, which were only open to certain officials before 1998, are now open to the general public.

"I was in Vienna with Hubertus in 2006, to meet Elisabeth Gehrer, the then minister of culture," Maria said. "Hubertus and I were talking in the lobby, and suddenly a sort of stern and stocky woman came charging into the room. She introduced herself and then told us she would be right back. She said something crass, like, 'I have to go hit the john,' or something. And she charged off out of the room. As soon as she left, Hubertus turned to me and said: 'And that is our minister of culture.' I could have died right there!"

Hubertus was at home embracing his wife one evening a few days later, when suddenly his body went limp, and he fell to the floor, never to get up again. He was only 50. At least he was able to see the paintings make their debut at LACMA in Los Angeles, just weeks before.

"I'll always remember how much I made him laugh. He couldn't keep a straight face around me. We had so much fun together sitting in my backyard just talking about life."

———◆———

I sit alone in the living room as Maria sleeps. There's something extra peaceful about an elderly person's living room. I've noticed that it's actually a few notches quieter than your standard quiet. In fact I wonder if there's a physicist out there who could prove that. I like to stare at *The Gold Portrait* hanging on the wall. I'd seen a copy of it a couple years ago, before I met Maria—my mother, an art history major from Vassar College, had shown me a book of Klimt paintings. It didn't mean much to look at it then, but now I know the history behind it, and I can daily hold the hand of a little girl who lived it.

I imagine Adele in the flesh posing for Klimt, who stands there in his smock with, as the story goes, nothing underneath. He paints her with the raw sexual fury that must have burned inside of him. They're in an old warehouse with splotches of paint splattered all over the floors; canvases stacked on the floor and leaning against walls, and books are piled on wooden tables. A basket of fruit rests by an open window that allows a whispering breeze through.

A young Maria—the very lady I'm watching taking a nap on the TV monitor right in this moment, nearly a hundred years later—stands hidden at the door in a little white sundress and little white shoes with the cute little black buckles, holding a teddy bear and sucking her thumb, wondering why Klimt is being so friendly with her uncle's wife.

*October 24, 2008*

(Maria and Chuck in Fall River in 1942)

*"You're not going to believe me, but do you know what the doctor's name was?"*

The story of the day was a wild one about a Saturday night in Fall River, Massachusetts, in September 1940. One-month-old Chuck had made his way out of his mother's womb in August. They were at home, amidst a huge blizzard. "The cars on the street looked like giant white potatoes."

Chuck suddenly started vomiting, and it didn't let up. "After a while there was nothing left for him to throw up." Maria dialed the doctor at his home, and calmly explained what was happening. The doctor reassured her everything would be okay and that he'd visit them first thing Monday morning. "He later told me that while I was on the phone with him he was already putting on his snow boots and hat, and looking for his car keys."

The doctor made it to the house within the hour. The vomiting had subsided, and all was back to normal. Then Maria asked me, "Do you know what the doctor's name was?" I shook my head. "Dr. Blood." I guess Dr. Vomit was snowed in.

Am I really done with this entry already?

*November 5, 2008*

*"Look. A bird shit on my car."*

We moseyed to Malibu for lunch this afternoon, to a beautiful seaside restaurant called Gladstones, which has a breathtaking view of the Pacific. We were meeting some old friends of Maria's who flew in from New York. One of them, Hanzi, uses a wheelchair. When he was in his thirties he was on a plane flying back to the states after spending a couple weeks in Paris on business. At the beginning of the flight he felt a tingling in his legs, and by the end whatever caused it had taken over his entire lower body. He had to be carried off the plane on a stretcher and taken to a hospital. He's now in his seventies, and has been permanently paralyzed from the waist down since that fateful flight.

"I've never heard him complain once," Maria said.

A few minutes earlier we walked out of the house. "Look. A bird shit on my car," she said as we both noticed a little white gift left for us on the windshield of the Klimt. Apparently the bird didn't know it was shitting on one of the great painters of the last hundred years—or at least his namesake.

Maria petted the dashboard endearingly as she got in and sat down, and said to it, "We've been through a lot together, haven't we?"

*Maria Altmann:* beloved niece of Adele Bloch-Bauer... renowned heiress to the Klimt fortune... proud owner of a 1992 Ford Taurus.

En route to the beach, we discussed that Cicada script I had written. She'd forgotten about it. I reminded her: "It's about a cicada named Simon who defies science and wakes up early to save the world from the first Global Animal War."

"A true story?" she asked facetiously.

"It's called *The Life and Legend of Simon the Cicada.*"

"Does he have a girlfriend?"

"Nope."

"That's why he can accomplish all those things."

While we were driving along the Pacific Coast shoreline, the subject switched to a guy both Tom and I know, named Jud. He has a rare disorder called fibrodysplasia ossificans progressiva (FOP). "What was his name again?" Maria asked.

"Jud," I said.

"Can he walk?"

"Very carefully."

"How porcupines make love."

It's estimated only 700 people in the world have FOP. It confines Jud to a stand-up wheelchair. He wasn't expected to survive past 25, and he's now 33. His doctors say they plan on making him the oldest FOP patient in the world.

When Jud was seven years old his bones began growing brittle, and by the time he got to junior high his arms were almost completely glued to his body and his knees were stuck in a locked position. He hasn't been able to sit down in nearly three decades, and he's forced to use special tools to do things most of us take for granted, like an extender on his toothbrush in order to reach his mouth to brush his teeth. He admits he has a recurring dream he's still a seven-year-old kid running up and down a flight of stairs.

It's part of my weekly routine to take his Australian Shepherd Snowball for hikes in the Runyon Canyon Mountains. Snowball is his only friend all day the majority of days.

"I just want my dog to outlive me," he said once. But to me, he's a cool dude who just happens to wear a helmet. I got past the physicality of it after our first meeting. He's got a great sense of humor, and honestly has a more positive outlook than most of my friends.

His mother, Mimi, who loves and cares for Jud more than her own life, was in town recently, and the power went out in Jud's condo in North Hollywood, so the three of us sat in the dark on the floor by the fire eating Chinese food. I wondered aloud which era we would live in if we had the choice. For Mimi and I it was between Paris in the twenties, Russia during the Age of Enlightenment, and Abraham Lincoln's era.

Jud said, "This age. My life is good. I wouldn't change a thing."

Jud and Maria are similar in this respect—both live in the moment, appreciating the good given.

Fresh Atlantic Salmon was on my mind as Maria and I walked to the restaurant to meet her friends.

"I love you like a son, and you shine like the sun," she said to me before we greeted Hanzi, waving contentedly at us in the distance in his wheelchair.

As we walked to our table Maria whispered in my ear, "I'm going to go home and find you a seventeen-year-old to make up for all these old bags you're forced to be with today."

I whispered to her I'd go to jail if I was caught with a seventeen-year-old.

She stopped and looked at me. "I'll bail you out. I can afford it."

*November 11, 2008*

*"At least they steal with a beautiful accent."*

The phone rang in the middle of Scrabble, and Maria continued staring at the letters without looking up.

"Sounds like Lily," she said with a scowl.

She decided to answer the phone. She told Lily she was busy, and hung up. "All she does is complain. It's ridiculous."

She crinkled her brow and stared curiously at a word on the board.

"What's a din?" she asked. I told her it was a loud noise.

She un-crinkled her brow and widened her eyes radiantly. "So Chuck is full of dins?"

Lily and Maria together are pure comedy. A few months ago, Tom took them to see the French film, *The Diving Bell and the Butterfly*. Maria had trouble seeing and hearing it (because she refuses to wear her hearing aid), and Lily was getting up to go to the bathroom every five minutes. Tom spent what seemed like the entire two hours chasing Lily down the aisles, and either shushing them or yelling at them what a particular actor just said in a subtitle. Maria and Lily both hated it. "It was the first thing they've ever agreed on," Tom said.

Lily's sight and hearing are virtually gone. One day on the phone I yelled at the top of my lungs so she would know when Maria was coming for dinner, and she plumb couldn't hear me.

"5:30!" I yelled, and she responded, "I can't do 1:30, honey, I have a hair appointment."

Even louder, I said, "No, Lily, Maria is coming at 5:30!"

She said back, "No, I need to know when she's coming for dinner."

I could do nothing short of drive to her house with a sign that read, "5:30," which she likely wouldn't have been able to see anyway. I spend a lot of time feeling for her, wishing I could help her.

Curtis Woodworth, our visiting nurse—whom Maria liked so much he was now being invited to family functions—paid us a visit this afternoon. He's a nice guy and all, but he's good looking, and sometimes that's all Maria needs. He does things like take Maria's blood sugar levels, her blood pressure, and gives her a weekly Vitamin B-12 shot, which if he wasn't so much of a looker would be that much more trying for everyone. His horse died this morning. He was very emotional about it and broke down in front of all of us. Maria comforted him by telling him what she tells everyone who tells her about a problem: "Everything will be okay."

Before Curtis left he mentioned that he was in Paris last year and had his wallet stolen on a train.

"At least they steal with a beautiful accent," Maria said. He laughed through his tears.

———— ◆ ————

Lily's 93-year-old sister Gerta was in town, and she and Lily were taking Maria out for dinner tonight. It was David's shift, so he arrived at the house at six to take the "Golden Girls" to town. I had Maria just about ready go.

The Klimt was idling in the driveway. Maria was powdering her nose in the hallway mirror, Lily was wandering off toward the open, empty garage for some reason, and Gerta was peacefully admiring the flowers in the front yard.

"You go get Lily, and I'll go check on Maria," I shouted to David, who bolted after Lily, who had nearly made it to Chuck's toolbox in the garage. Maria suddenly materialized at the front door crunching on a cracker. She looked curiously over at Lily.

"What is Lily doing in the garage? David? The car is *this* way, Lily!"

Then Maria joined Gerta at her flowerbed, proudly pointing out the work her gardener, Javier, was doing. David finally grabbed hold of Lily, whirled her around like a wind-up toy and guided her to the car. Gerta quietly found her seat in the back, and stared out the window in amusement. I helped Maria into the front seat, and, alas, the final shut of a door left David and me standing there in the driveway taking a simultaneous deep breath. I suggested they ditch dinner and go straight to Vegas.

# 2009

*February 18, 2009*

*"I have to go to the doctor on my birthday?"*

Today is Maria's 93$^{rd}$ year of elegance. We had an appointment with her eye doctor, Dr. Stoll. Someone had scheduled it without considering the fact that it was her birthday, and it was too late and important a visit to cancel. Of course she rose to the occasion with the gusto that shot her out of bed the morning of her escape from Vienna.

While we sat in the waiting room, a large woman with large breasts stomped by. I watched Maria intensely studying her as she disappeared into a room. I knew it was coming. And it came. LOUDLY.

"She could throw her boobs over her shoulder." When I showed her I was at first amused, she became amused, but then I rolled my eyes, which made her even more amused. I can't take this woman anywhere.

Maria visited the bathroom before we left. I wandered down the hallway to flirt with the cute nerdy Latina secretary at the front desk. Suddenly I heard, "Gregor! Gregor!"

I booked down the hallway and through the bathroom door to find her sitting on the toilet seat, struggling to lift herself up. Whoever designed these toilet seats must have been a dwarf. It was less than a foot from the ground! I crouched down, bear-hugged her from the front, and deadlifted her to a standing position. She was really embarrassed.

Later we sat at the kitchen table drinking wine. Maria raised her glass and said, "Here's to getting me off the toilet."

———— ✦ ————

Guido's is an Italian Restaurant in Santa Monica. The Altmanns rented out an entire room to fit the 30 people attending Maria's birthday party. I gave a speech in a dimly lit room full of old dusty wine bottles resting on mahogany bookshelves. It was the first family gathering at which I spoke. I honestly don't remember what I said because I was in the "zone." It's like the acting zone, when you're so present and in the moment that afterwards you have no idea what you did, what you said, or how long you said it. All I remember saying was something like, "I owe a lot to this family." I couldn't finish because I welled up. I don't like Maria seeing me get emotional. I'm supposed to be the guy who keeps it all together.

*March 2, 2009*

"*I think those... what do you call them? 99-Cent Stores?*
*Well I think they are just fabulous.*"

Maria Victoria Bloch-Bauer Altmann is a multi-millionaire scion of one of the most cultured and influential families in Austria at the turn of the twentieth century—yet today she was skipping around the Goodwill store on Eighth and La Brea as if she were Cinderella in a bridal gown shop.

At one point she became enchanted with a sweater listed at a buck-fifty. She looked at the price tag, suddenly widened her eyes, and turned to me and implored, "Do you think this is right?"

I nodded, and she exclaimed, "I've seen it all!" She flung it over her shoulder and was off to the next item, a table lamp. "Do you need a lamp, my love?"

I stood back a couple feet, fielding friendly stares from customers and employees who looked at me like, "Grandma's first time, huh?" *If only they knew.*

As I put back the clothes she kept pulling off the racks for me, I reminded her we were here to find a couch for my new apartment in Hollywood.

"Of course. A couch. We're going to find you a beautiful couch."

We found a surprisingly clean and comfortable one for $50. Boy, she couldn't stop talking about what a deal we got. You'd think this $50 couch from Goodwill was the biggest news to hit Southern California in years. Tom showed up in his pick-up truck to help us haul it to my apartment.

"*Mein Geliebtes,* get Margie on the phone, I want to tell her about this fabulous store," she said as we met Tom in the parking lot.

I dialed her daughter in Hawaii and, always finding this quite amusing, I handed an iPhone to a 93-year-old.

After hearing about her mother's discovery, Margie said, "Mother, I can't verify it now, but I think you might be the first heiress to ever set foot in a Goodwill."

As if the rain gods were waiting for us to be on our way, it began to pour five minutes into our drive. I looked anxiously in my rear view at my brand new couch getting royally soaked in the back of Tom's pick-up truck. It was too late to do anything about it.

When we arrived at my apartment we heaved it through the door, and you'd have thought we fished it out of a lake. I fetched my tiny ten-dollar Walgreens fan, propped it on a thick atlas on the floor and pointed it up at the couch, and the three of us sat on my bed in silence staring at the David of fans slinging its pathetic little stones of cold air at the Goliath of couches—it just sat there with its arms folded, dripping.

Maria looked at me, I looked at Tom, and the three of us howled with laughter. When I got home that evening the couch was dry as Steven Wright. It seemed to defy science, and only added more character to an already memorable afternoon. It was all part of the pilot episode for my new sitcom, *Two Guys, a Girl, and a Goodwill Couch.*

Dear all;

Tonight was the world premier of my new film, *Night Before the Wedding!* What a treat, seeing Maria walk up the red carpet. David, who directed the film, and his fiancée, Karen, posed with her as the cameras flashed.

Last night Jesell asked Maria if she was sure she wanted to see it, since it was such a raunchy movie. Maria said, "Well... I think I'm old enough now." Curtis was there as well. I introduced Maria to some of my friends, who had no doubt heard plenty about her already. She was a pro, saying hello to everyone as if she had known them for years. I was nervous enough to show the film to 200 people, let alone more nervous for Maria to see it! David got up before the film to give a pre-screening speech, and dished out a warm shout-out to Maria and the entire Altmann family.

I tried to watch Maria's reactions during the film but it was too dark to see her expressions. As the credits rolled I ran up to her to thank her for coming. She told me I was "fabulous," and that I was a "natural." I asked her if she was able to hear it okay, and her response: "I heard every fucking word!" (There are a lot of "fucks" in the movie).

G

# *March 11, 2009*

(Maria and her parents in Salzburg in 1936)

*"Let's go have a drink, and then we'll get married."*

Claudia Schmied, the current Austrian minister of arts and culture, and her chief of staff, paid an impromptu visit today. The polite Austrian knock came around three, and when I opened the door I knew right away at worst the visit would be tolerable for Maria, because her chief of staff was a tall, handsome man.

Frau Schmied was terribly nice, unlike, from what I've heard, her predecessor (Elisabeth Gehrer). As expected, Maria was a hit across the board. That such a high-profile politician—from a country who was still understandably stunned and saddened about the loss of the Klimts—was honored to visit Maria, was, I thought, a commendable thing.

When they left us, we sat in the living room amidst her parents' antique clocks and baroque angels from prewar Vienna. After a few moments of silence, Maria said, "Let's go have a drink, and then we'll get married. People might talk, but I don't care."

It's interesting that Peter has mentioned to me that "Mother" is a lot "freer" in her speech in her later years, and he largely attributed that to me specifically. I didn't know her in her early years, of course, but no matter how "free" she gets I've never met a more classy lady in my life. I'll show you. I've got video now!

Once we migrated to the kitchen, I brought Maria a Bourbon and soda and a hard copy of an email Randy had forwarded me last week to give to her. It turns out one of the Gestapos who stole Ferdinand's porcelain collection in 1938— much of which ended up in Hitler's private home in the Bavarian Alps in Germany—contacted Randy to tell him he's decided to sell what he was able to keep for himself all those years before, and out of the goodness of his heart he's offering to give Maria a portion of the profits.

"I'm not interested," she said with an ironic chuckle, and handed me the paper.

Dinner included creamed spinach, chicken breast, yellow rice, and white wine. I apologized up front that the creamed spinach was a little cold, and Maria said, "Little? One could ice skate across it!"

I was happy as I left tonight, because Super Dave strode through the front door with his magical machine. Maria would be visiting her Cyber-Plácido tonight.

It's been written that if Abraham Lincoln was impelled to write an angry letter, he would go ahead and write it, then set it aside, go to bed, and if in the morning he was still angry, he'd send it. He'd usually end up throwing it away. I'm no Abraham Lincoln.

Dear Altmanns:

Curtis was out of town this week, and the company sent a girl. She called me to connect, and greeted me with a "What's up." That was the first red flag. Then she refused to turn down the music in her car. I should have asked for another nurse at that point, but I didn't.

She arrived at the house 15 minutes late, and pulled into the driveway. I asked if her if she could please park on the street, and she said through her window, "Don't worry, I won't be long." She sashayed through the open front door, I brought her to the kitchen, and she barely introduced herself to Maria, who was sitting right in front of her. Maria immediately shut down her personality, which she doesn't do unless she's truly beside herself. Maria even looked at me like, "Who the hell is this rude girl in my house?"

She went to prick Maria's hand, and it started puffing up, and, I kid you not, the girl said, "Oh shit, that's never happened." I said, "Well what should we do?" And she said, "Do you have any gauze?" I wanted to strangle this girl to death. We finally stopped the bleeding.

This has been TWO "nurses" sent here who are in a caring industry, who have no idea how to care for someone. Come home, Curtis!

*March 19, 2009*

*"Goodnight, my love."*

Jim will call his mother to chat, and then he'll find out what I'm making for dinner, and tell me, "Be right over." And sometimes he'll bring his girlfriend Jesell with him. So it's a good thing I always buy extra meat items. Tonight he barreled through the front door, went right for the fridge, rooted around like a bear at a campsite for a good two minutes, and walked out of the kitchen wielding a beer and a piece of sausage. Then he was on the prowl for something to fix. I told him his mother's walker had been squeaking for weeks. He found it was the tennis balls that needed replacing. After he hollowed out a couple new ones, he proudly presented it to her.

"Look, Mom... Mr. Walker has new balls."

She sized it up and responded, "Mrs. Walker's gonna be *very* happy!"

———— ♦ ————

Some priests are just way too cool to be men of the cloth. Like Father Sweeney. He joined us for dinner. He's been a friend of the Altmanns for 30 years, and hasn't seen Maria since he retired in Los Gatos, California last year. When I first met him at the house mere months ago, he was vivacious. He pranced. He sparkled. Today he was a different man entirely. There was a life that had left him. He walked slower, and he snuck little winces in when no one was looking.

He and Maria sat very close to each other in the kitchen drinking wine, rubbing each other's wrists and telling old stories about Jimmy and how big of a heart he has. When it was time to leave, Maria walked with him to the front door, and, something she doesn't do with anyone besides her kids, continued with him down the sloped driveway. They embraced at the bottom, and with unusually intense interest she studied his every move as he hobbled into his car and drove away.

As he disappeared down the street she turned toward the house and said, "Good night, my love," and we walked to her bedroom in silence.

*March 23, 2009*

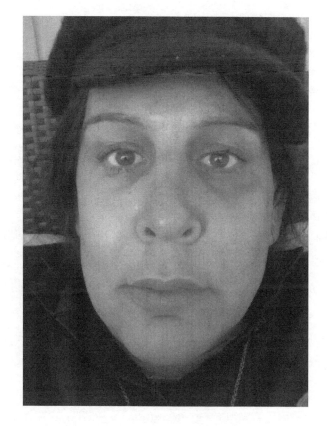

(Tom)

*"I'm not your typical call girl. I'm 93."*

When it comes to Maria's medication, Tom is like northern Renaissance painter Albrecht Durer—a master of his craft. After years of doctors in white lab coats behind desks prescribing drugs without knowing the real heart of the patient, Tom, the doctor-in-shining armor, strode through the door in 2007, with not only every bit of knowledge as a white-lab-coated doctor, but with that all-important missing ingredient: genuine love of the patient. And for that reason Maria's years on earth have been extended. I owe him this job. I owe him everything.

This evening Tom picked up Maria Harris and her husband at the airport and brought her to the house. Maria Harris is Nelly's daughter and Luise's granddaughter. She was visiting from Vancouver. There was a funny moment with her husband, David, who is British, as he stood in the middle of the kitchen holding a teacup full of cold water and a teabag. I told him to "Just throw it in the microwave."

He stood there and glared at me for a long comical second, before saying, "You're telling a *Brit* to put their bloody *tea* in the bloody *microwave?* How dare you!!"

Maria Harris and I sat in the den alone while Maria Altmann and David Branin were in the kitchen watching YouTube clips of actress Hedy Lamar (Maria knew Hedy back in Vienna). Knowing Maria Harris went through the same with Luise—whom she considered her best friend—I told her I was concerned I wouldn't be able to handle Maria leaving me. "She'll be with you forever, that's what's so great, Gregor."

My heart soared and sank simultaneously.

*April 7, 2009*

*"He's so short!"*

Tonight Maria was meeting Stephen Lash, the chairman of
Christie's Auction in New York, at the Beverly Hills Hotel.
Stephen likes to let Maria know when he's in town on business,
and always offers to take her out to dinner. We were a little early,
so we sat in the lobby. I spotted actor Michael Douglas leaning on
the front desk talking to the concierge, and I told Maria, who
widened her eyes and didn't believe me until I pointed him out
and insisted it was him. I asked her if she wanted to meet him.

"Don't be ridiculous, of course I don't want to meet him."
Then she discreetly pulled a pocket mirror out of her purse and
began fixing her hair and makeup.

Michael finished at the desk, and I stood Maria up and
pushed her toward him. He paused.

"I want you to meet someone, Mr. Douglas. This is Maria
Altmann. She's from Vienna."

He smiled and shook her hand. "I hope you are having a
nice stay in Los Angeles. It's a pleasure to have met you." Maria
couldn't contain herself.

"You're a fabulous actor, and so is your father!"

Michael thanked her, turned to leave, and was no more
than five feet away when she whispered to me loudly (as if she
knows another way to whisper): "He's so short!"

Michael paused momentarily without turning, cocked his
head to the side, and disappeared into the elevator.

It was that *Romancing the Stone* cock. When he meets
Kathleen Turner at the broken down bus and she pleads with him
to help her get to Cartagena, then she mentions a dollar amount
that speaks his language, and he stops in his tracks, and cocks his
head to the side. That cock. I couldn't help but fantazise about
asking him on set one day if he remembered meeting a very loud
and inappropriate woman at the Beverly Hills hotel in 2009. He'd
probably say, "There's been so many—which one?"

Stephen Lash arrived polished and snappily dressed, the
kind of guy who must have come out of his mother's womb in a
suit. While we dined he told a story about a man who was
interested in a painting at Christie's last year. The man called in
by phone and was assigned to a bidder. When the auctioneer
began his work, the bidder described to the man on the phone the
painting on center stage. The man on the phone showed interest,

and the bidder asked the man for his first bid. The man gave it to him. As the bidding continued, the bidder had trouble getting clear, concise responses from the man, who seemed distracted.

After a while the bidder said to the man on the phone, "Sir, you are going to have to bid quicker and clearer."

The man apologized, but the pauses and delays continued throughout the bidding. Now concerned, the bidder asked, "Sir, you seem distracted, are you okay?"

The man on the phone said, "I'm terribly sorry, I'm in surgery right now."

After dinner I had to rush to cater for a late party at The Music Center, so David came to steal Maria away from Stephen. Plácido was giving a speech over a dinner. I hadn't seen him walking the Music Center halls in awhile, and I'd never had any reason to pull him aside. But tonight, I had good reason.

Near the elevators before the dinner began I saw him chit-chatting with a couple of men in suits. When they split up I trailed him, and when he noticed me following him he turned to acknowledge me, and continued toward the elevators. "Mr. Domingo," I said, catching up as he pushed the elevator button.

"I just wanted to tell you that I'm one of Maria Altmann's caregivers." At this, he stopped what he was doing, and I assure you I'm not exaggerating: his eyes did the tango. He stepped inches from my face and stared through my pupils.

"I was just talking about her the other day and we were wondering if she was okay!"

I told him she was doing great and would love to hear that he asked about her.

"Give her my best!"

And he got into the elevator and disappeared.

At the end of the party I was cleaning up the coffee station and I felt someone's presence behind me. I turned around, and how often can you say that the premier opera star in the world is standing behind you waiting to speak to you?

He said, "I was just thinking about Maria, and I would love her to come by for our dress rehearsal next week."

He bounced off with his entourage. I looked up at the other caterers, and my boss, who all stood there speechless. I said nonchalantly, "He and I go way back." Then I turned to finish cleaning the coffee station.

## *April 12, 2009*

(Plácido)

*"You think Wagner was anti-Semitic..."*

The following is an email I sent to multiple recipients after a night at the opera. Since there were fresh eyes and possibly even the eyes of the man who made it all possible, I decided to refer to him as Mr. Domingo. Maria was spoiling me at home calling him Plácido.

Dear Maria Admirers;

There's really no word to describe tonight other than magical. And to think it all began when I told Mr. Domingo I'm one of Maria's caregivers.

Maria, Chuck's friend Kirk, and I, arrived in the Klimt at the Music Center valet. A man named Mitch swooped us up and escorted us to our seats. The road was on the show.

It was 5:55 pm, and we had about twenty-five minutes to make a pit stop at the second floor ladies room before finding our seats in time for the show to begin. A woman offered to help Maria into and out of a stall. I took over after that—with Kirk running ahead, parting operagoers and opening doors—and we stood waiting for Mitch to tell us where to sit. As we waited we were accosted by a friendly man named George—one of the Music Center people who helped organize the event—and his pretty date, to whom Maria went out of her way to say, "You have a splendid figure." Then an elderly lady walked by and noticed Maria, who happened to be an old clothing client. They talked for a good five minutes.

Friends were coming out of the woodwork. Randy and his mother, Barbara, showed up, as well as Harold Rosebush and his wife. I noticed a guy near the elevators who looked like a younger, more compact version of Mr. Domingo, and it turned out to be his son. I left Maria for a moment to get a drink of water, and I returned to find the two already in an animated conversation. We discovered our seats were right next to the entire Domingo posse.

Maria was, shall we say, a little confused by this rendition. They tried out a new thing tonight. The creator of the production must have said in his pitch: "Think Die Walkerie... IN OUTER

SPACE!" All the characters wore heavy, Tim Burton-esque make-up, and it had the feel of somewhere in between a David Lynch film, a Michel Gondry music video, and a Salvadore Dali painting. I'm sure Wagner would have been confused as well.

Maria has earned the right to misunderstand this altered version, after all, she's been attending classic opera in Vienna for seventy-plus years. Mr. Domingo himself can't even say that. I mean, Maria's mother KNEW Puccini, and her father KNEW Brahms. Legitimately.

Even though it was my first opera I could already see Wagner wasn't my favorite composer, but I was so honored to be there. Maria was concerned I was miserable. She leaned over to me at least every five minutes during the first act, moaning, "You're never going to want to go to the opera again." Halfway through the second act, she whispered, "I want to go home." I fired back right away, telling her I did NOT come all this way NOT to have her see Plácido Domingo. She shook her head and faced the stage. I sensed she was coming under the weather.

Later in the act, she turned to me heatedly: "I have nothing against blacks, but Wagner would be rolling in his grave if he knew a black man was playing Sigmund!" I told her Sigmund (played by Domingo) wasn't supposed to be "black." She winked at me, and said: "You think Wagner was anti-Semitic, you should have met his daughter."

Mr. Domingo planned to meet us immediately after the second act. When it ended, I had to rush Maria to the bathroom. When we arrived at the ladies room, the short line I fantasized about was a very long one. Fifty people who had no idea we were in a rush to meet Plácido Domingo, selfishly stood there as if they didn't care. I shook my head. There's no way this is gonna work. The whole evening was a bust.

Suddenly a woman saw our urgency and paved us a path to the front of the line. I walked right into the "danger zone" with them, and stood leaning against the wall intently staring forward so as not to reveal the slightest bit of evidence I was some creepy guy peeping into ladies room stalls, even though, c'mon, I'm only human. "You look very comfortable in here," a woman said, breaking the silence. "It's because I do this often," I quipped, as I continued to stare forward. If you've never made a bathroom-full of opera ladies laugh...

When Maria was finished we plopped her into a wheelchair and sped her back downstairs. Just as we got off the elevator, as if we had now entered a marathon race, George and Mitch frantically waved their arms at me to keep going. I pushed the wheelchair in and out of stagnant operagoers as fast as I could without scaring Maria. I left her sitting and ran ahead, and suddenly I saw Mr. Domingo peeking out of a side door looking around. You could barely recognize him under all the make-up. I ran back and told Maria he was waiting for her, and quickly lifted her out of the chair. She was ADAMANT he not see her in that wheelchair.

He went right up to her, got really close to her face, put his arms on her arms, and said, "Oh, Maria, it's so good to see you." Since I've known her I'd never seen a wider smile, and we're talking about a wide-smiling lady. We were causing quite a commotion. I'm sure many wondered who this woman was and why he was spending so much time with her. Maria kissed him on both cheeks, and blew him some as well. She really blew him some! When he left to go perform in the second half, Maria stood there at a loss for words.

Thank you so much to Mitch and George and Richard and the whole gang for rolling out the red carpet for us. Maria will live at least another ten years because of this night.

Gregor

## *April 13, 2009*

(Maria, left, at an opera in Vienna in 1934)

*"You don't want to go there, they all look like men."*

I never met my grandparents on my mother's side, and those on my dad's side died when I was around thirteen. My paternal grandparents were Christian Scientists. I didn't see them often, but when I did they were nice to me, and hugged me, and made sure to smile at me so convincingly. It wasn't until years later when I realized underneath their cloying smiles they never really liked me. I never felt I was the person they wanted me to be, that I thought the way I was supposed to think, or acted the way I was supposed to act. I wasn't "one of them." I was secretly shunned and I didn't even know it. But it makes sense now.

As a result of this, along with, I'm sure, many other things, I'm an adult with a finely tuned bullshit meter, and I walk the earth seeking and cherishing genuineness, and shunning and abhorring phoniness. Maria was the first elderly person in my life—maybe even the first woman besides my mother—who took me under a wing and genuinely loved me.

With Maria I've seen the upside of age, and I've seen the downside. The downside ain't pretty: the "forgetting what you had for breakfast" thing: the "needing to rest every 50 feet on a walk not to mention every five minutes to use the restroom" thing: the "having to speak extra loudly and not being able to enjoy a quiet, subtly humorous moment in public" thing... There's a whole laundry list of unglamorous-ness. Yet the more I'm exposed to these inevitabilities the more I love her. I'm pretty sure that's the definition of true love.

This morning and all day, the house was the locker room of the winning Super Bowl team. Phone calls were fielded, champagne was opened, and visitors were welcomed. The flu symptoms she was showing last night during the opera have now become the full-on flu, and how fortunate for us all it arrived this morning rather than last night.

I shared pictures from my trusty disposable camera. Maria was so full of whimsy reliving all last night's moments through the pictures—she forgot she was even sick. I left her alone in the kitchen to make sure Javier was tending to the new flowers Maria had been nagging him to plant near her bedroom sliding glass door. While I was talking to Javier, I heard through the open kitchen window: "Look how *into* him I am!"

Javier and I walked into the house to see her engrossed in a picture of her staring lustfully into Plácido's eyes.

"I have nothing against Blacks," she began, but I cut her off. She had already explained this.

Save Margie and Myron, none of Maria's kids go as gaga over opera as their parents. When Chuck was born, Maria was convinced he would be her tenor. When that didn't work she attached her hopes to Peter. Her story of what follows explains how that went...

Fritz took Peter to the opera for the first time in the late 50s. Peter wasn't appreciating it as much as Fritz hoped he would: he squirmed and complained the entire evening. As they walked to the car after the show, Fritz yelled, "That's it! I am never taking you to the opera ever again!"

The ride home was agonizingly silent. Peter stormed out of the car and into his room.

Later, his mother walked in. "So I heard Daddy's never going to take you to the opera again."

Between sobs, Peter replied, "He may forget, but I shall always remember!"

I've decided to start mentioning my book to Maria. My goal is to finish it while she's still alive. "I'm writing a book on you," I said.

Her face lit up. "Will anyone read it?"

"I'd read it."

"What's it about?"

"Our relationship."

She slyly raised her right eyebrow. "We can increase it, you know."

By the end of the day Maria's flu had worsened. Last night had been exhausting enough for her, walking up and down stairways, going in and out of bathrooms, and meeting preeminent opera stars. Dealing with the flu was too much. I helped her into bed.

She looked up at me groggily and said, "Do you know where the word lesbian comes from? Greece. The Island of Lesbos."

I told her I'd like to go there. "You don't want to go there, they all look like men."

Her eyes were starting to close. I pulled the covers up, she clasped them, and pulled them up to her chin.

"I hope I don't croak in a way that inconveniences you."

Then she snuggled deeper into her sheets and closed her eyes. On my car ride home I cried at the thought of being without her.

## *May 10, 2009*

**"I don't plan to give you up that easily."**

Maria and I were off to visit Peter in Tacoma today. He's spent the last few years building his boat from scratch, and it was officially ready for its unveiling. He wanted his mother to come break a bottle of champagne on the bow. I was in Cheviot Hills extra early so I had time to lie to her about the time. Last year when she flew up with Tom (before I started working here), she thought it was perfectly okay to leave the house 45 minutes prior to the plane leaving the ground. So the clocks were an hour ahead of the actual time today.

Cane? Check. Walker? Check. Portable wheelchair? Check. Her suitcase? Check. My suitcase? Check. I should have been an octopus.

Tom drove us to the airport in plenty of time, thanks to my clock obsession. I unfolded the wheelchair and pushed Maria through the gate, as Tom helped me with the bags.

I had a nice thing going with the friendly lady I met at the Virgin America check-in desk. When Maria needed to use the bathroom, the lady and I would make eye contact, which meant I was taking my "grandmother" to the bathroom and needed her to keep an eye on our stuff. We played this game a few times. When we arrived at the ladies room on the first trip, I looked around anxiously for a solution, because the issue of getting her into it didn't occur to me until I got there.

Maria let my hand go. "I'll be back in five minutes, darling."

*Oh no.* There was no way I was going let her walk into that crowded bathroom alone. I stopped her in her tracks. A woman saw our dilemma and offered to help walk her in while I stood guard. The two were socializing before they even made it to the stall. The woman was so delighted as they walked out that she seemed not to want to leave us behind.

We were in first class. This was kept hidden from Maria until now, for fear of tension because of her obsession with not appearing better than anyone else. I was nervous she'd put up a stink about it, but as we lounged in our comfortable chairs, I looked at her and she smiled and said, "Are you excited, my love?"

Maria read the *Los Angeles Times* during much of the flight. She found a story about a minor earthquake that occurred around the Palo Alto area this morning. She lowered the paper to show me the article, and said, "You see, in Vienna we didn't have quakes... we had national socialists, but not quakes."

Keep up the good work, Virgin America, and by good work I mean the hiring of attractive flight attendants.

————— ♦ —————

When we got to Peter's house he was eager to show his mother her room. He had been telling her since last year, "You'll be sleeping in the Domingo Room when you come up to Tacoma."

When we entered a giant banner of a grinning Plácido filled the entire wall behind her bed. Now, after years of professing her love to him from afar, Maria could officially say she slept with Plácido Domingo all night, every night, for a whole week. What happens in Tacoma stays in Tacoma.

Peter knows a lot of people who are so friendly they would give Tom a run for his money. Nearly a hundred partygoers packed into his house. In the backyard a band played jazz and country music, while a couple of chefs barbecued the most succulent spare ribs, corn on the cob and chicken this side of the Puget.

I spent most of the evening sitting with Maria on the couch, serving as her eyes and ears. People would greet her as if they'd known her their entire lives (which many times they had). Maria would follow their lead, and half the time after they walked away she'd turn to me and say, "Who in the heck was that?"

I finally met Peter's Donna, who is as sweet as Peter.

After the festivities Maria went off to sleep with Paper Plácido, and I went to my room, which was directly across the hallway on the ground floor. I cracked my door so I could hear if she needed me during the night.

She got up around two. I snapped awake. I lay there listening to her fumbling around her night table to turn on the light, and then her feet slapping against the hardwood floors, and then her scuffling toward the bathroom. But the footsteps were going, rather than coming. *Hmm.*

I sat on the edge of my bed to get a better ear on it. Wait a minute... *Is she walking down the hallway?* I stood up and as I craned my neck out the doorway I saw Adele Bloch-Bauer's niece about to walk out the front door.

I caught up to her just as she was reaching for a doorknob that would land her in the middle of a boulevard. I lightly touched her on the shoulder and she whipped around not knowing who could possibly be behind her at such a late hour.

"What are you doing up so late?" she wondered.

"I'm asking the questions, here. Where are you going?"

"I'm going to the bathroom, why?" She turned to continue back to the door.

I grabbed both her shoulders, turned her around, and pointed her back in the right direction. Thank God I'm a light sleeper.

There were twenty people on Peter's boat the next morning. I had never been to the Northwest or the Puget. Maria said the trees and lakes reminded her of Vienna.

Her granddaughter Alana is so sweet with her. She sat next to her hugging her the whole way to the waterfront where we'd be having lunch. I think about their relationship and how I didn't have that warmth of family growing up, and how those secret cravings for this sort of thing over the years seems to have yielded the Altmanns. The trip brought me closer to Alana, knowing we're both equal adorers of the same girl.

We were boating to Jim Valley's house for brunch. He's a former member of the popular American rock band, Paul Revere and the Raiders, who has been friends with Peter for years. We coasted right up to the sandy beach.

When we docked, we were immediately faced with getting Maria off the boat. The closest we could get it to shore was about three feet from the dock, with fairly deep water between Puget and land. It looked so bleak that we considered turning the boat around, bringing Maria home, and driving her back. But Peter returned with a two-by-four, and with the help of five people we managed to coax Maria to walk the plank to solid ground, where a chair awaited her. There was a raucous round of applause for what was a great team effort.

Peter unveiled champagne, passed around glasses to everyone, and amongst the crashing waves and howling wind on our own private beach, we all toasted to Maria.

———◆———

Packed and ready to return to Los Angeles, Maria and I were sitting on the couch. I gave her vitamin pills with a glass of water, and turned to walk toward my room.

Suddenly I heard choking. It was a mad dash back to the couch. She began flailing her arms, searching for air that wasn't there. I got behind her and pumped her stomach with all my might, my actions the result of watching *Mrs. Doubtfire*. Only it wasn't a shrimp in her throat, it was a giant horse-sized pill.

Maria's face was turning purple. I screamed for help. Peter and Donna ran downstairs. I ordered them to stand back. I pumped her stomach. Out popped the pill.

She doubled over, coughing and wheezing like she was drowning.

When she regained her composure she turned to me and said, "If you would have played a paramedic in a movie you would have killed me." Between coughs she added, "Thank God I'm not a soprano, I'd never work again."

I was sure I'd pumped too high into her rib cage, and that she would have permanent bruises. But she was alive.

Before we were off to the airport she looked up at me, rubbed my cheeks, and said, "I don't plan to give you up *that* easily."

Peter took a deep breath and smiled gently at his mother and then at me, as if to say to us both, "I sure am grateful that you two have each other."

# 2010

# January 1, 2010

*"Look at how she's flirting."*

My life has kept me from writing the last few months. A second film David and I shot called *Goodbye Promise* has been calling our names to finish, and I've begun writing a screenplay with my friend Andrea.

Since that horrible incident in Tacoma we've been giving Maria her vitamins in liquid form, which seems to be working just fine. According to Tom, her increasing difficulty swallowing is a sign she's "turned a corner" with the "d" word.

The choking incident made it clear I had no idea how to perform the Heimlich Maneuver. In fact I didn't know how to do a lot of things I should know as a caregiver. Back in June I suggested to Peter that Tom, David and I take a class and get certified with the American Heart Association. Tom was already certified, but he felt it was a good time to brush up. A representative came to the house and we cleared out the den to make enough room for the dummies we'd be pumping and kissing.

At one point Maria, who was not told about this class and who was supposed to be napping, walked by the room as we were kneeling on the floor with our faces glued to dummies. She stopped and peered in with squinty eyes, and we all looked up at her simultaneously frozen in our positions. The awkward scene didn't seem to faze her in the least. She said hello, and continued to the kitchen. She never asked, and we never told.

I predict a banner year for me, by the way. I'm like Denzel Washington, a Man on Fire. I'm like Martha Stewart—I was incarcerated, and now I'm free. I'm like a Nike freight train—you best get out of the way, because I'm just doin' it. I'm also like a homeless guy, and bear with me on this one: I realize acting is a numbers game, and the angrier I get at each person (casting director) who decides not to give me "money," the fewer chances I'll have to make money.

Ernest Hemingway said, "Nothing good gets away." But how do I know if what I haven't yet achieved is what I should still be fighting for? So many questions, so little answers. But the truth is always in the now. And the now includes Maria. And that's all that matters.

Andrea's been at the house often in recent weeks as we try and get through a first draft of our script. She had recommended months ago that I see *Harold and Maude*, a film made in the 70s about a teenager's "unusual" bond with a 79-year-old woman. I went in thinking I'd be watching Maria and I on screen, but their relationship was completely different than ours, on so many levels. The one scene I could truly relate to was when Maude yells, "Harold, you make me feel like a schoolgirl!" I feel like Maria would have yelled that to me, of course substituting "Harold" with "Gregor."

Dear Everyone;

Lily's daughter, Jackie, Maria, and I, went to Picolo Paradiso for dinner. At the end of the dinner, a man of about 40 approached our table and said, "Can I just say you are the most charming, attractive family I have seen in quite some time." He sat next to Lily and asked how old she was. She responded proudly, "98." About 30 seconds later, she said again: "I'm 98." She did this adorable bragging routine at least two more times. "Look at how she's flirting," Maria said, feeling a little left out.

On our way out I thanked the man for being so gracious, and I told him Maria had a great time. It suddenly occurred to him— "Wait, that's not Maria Altmann, is it?" I confirmed it was, and he exclaimed, "No way!" He went up to her and said, "You were so brave to get those paintings back! You should be so proud!!" Maria spoke to him for a good five minutes. He gave me his card. He's in the art acquisition business.

G

**January 13, 2010**

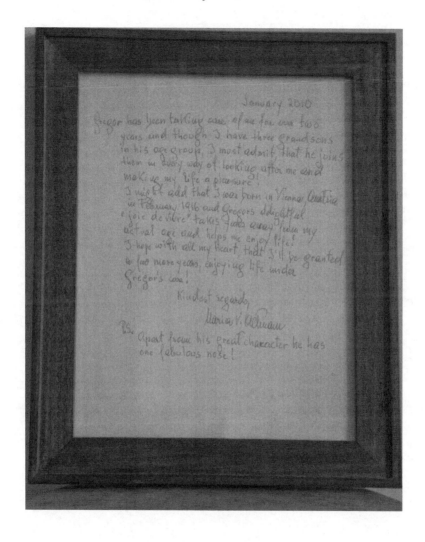

January 2010

Gregor has been taking care of me for over two years and though I have three grandsons in his age group, I must admit, that he joins them in every way of looking after me and make up my life a pleasure!

I might add that I was born in Vienna, Austria in February 1916 and Gregor's delightful "joie de vivre" takes decades away from my actual age and helps me enjoy life!

I hope with all my heart, that I'll be granted a few more years, enjoying life under Gregor's care!

Kindest regards,

Maria V. Ullman

P.S. Apart from his great character he has one fabulous nose!

*"I haven't seen something this unappealing since The Holocaust."*

Word just came that Father Sweeney died. I think back to his last visit to the house just a few months ago, and how they gave each other that extra dose of love, and how Maria went out of her way to walk him down the driveway and wistfully watch his car drive out of sight. It's like they both knew it was the last time they'd see each other.

He was only 77, which seems young to me now. I'd only met him twice, but since death is so unfamiliar to me his is really vexing, which has me frightened of what will eventually happen to someone *really* important to me. The truth is, though, it's a selfish fear; a fear of what will happen to me, not Maria.

Maria has checked into the hospital again, complaining of chest pains. It turned out to be a serious lung clot. Again, this happened during Tom's shift. I don't know why these serious health issues keep landing on him, but with Tom having such a brilliant medical mind I'm not arguing with the universe. The visit turned into one big Jewish stand-up routine. I even forgot she was at the hospital, and she seemed to as well.

"This meal is an offense. You really have to try hard to cook something this bad. I wouldn't feed it to a cat—and I hate cats. Will you take a look at this?" She pointed to what appeared to be a piece of chicken. "I haven't seen something this unappealing since the Holocaust. Now the food at Cedars-Sinai is delicious. They must like the Jews better there."

For some reason while Maria was in her hospital bed she was intent on writing David, Tom and me a job recommendation. It was one hundred percent her idea. She made it clear it wasn't an excuse to leave her. I can't imagine I'd ever use it, but she was insistent about writing it. I framed it. What a keepsake.

# January 17, 2010

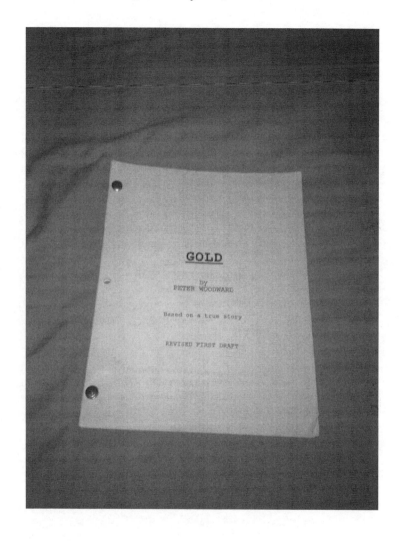

*"Why on earth is he crying?"*

Today was tricky. I had an audition for a guest star on the TV show *Fringe*, in Studio City off of Ventura, and here I was all the way in Cheviot Hills, script in hand, staring at a 93-year-old woman reading the morning paper who had no idea of my predicament.

Chuck was at a doctor's appointment, Tom was in the Valley, and I'd been trying to reach Lisa all day. I began to find peace with the worst-case scenario—or was it the best-case: having to take Maria with me to the audition. I'd bring her in the room and say, "Mind if my grandmother sits over there in the corner?" She'd be so charming I'd book the job and be the talk of the town, and then I'd be approached to the tell the story on Leno, and I'd say, "No, I want Conan."

Lisa called and derailed my plan. *Phew.* She ran over.

I drove an hour and a half in traffic, literally sprinted into the casting waiting room, sat for two minutes staring at three actors who looked exactly like me, was called in by a cute assistant casting director named Pam, read two lines, had the casting director say, "You're a really good actor, wow," then dashed out to my car, and raced back expecting all hell to have broken loose. Maria was sound asleep, and Lisa was reading *The New Yorker* in the den. Three hours to say two lines. Welcome to Hollywood.

———— ◆ ————

Humans are like the engine of a car, starting off fresh and ready to face the road, and over time wearing down and eventually it's either get a tune-up or be hauled off to the scrap yard. But I'm in no need of a tune-up. You'd think after nearly two and a half years I'd need one. I've seen this woman's face more than I have any other face since 2008, and on top of that I have a history of not being able to tolerate the same woman for extended periods of time. Say I'm sitting in the kitchen and I hear some weird noises coming from her room, or she asks me for a cup of tea when I'm in the middle of my toast, or we're sitting together and she wonders if the mail has arrived yet. It would be natural for me to blow her off just once. But I don't. Maria is an oil well, and I am the oilman.

———— ◆ ————

Because of my running around this morning, I couldn't make it to the post office to buy a stamp and mail a bill. Maria wasn't up to getting dressed, so I convinced her to come with me in her bathrobe. I snuck her out of the house because I didn't have the time to explain to Chuck why his mother was going out in public in her bathrobe. She just was. I left her in the car while I ran in to buy the stamp, mailed the letter, and then decided to go to Jersey Mikes, a sandwich place on Beverly.

I illegally parked in an alley, and as I ran in I thought how cool it was that a real-life Bloch-Bauer was sitting in my beat-up Toyota Scion, in a bathrobe, slippers, and sunglasses. Then, while waiting in line for our sandwiches, it occurred to me that I have a scion in my Scion. We were so hungry that we decided to eat right there in the car.

We had to rush home to meet British actor/screenwriter Peter Woodward. He had contacted Randy about a feature script he was writing based on Maria's life and case. He was gracious to Maria, who gave him her full endorsement of all things British.

"We had such a great time in Liverpool during the war," she said, and offered him a seat in the living room and gave him every ounce of her charm. They hung on each other's every word. I brought cheese and crackers and sat off to the side enjoying a Viennese accent and a British accent running around a playground together. Occasionally Peter would look over at me after Maria would state a fact that sounded too good to be true like the story about Poldi and "Hitler's Nephew," and I would nod and affirm it was true. I felt like the Sommelier of Maria Altmann.

Peter knew her general story, and—the mark of a gifted screenwriter—was mainly interested in the tiny little details of her life and escape, those little touches that add flavor to a story. I hold near and dear to my heart certain facts about her life that no one on earth knows except you. I wasn't about to give them to him. I'll keep you abreast of any developments with the script.

After Peter left, the paper made a late appearance due to the busy morning. A while back Governor Mark Sanford admitted to having an affair with an Argentine mistress. His name was mentioned in an article, and I showed Maria a picture of him on my phone with his head buried in his hands, sobbing.

"Did you hear about this guy?" I asked her.

She squinted at his picture. I told her he was a politician who was unfaithful to his wife with a gorgeous lady from Argentina.

She removed her glasses and looked up at me sincerely.

"Then why on earth is he crying?"

*February 10, 2010*

*"This will be our own private park."*

I walked into the kitchen this morning, and Maria was sitting astutely, fully dressed and perfumed, reading the paper. In two years, this was a first. I got the feeling she wanted to impress me, just around the corner from 94. I brought up my book again.

"It's called *Conversations with Maria*."

"How long is it?"

"About 150 pages."

"I converse that much?"

We read in the paper that Plácido was recovering from colon cancer surgery, and set for a concert in Milan to perform Verdi's *Simon Boccanegra*. I sat and watched her read for a few moments until she noticed. Then she put the paper down and dramatically jerked her head to the side to show me her profile— her way of telling me to show her mine.

I just sat there and stared at her indignantly. "I'm going to start charging you for profiles," I declared with a flare of arrogance.

"How much?"

I considered it for a comical moment. "One hundred dollars per profile."

She reached for her purse. I stopped her.

Now that she was all dressed with nowhere to go, we decided to christen a little park we'd always talked about visiting, just south of the Beverly Hills Hotel—where we had met Stephen Lash and Michael Douglas that one evening. We found a bench in front of the fountain spewing out water, and watched the little fishes and ducks swimming around it. I helped her sit down on a cold bench. We looked around. We were alone.

"This will be our own private park," she said.

"I like that," I said, and nothing else needed to be said for a good minute.

"You've awakened in me what I thought wasn't there anymore. I'm enjoying life with you like I did when I was young."

All the potential of the universe was in my hand as I placed it on her knee and kept it there. What a beautiful world.

Hi Richard;

It's Gregor, Maria Altmann's caregiver. I had taken her to see Plácido last year.

Is there any possible way on earth he is in town on February 20, and able to pop in on her birthday celebration at Jim's house in Agoura Hills next week? I look forward to hearing!

Gregor

**February 18, 2010**

*"My kids don't even know about this."*

For Maria's 94th I wrote a poem I read aloud at the gathering at Jim's house:

> A charmed and fairytale life she's had;
> From Klimt to Adele to her wonderful dad;
> From butlers to opera to her dear Uncle Ferry;
> To the smart handsome man she'd eventually marry.
>
> From Satan to rabbits to the horses she'd pity;
> Who'd slip on the ice that surrounded the city;
> From weddings and parties and galas galore;
> To the roaster of chestnuts she'd love to adore.
>
> There's no end in sight to the people she's known;
> To the places she's been and the courage she's shown;
> And yes one more thing I have failed to yet mention;
> A case so supreme that it gave quite a pension.
>
> But strip away all the above that I've told;
> The fame and the fortune... The Lady in Gold;
> And that which remains is a powerful light;
> The most wonderful, whimsical, grand dame in sight...
>
> ...AND I KNOW I'M RIGHT!
>
> -GC

She looked up at me standing before her holding my crumpled piece of paper, and she reached out her hand and I gave her the poem. We all watched her as she read it over and over again to herself as if she couldn't believe it was real.

Then she put it down and removed her glasses, and with her hand resting on her heart, she spoke into mine.

"How did you know all these things? Satan? And the horses? My kids don't even know about this."

It was the first time I saw Maria Altmann cry.

*April 16, 2010*

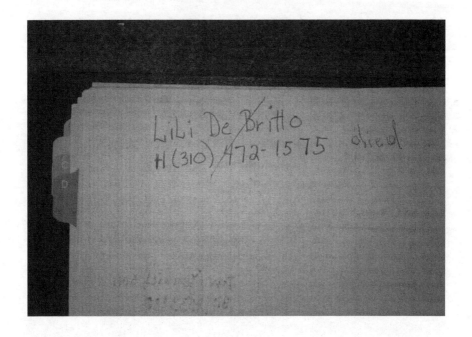

*"Fritz had a rule to never go to funerals in your 90's."*

Lily De Britto was supposed to be a Centenarian. Every other week I'd hear she fell again, yet when I showed up with Maria for their weekly dinner in Brentwood the same four-foot-ten-inch, ninety-pound lady swung open the door before we could even ring the bell, greeting us in the middle of a frenetic sentence, pushing her walker around her house like it was a lawnmower headed down a steep hill.

David and I were standing in Maria's kitchen just last night talking about how Lily was going to be 99 later this year. It never crossed our minds that anything would ever stop her. We had a laugh remembering how one day she refused to go shopping with her grandson Mark because he hadn't shaved that day. We talked about her making sure the maid dusted her books, which Maria thought was "so pointless." We talked about how she still wore Prada shoes, and still wore Chanel #5.

After I hung up with David I dialed Maria, and told her I'd heard the news. "Lily had one last wish, and that was to never die suffering. She got her wish."

There was a silence before she continued. "Lily was always afraid of dying."

That startled me. *Lily feared the final surrender.* Then Maria bookended it with her usual flare for levity: "She's probably already driving those people crazy."

She was torn about whether to go to the memorial service. "Fritz had a rule to never to go to funerals in your nineties. But I don't know if I could do that to Lily."

Then she brushed it all aside and asked if I was having fun on my day off. She had to be battling her own mortality, knowing her oldest friend is now gone. Her friends were being steadily checked off the list. She lost her best friends Peter Koller and Maria Reitler in 2006, along with Hubertus Czernin, then Father Sweeney, and now Lily. Edith was her only remaining close friend.

I had seen Lily just two nights ago when I dropped Maria off for dinner. She answered the door mid-sentence of course, and was in excruciating physical pain. She struggled to stand in the doorway to greet us, her body shaking from head to toe, her voice so frail and weak. She was still pushing her little walker like a lawnmower, only now she was struggling to push it *up*hill.

The last two months she showed off a new injury to me every week. She had a fresh bruise on her arm that evening, and bruises on her face and neck. I felt so horrible for her, but there was nothing I could do. And the maid just stood in the corner. All poor Lily had in her final days, final months, final years, was a maid who stood obediently in the corner awaiting her next direction. I wished I could have kept her company, even for an hour a week. I could have done it. Why didn't I do more for her?

Maria and I made our way to the sofa with Lily after dinner. I left Maria's side to help Lily make it to the couch and she was grateful. I asked her what happened to her arm, and she said she injured herself in bed. Then I asked her if a gentleman caller was to blame, and she smiled and said, "I wish." It was a treat to see Lily smile. It didn't happen often.

I knew she used email, so that night I asked her for her address, and she wrote it on a sheet of paper for me. I kissed her on the cheek, noticing a hint of jealousy on Maria's face. I informed the two old friends that David would be picking Maria up at 8. Then I left. It was the last time I saw Lily DeBritto.

When I got home, mere hours before she died, I logged onto my computer and sent her an email. "Hello, Lily! It was great seeing you tonight. I hope you have a wonderful evening."

I will always wonder if she opened that email. Maybe one day I'll check my inbox and see that there's one from Lily, telling me she was sorry she couldn't respond because she had her hands full with the whole "final transition thing."

Rest, Lily. You deserve a peaceful rest.

*April 21, 2010*

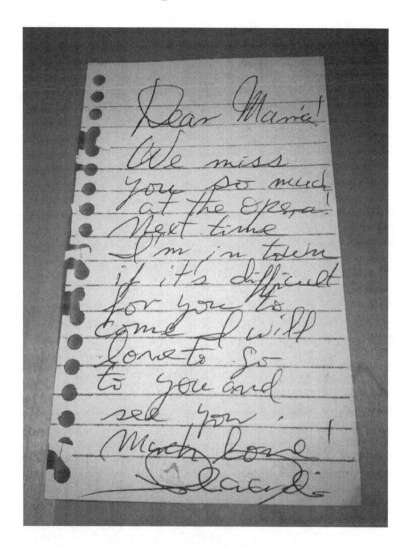

"*If Lily would have known croaking would have gotten her into the paper, she would have croaked a lot earlier.*"

Maria said the line on the previous page as she read Lily's obituary in the *Los Angeles Times*. She set the paper aside and stared off into the backyard. I got up and stood near the fridge where she couldn't see me. What was she thinking about? When she and Lily were kids? About death? Her own mortality? Emma? Her father? Me?

Every moment of every day she lives to engage others, to see other people enjoying life, with nary a moment of a self-reflection, nary a moment of self-analysis. She makes life look so easy. What does this woman struggle with inside? I stepped into view and she acknowledged me standing over her, snapping out of her trance. I sat.

With a sudden, sage smirk she asked, "What are you gonna do after I croak?" I left her in the kitchen with the question.

————◆————

Chuck's having "minimally invasive" back surgery this afternoon. Maria's been nervous about this for quite some time. We're visiting him later at the hospital. A lot had to happen before we could leave the house. For one, Monika Henreid, actor Paul Henreid's daughter, was coming over in the late morning hours to visit. She arrived bearing a small note for Maria, signed by a man she would be delighted to hear from.

When Maria finished reading it, she studied us through her reading glasses, went back to note, then set it aside, and removed her glasses.

"This is fake," she decided. Monika assured her it was real and said she had just had dinner with him and his wife last week.

Maria read it again with more interest, then decided Monika was telling the truth. She was utterly enthralled with the massive, flamboyantly-written "P" in Plácido's signature. She looked at us with fire in her eyes, and said sarcastically, "Look at that extravagant P! He thinks nothing of himself. *Absolutely nothing!*" This note, of course, made her day, and helped her forget about Chuck's back. I put it on the fridge under a magnet, and texted the image to the family.

Edith brought lox and cream cheese bagels for lunch. She and Maria had gone to the same elementary school together in Vienna, and like Maria Reitler, they both inadvertently ended up in California decades later. Edith is sharp as a whip, if a whip needs to be sharpened, and always genuinely interested in my life and my pursuit as an actor. She looks amazing at 91. Seeing her from behind you would think she was a woman in her fifties.

"Edith is a real lady," Maria said after she left. In the past two years I've come to know what a real lady is.

Left alone in the kitchen, I brought up my book again, which I've decided to call, *I Just Met a Girl Named Maria.*

"I can't wait to tell the world that you've become a friend, a mother and a grandmother to me."

As if disappointed, she said, "Well what about mistress?"

## June 15, 2010

*"Just a few years ago I visited Uncle Ferry's home in Vienna. They gave me a key for the day. I wanted to take something back to California with me—a memory, maybe something had fallen to the ground—anything that would remind me of my youth. Let me tell you, there wasn't even a doorknob left to take. Everything was remodeled. It was nothing like it was. Very sad."*

I just returned to Los Angeles after spending a weekend in New York to see *The Gold Portrait*. The last time I was in New York was on New Year's Eve in 1998 with my parents and my brother to see *Phantom of the Opera*. As far back as I can remember my parents exposed us to the arts. While the other high school kids were at home watching *Saved by the Bell* or at the track racing Go-karts, Christian and I were in slacks and sweaters strolling around Phillip's Gallery in downtown DC, looking at the mere 36 Vermeer paintings in existence. I appreciated it then, but looking back I am terminally grateful for that art exposure at such a young age. If I ever have kids they'll be in slacks and sweaters strolling around plays and art galleries. Well, maybe not sweaters.

Weeks ago when I told Maria I wanted to go to New York to see Adele, she picked up the phone, and five minutes later her 93-year-old cousin Ruth Rogers-Altmann told me I could stay with her for as long as I wanted. She lives in a prime spot on Park Avenue near Grand Central Station.

Ruth was yet another impressive woman in her 90's, who, like Edith, whisked around town like a woman half her age. She was born in 1917, the daughter of well-known Austrian architect Arnold Karplus. At a very young age she became interested in art and skiing, and her love of both led to a career in fashion design.

She was responsible for two very important advancements in apparel for skiers. After she bought some stretch fabric for ski pants in Paris and realized the States had not seen anything like it, she introduced the fabric to America. In 1938 she designed the first ski jacket that had a concealed hood built into the collar. In Florence in the 1980s she was knighted for her contributions to the fashion industry.

And in 1998, at the age of 81, she competed in the Gerald Ford American Ski Classic, where she faced an opponent in her twenties—and won. She goes to the East Hamptons to paint every summer.

I walked 46 blocks to the Neue Galerie from Ruth's apartment. The gold carpet was rolled out for me, thanks to Renee Price, Ronald Lauder's right-hand-woman. I met the kind Swiss gentleman, Bruno, who manages the bookshop, and a sweet woman whose name I wish I remembered gave me a formal tour of the museum.

Seeing Adele was as strange as it was a thrill. So accustomed to seeing copies, I stood admiring what they told me was the original, insisting to myself, "This is just another copy. It has to be." It didn't sink in that it was the original until I had time to think about it later. It was much larger than I envisioned it being.

Simply being in the same room with Adele was worth the trip. I had spent the last two years getting to know her niece and only hearing second-hand stories about her short and distinguished life, and now I was as close to her as humanly possible, able to really feel her in my bones, imagine her actually being painted by Klimt, and consider more meaningfully her place in history.

(Adele shushing one of her German Shepherds in 1920)

Now I'm back in Los Angeles doing the things some audacious Los Angelenos do, like giving my headshot to my drycleaner. The owner's name is Bob, a Chinese man in his sixties. One day I walked in and there was a pile of clothes on the counter, and he said proudly as if he were showing me his son's straight-A report card, "Angelina Jolie and Brad Peet clothes. Right here."

He has a row of headshots on the wall, everyone from Mel Gibson to Sylvester Stallone, and I figured he needed Gregor Collins to really make it legit. I handed the headshot to him and said, "This might be worth some money someday."

I looked at him and imagined him laughing uncontrollably. Just once. He must have read my mind because his dour face lit up like a liquor store sign at night. It was the first time I had ever seen him smile, let alone laugh. You should visit him. He's on the corner of Franklin and Canyon, in Hollywood. Find my headshot (in the trash), point to it, and say, "That guy says hi."

*June 17, 2010*

*"I know exactly where I was when Kennedy was
shot. I was walking out of my front door and a little
boy was running down the street yelling, 'The President
was shot! The President was shot!' For him it was
a tremendous excitement."*

I received a phone call today from Tom. He told me he had a hunch a "big event" would happen within a year. He spoke of Maria's irregular heartbeat, and how it's getting more irregular every day.

"Thanks," I said. I hung up and sat on the edge of my bed and chewed the edge of my iPhone until I felt the tears coming.

*Maria is dying.*

*"Isn't there some species of animal where the
male has sex with the female and then kills her?
Well anyway, it's a good idea."*

Poldi was a top-ranked golfer in Vienna in the twenties and thirties. Golf has played a big part in my life. I picked up a club for the first time my freshman year of high school in Northern Virginia, and within weeks was at the driving range every day whacking balls over the fence. I started to hit them so well and so far that the range's pro shop would get regular phone calls from homeowners over the back fence, complaining of little white round balls pelting their garages and windows, and threatening to sue if it didn't stop. Whoever was working the desk didn't think twice before leaning their head out the door to yell, "Put the driver back in the bag, Gregor!"

I tried out for the school team and became Centreville High School's number-one golfer, and would maintain that status through the end of my senior year. Along the way I was able to land a few write-ups in the local papers.

It made sense to consider pro golfing as a career path, so I applied for a scholarship at several small and medium-sized schools. I received a grant at a small one—Ohio Wesleyan University—where I played third seed my freshman year. It was during a practice round at the local course in Delaware, Ohio that I shot my first ever 68—and that was with bogeys on the last two holes. For you non-golfers, that's pretty awesome.

But soon my desire for a school with a more social environment became more important than my desire to play golf. My best friend Magnus and I decided to transfer to Miami University of Ohio, near Cincinnati, at the time ranked sixth on the list of "American Colleges with the Hottest Women."

We did what young men were supposed to do at college: join a fraternity, drink beer, and chase top-ranked women. After our sophomore year, Magnus stayed behind, but in my continued quest for why I belonged on earth, which was, apparently, at least partially, to meet a Holocaust refugee in 2008 in Los Angeles, I transferred yet again.

Before enrolling in a new school I decided to work for a television program called *World Business Review* with Caspar Weinberger, taped in Southern Florida and filmed in DC. Golf officially fell down the priority list. I worked at the show for a year as a production assistant, amassed knowledge and experience behind the camera, and applied for in-state tuition at the much-sought-after Media Production Department at Florida State University. I finished at FSU with a degree in Media Production and a minor in Spanish.

Lucky for me, I befriended a teacher, Mr. Sawyer, who went to FSU with the creators of a new dating show produced in Los Angeles, called *Blind Date.* He made a phone call to one of these creators, David Garfinkle, and set up an interview I ended up flying out for and nailing. I flew back to DC, packed up my bags, and drove three thousand miles back to LA to make it to my first day of work as a tape librarian.

One day at the *Blind Date* offices a beautiful, green-eyed blonde, ten years older than me, poked her head in the tape library looking for the casting office. I showed her where to go, and after she was finished auditioning she returned to the library. I walked her out to her car. Caroline became my first girlfriend in a decade. It was my most healthy relationship to date. She's married now.

In its freshman year on the air, the executives at *Blind Date* decided to organize the first annual golf tournament they were dubbing the *Blind Date Invitational.* Word had spread around the office that I played golf in college, and there were some producers who felt threatened, knowing they'd been playing for years and there was no way in hell this hotshot from the East Coast was going to come in like he owned the place. The office was abuzz with chatter. There was a lot at stake for me. And my golf game was a rusty gate.

On the big day I stood at the driving range hitting balls. I was playing "military golf": left, right, left, right. The ball was going everywhere but down the middle. Employees wrote me off before I even stepped onto the first tee.

I walked onto the first tee, as nervous as I was during a real tournament. I teed the ball up, did a few waggles, swung for the fences, and looked up. There was no white ball whizzing down the middle of the fairway. Instead it was dribbling down the dinky little hill right in front of me. I was humiliated.

One producer—we'll call him John M—stood off to the side with folded arms and the most satisfied expression you can imagine. My heart was in my shoes as I slumped after my ball, resting twenty yards in front of the tee box.

When I reached my ball I pulled out my trusty two-iron, gave it a good whack, hit the green about 200 yards away, and three-putted for bogey. Seventeen holes later I stood over a six-foot birdie putt to shoot a two-under par 70. I sunk it.

A trophy awaited me as I walked to the clubhouse, and John M materialized, shook my hand and said, "Great round, Gregor." My reputation around the office skyrocketed.

So anyway, golf for me is like riding a bike.

Maria and I have been talking for months about a golf date. This afternoon we went down the street to Rancho Park Golf Course. She was going to see how good I was. But what I'd envisioned for the months leading up to the day was different than what actually happened. She could barely see me swinging because the only open bench was two stalls over. She definitely wasn't close enough to notice or appreciate the extraordinary intricacies of my swing. And she was weak today. Not at her best. At least Poldi was able to see that he has some stiff competition.

*July 16, 2010*

*"I wouldn't like that as a man <u>or</u> a woman."*

I didn't tell you that last year I tried to organize a pool party at Maria's house. I sent out an impassioned email to the select few I considered worthy of attending, people who I knew would appreciate meeting the most important person in my life. Half responded, and among those only two or three could make it.

It stung. It was like not hearing back from a girl the day after you just knew you rocked her world. In hindsight I should have written, "Come to a barbecue at my friend Maria's house." But no, I had to get all emotional and write a bunch of self-important histrionic horseshit. Par for the course.

I ended up cancelling the whole event in disgust, and was tempted to take the people who never responded off my good friend list permanently. So this year I only made phone calls.

Maria looked great. She wore a blue and green flowery blouse, pants as white as a Republican, and her red-rimmed Prada sunglasses that make her look like a movie star. We had a cellphone photo snapped of us on the back terrace, taken more as an afterthought, but it ended up looking perfect enough for a book cover.

I was the head chef, grilling up fresh German deli fillets. She gave my friends the love I knew she'd give them. Unfortunately there were too many people milling about for everyone to have sufficient time with her. But even if they had ample time they'd never know the Maria I knew. At the same time that delighted me, it saddened me to know that I could never fully communicate to anyone all the little nuances and delicacies of our relationship.

My friend Doug monopolized her. With him she was a pig in dirt, because he, according to the "profile guru" herself, has a wonderful profile. She couldn't stop making sure he knew this. Chuck rolled his eyes at me as we both watched her flirt with Doug.

Darkness fell, and Maria—who hadn't had a nap all day—was still going strong on the back terrace with Archie, his charming new girlfriend Anne, Andrea, and another gal named Amber. We decided—well, I decided—to give Maria her first ever shot of tequila. She took a baby sip, winced and made a choking sound, and pushed it away.

"Don't give me any more of that, please."

Naturally, everyone was interested in Maria's life. When asked about sports she said, "I was never very athletic. I was always more into the ski instructors than the actual skiing."

Later Archie opened the Facebook app on his phone and showed Maria a picture of a friend he wasn't sure was a man or a woman.

Maria studied the photo and said, "I wouldn't like that as a man *or* a woman," and handed him back his phone. The porch erupted in laughter.

Later Maria called Margie to tell her about the barbecue. Naturally, I was listening outside her door. Toward the end of the conversation, she said to her daughter, "He's everything I always wanted."

*August 23, 2010*

(Ronald Lauder's Assistant Renee Price, her dog, me, Maria, and
Edith, outside Shutters Restaurant on Santa Monica Beach)

**"I think Shaquille O'Neal is just fabulous."**

The closest I've been to seeing death was when my friend from elementary school, Noah Eig, died after being struck by lightning at a school football game. This year, though, call me Dr. Death. There have been many that have rocked me to varying degrees. There was Lily, Father Sweeney, and David's fiancée Karen's cat of nearly two decades. There was a trainer at my gym who was broadsided by a truck on her way to Vegas for the weekend, a girl at Patina who committed suicide, and a daredevil colleague I used to work with in reality television, in a motorcycle accident. And now at 91 years old, Maria's last friend on earth, Edith Mestner. The friends are all gone.

Edith was at the house for the lox-and-bagels lunch just a week ago. She was rich in spirit, healthy, and happy. I got a call this morning from her daughter. Within the last six days she'd had a stroke and died in the hospital. While I was on the phone, David and I made contact, and he slumped into his chair. Everyone was fond of Edith.

I felt sick imagining telling Maria her last friend on earth was gone. I pictured her staring out the window wondering if life was worth living anymore. Tom told me that Lucille Ball— towards the end—did an interview where she suddenly started crying, and the journalist asked her what she was crying about, and she said, "It's just that all my friends are gone."

I was afraid Maria would respond in a similar way, and I wanted to spare her that pain.

The consensus was that we should tell Maria. Jimmy offered to take her for the weekend in the mountains, and tell her there. Then Chuck sent out an email suggesting—well, Chuck doesn't exactly suggest—that telling her would accomplish nothing. The truth is, though Edith was a good friend and they were very fond of each other, Maria rarely saw her and rarely spoke of her. Chuck was right. What she wouldn't know would never hurt her. There are times that ignorance is bliss, and a woman who's lived on this earth for 94 years deserves bliss.

*September 11, 2010*

*"Everyone forgets I'm 94!"*

Today is Peter's wedding to his girlfriend Donna Hansen in Maria's backyard. If you can believe it, not only is her name Donna, like Chuck's Donna, but her middle name is Marie, like Chuck's Donna. What are the odds of that? The way we've agreed to tell them apart is to call Chuck's Donna LaDonna, for Los Angeles Donna.

My first question to Peter was why they chose September 11 as the wedding date.

"It was my idea. I wanted to give the day a more positive light." This says most of what you need to know about Peter.

The ceremony didn't start until the afternoon, so I slipped in a quick hike in Griffith Park. I got a text on the way from Peter, who had just arrived at the house from Tacoma.

"If you're close, stopping by would be helpful."

I had no idea what it was referring to, but in "Peaceful Peterland" this is an extremely urgent text requiring immediate attention. I was at the house in twenty minutes.

When I arrived I was warned that because of Maria's anxiety about the wedding and all the dozens of people who would be swarming the house, she was distressed, and was refusing to work out with Tina, who was due to arrive at the house any minute.

I walked into her room to find her staring into the bathroom mirror brushing out the knots in her hair. I put my arm around her and waited for her to make eye contact with me through the mirror. She forced a pouty smile.

"My hair just refuses to cooperate." She handed me the brush.

I slid it through her hair like I was her mother and we were getting ready to receive guests for dinner. She allowed me to comb for a few moments and it appeared I was doing a good job, but she got so discouraged with how it looked that she took the brush back. "It's not you, darling, it's this damn hair." She resumed for a few moments, then tossed it in the sink.

"Everyone always forgets I'm 94! I don't want to work out."

"I know," I said, comforting her.

She exhaled and put her arm around my shoulder. I reminded her Tina was coming in a few minutes.

As I went to open her closet to lay out her clothes, she said, "It will be better when I croak because then I'll be in a much more favorable position to bug God to be good to you."

An hour later she stood in her room showing off in a gorgeous pink dress LaDonna had bought for her from Macy's. I told her she looked like a princess, and this excited her enough to ask me to marry her. I promised I'd ask Peter if we could make it a double wedding.

Seventy people showed up at the Altmann house. Peter wound Christmas lights through the branches of every tree in the backyard, and white chairs were set up around a flower-studded wedding arch. Jimmy spent the entire morning nailing plywood down around the edges of the pool to prevent any unwitting tumbles.

Peter greeted guests wearing a black top hat. How perfect. I always viewed him as Lincoln-esque, so for his wedding gift I had gotten him one of my favorite books, *Team of Rivals: The Political Genius of Abraham Lincoln.*

Peter announced to the crowd that his father, Fritz, had worn the hat at his own wedding in 1937, and it had belonged to Fritz's father. This hat had been around since 1862. Randy's father, Ronald, a retired judge, officiated the ceremonies. During the exchange of vows I suddenly felt little droplets of water sliding down my cheeks, and I looked up. It wasn't raining. The tears were easy to hide because I was mainly on the outskirts of the crowd shooting video.

After the ceremony Peter pulled me aside and led me on a silent walk down the driveway. I trailed him until we stopped at my car.

He found his words fairly quickly and easily. "A year ago my mother said to me, 'Take care of the little one when I'm gone.' I'm just getting around to telling you."

He hugged me and looked at me lovingly and I understood everything I needed to understand.

*October 1, 2010*

*"You're going to leave me now."*

Last week I was in the Empire State again, this time for our New York premier of *Night Before the Wedding*. I thought of calling Maria to say hello, but my trip was chock so full of activity I didn't even call my old friend Ruth, who was just down the street.

I expected a tough crowd in NYC, but they laughed at all the right places, even at some of the wrong ones. Upon my return to Los Angeles there was no reason to expect anyone but the jovial young girl I had left behind. But instead an old woman struggled to push her walker down the dark hallway.

She was in pain. On our walk to the kitchen she stopped to favor her wrists. "I used to be so proud that I never had any physical ailments. Now they've all come at once."

Seeing her this morning made me never want to leave town again. Everything I've ever done in my life has led me to this neighborhood, to this house, to this woman. I need to be here.

She had an appointment with Dr. Stoll today. Her eyesight has been getting steadily worse. Her right eye is nearly blind, and her left eye has been showing signs of elevated macular degeneration.

Getting dressed was more of a chore than usual. Putting on her socks was so difficult she had to rest between feet. And they've become so swollen that I couldn't get her shoes on. I called Tom. He told me to take her blood pressure. I took it, and called him again. He was concerned enough to tell me to take it once more for safety in an hour. It stabilized. I finally forced her shoes on. *Her legs are so swollen and sensitive right now.* I can feel her pain. Now I know how truthful people are being when they say to loved ones, "If I could transfer all your pain to me, I would."

I found a spot in front of the doctor's office. As I got her out of the car, she told me she felt funny. I suggested she do a stand-up routine, but she didn't laugh. I immediately knew something was seriously wrong. I led her into the building as swiftly as I could, but as we entered the waiting room her body suddenly turned into dead weight. She collapsed to the floor. I hoisted her up under her armpits and dragged her toward the chairs—they were all filled. One woman stood up and offered hers, and even in the throes of her dizziness Maria thanked her profusely.

We caused quite a stir in the office. I ran to get a cup of water, and when I returned her hands were buried in her face in shame.

"You're going to leave me now. I'm too much trouble."

I leaned over to her and said firmly, "I am not going to leave you, Maria."

We cancelled the appointment and I got her home and into bed. Tom arrived for his shift and I left him to a resting Maria. Halfway home I got a call that he was taking her to the ER. It was another bladder infection, this one "severe." Another couple days and it would have been fatal.

We're all saving her life in different ways. Tina with humor and exercise; Tom with boundless love and charm, but more than anything, medically; David, with his superhuman humility and grace; and I guess I'm doing whatever it is I'm doing, which is more than I've ever done for another human being.

*October 13, 2010*

*"When you're pretty one day, and you're ugly the next, and someone has to help you shower, it's very hard to accept."*

Why does the majority of physical discomfort have to happen when you're old? Why must such fragile frames be forced to endure such abominable pain? Give the pain to the young—the limber ones with hubris who think they have it all figured out. Better yet, life would make more sense if we were given the choice when in our lives we wanted to endure the pain the majority of which would come near the "end."

Mr. God, let's give every newborn a printout showing a chart indicating how much physical pain (aside from the pain they might cause from their own carelessness) they can expect to endure in their life—some destined more than others—and at any point in their lives they have the option to say, "Okay, I have a couple weeks of vacation coming up at work, it would be the perfect time to get all this pain out of the way now. I'm young and strong and can take it."

And why can't the sense of smell go first... or the sense of touch? Why does it have to be the eyes and the ears? There is no justice in the intangible world.

One day Maria's donning my favorite purple velvet jumpsuit, doing windmills and knee bends with Tina in the living room, and the next, she's lying in a hospital bed fighting for her life. I think about the good old days when we'd mosey to Malibu, trek to Tacoma, or prance to the park. No more moseying, trekking or prancing. We're mostly around the house now.

Her frail frame, a once sleek red Ferrari, is now a weathered brown Volvo. She retreats to bed more often. She used to take one nap and sometimes none, but now she's averaging three. It appears the Scrabble ship has sailed. I pulled out the board this afternoon, only to make it through ten minutes before she became confused, uninterested, and tired. It was clear it was our final game. The tears are flooding as I write.

Yet we tread on through the blizzard. Maria, David and I watched *Guys and Dolls* tonight. It was one of Fritz's favorites. David had discovered the copy in a drawer in Chuck's office. As we watched it she sang along with the choruses.

"Fritz used to sing it all around the house."

She periodically looked over at us sitting on the couch in the dark to see if we were enjoying it as much as she was. At one point she looked over at us feebly, frightened we had left her there alone. I reached into the light and touched her shoulder, and she returned to her state of calm.

The one boon of her determined and unstoppable journey down Dementia Lane is that she trends to forget about recent, unsavory episodes. We hired a nurse to visit the house to help Maria shower. Lately we've noticed she just stands under the water, letting it trickle down her body. There needs to be more scrubbing. So last week, when the nurse showed up for the first time, Maria was incensed we hadn't told her she was here to help her shower. It was strange to see Maria angry, I'd never seen it. Underneath was a kind of hurt.

"When you're pretty one day, and you're ugly the next and someone has to help you shower, it's very hard to accept." A brave admission from a brave woman.

I'm still shocked by her fits of incredible memory. When I first met her I invited her and Peter—who was in town—to see a theater production I was in. I played three different characters, one of whom was half-naked throughout the entire first act. I don't know what I was thinking, inviting them to see that so early in our relationship, let alone at all. Nearly three years later—just last week—she asked me, "Am I crazy or were you half-naked in a play?"

Since Maria is too weak to leave the house right now, the salon came to her today. Margie arranged for Maite to pay a "surprise" visit to do her hair. We told Maite to tell Maria it was a surprise, so Maria wouldn't feel guilty she came all the way to her house (which is only a couple miles). She was thoroughly convinced Maite had decided to drop by unannounced.

Maria felt so energized after the visit, she dialed Lisa. "Lisa, my love, I just got my hair done, and you're going to want to come over and rape me."

A few minutes later she was out like a light.

I wandered into the den, and pulled from the shelf a VHS tape from 1987, labeled "Maria and Fritz 50 year Anniversary."

I watched Maria "on stage" at age 71 looking and acting and moving like she was 41. As she worked the crowd giving a speech to her family on the television, I turned to the monitor showing her in present time sleeping peacefully in her bedroom. Then and now, past and present.

I cried at the tragedy of time passing, at a woman so in control of herself and her life, and now a woman with no control over anything but her love. I think of Leo Tolstoy's quote, "All, everything that I understand, I understand only because I love."

Such a deep and profound truth only amplified by tears.

*November 6, 2010*

*"Luise turned 90 around the time that
whole Monica Lewinsky thing came out. She was
so proud, she said, 'I don't know what the big deal is,
I would have given him a blow job.'"*

I believe I was born with a heart unable to regulate the intake and outflow of love. I'm not sure why I think you should know this, perhaps because you probably already do. I've come to the conclusion that I will always be a ball of pent-up love that I'll never know what to do with, when to use it, or who to use it on.

The love I give pours out not in cups, not in buckets, but in large, master bedroom bathtubs, the kind you'd have found in Uncle Ferdinand's Czechoslovakian castle. I don't know what else to do with someone in whom I've placed my trust, than to give them all the keys to my kingdom—you can call me the Janitor of Love. On January 30, 2008, I met my love match. Maria and I have given each other our keys. And it's a beautiful thing.

But did God purposely not build a dam or a little doggie door, or a car washer flap, to regulate this outpouring? I like you, God, you know that, but I hate that you created a heart that forced me to want to profess my love to someone who's too young to handle it. You'll meet her in the next paragraph.

There's this girl from New Jersey. *Jersey girl.* She took the train into New York to see *Night Before the Wedding* last month. She found me on Facebook weeks before the premier and would check in with me once or twice a week to say things like, "LOL, OMG, LMFAO." I didn't believe she'd bother to take the train in from Jersey to see the screening as she kept promising, but she did.

We hung out in a large group afterwards. I kept asking myself what this girl wants from me, why she's so into me. I gave her my phone number. Later that night after we parted ways, she started texting me, calling me, and I found myself sitting on a plane ready to fly back to Los Angeles responding to every text she'd ever sent, and there were dozens. I finally couldn't contain myself. The doggie doors were opening, the car washer flaps were beating in the wind, and the keys were making their way out of my pocket.

Two weeks later I sent her a text that was a novel, even though it was very nonfiction. It said, among many other stupid things I must have gotten from the movie *As Good As It Gets*, that I wanted to make her a better woman, and I wanted her to make me a better man. After I sent it, there were crickets. No response. I felt betrayed. Angry. Enraged.

Honesty is great for love, but it's also so fucking bad for it. Girls want love, and yet when they get it they decide they don't want it. Just because Maria came into my life to prove me wrong doesn't mean that it doesn't hurt to love.

It's been said that if you give nothing, you get nothing. I say if you give everything, in the end, you still get nothing. I have a real problem with you, Love.

*November 8, 2010*

(Mom)

*"I don't believe in ghosts, but that doesn't mean
I'd be happy with one in my room."*

Right alongside Maria, my mother, Kathryn Grant, is the strongest woman I know. She was born in 1947, and grew up in one of the most crime-ridden neighborhoods in America at the time, the South Side of Chicago. Her parents were Sicilian, and her brothers dabbled in the mafia, and were in and out of jail most of her youth. At fifteen she landed a job herself as an intern at the *Wall Street Journal*. At sixteen she packed her bags and ran away from home, and would never speak to anyone in her family ever again.

She put herself through Vassar College by waitressing at the Lobster Inn in the South Hamptons during a summer, and graduated cum laude a year after Meryl Streep. Then she got a job again at the *Wall Street Journal*, this time in Philadelphia. Desperate for the peace and normalcy she lacked from her family, she moved to DC to marry a tall, gentle journalist named Keith Collins, who gave her the TLC she so desperately needed. He became my father. They called it quits when I was 21.

I remember fifteen years ago when her mother died. I asked her about it, and she shrugged it off. Later she confided: "My whole life I've been running away from my past."

The above is all I know about my mother.

Though Maria is one of the few women I've met who I can trust, I still have a general distrust of them. And for most of my adult life I assumed it was because women were actually untrustworthy. I'm having epiphanies.

We'll pick up where we left off: Jersey Girl cut off contact. How could she just stop contacting me? Another girl who had proven she couldn't be trusted.

I went on a lot of hikes and looked at a lot of sunsets. Even dogs would depress me. I would assume they were depressed too. They must be agonizing through life knowing it will end in a mere decade. They must have just as bleak an outlook as me. *But no dog ever committed suicide.* I concluded all this disjointed emotion was a sign I either needed a girlfriend, or therapy. I wasn't sure which. Probably both.

At the height of my low, as I sat slumped against the wall in my bedroom, I tried calling my brother. He didn't answer. Then I tried Archie. Nothing. Then, for some reason I decided to call my mother. Perhaps spending so much time with Maria's family made me want to reach out to my own. She was never the one I called when it came to women. I dialed her. Only rings.

My phone rang 30 seconds later. Mom was naturally concerned I was calling her so late. I told her how depressed I was, and that I was sure it was spawned by a stupid girl from New Jersey whom I barely even knew. She said I should thank my lucky stars I met her to reveal issues I needed to face. She was loving and listened—just what I needed. We hung up.

The phone woke me up twenty minutes later. It was Jersey Girl. It was the first time we spoke in a week. I decided to be brutally honest, admitting I was a mess because I hadn't heard from her, and that I was needy, and that I spend so much time working that I deprive myself of women, which is just an excuse to avoid issues I'm frightened to confront. I told her she was seeing me at my absolute emotional rock bottom. Then my trust issues with women arose.

"That stuff all goes back to your mother," she said.

After we hung up I thought about this. I was never one to pull the "victim card," but the more I thought about it the more I acknowledged that my mother was one tough cookie who endured a lot of crap in her life. Due to her tough upbringing she wasn't the kind of mother who overdid the doting. She wasn't a coddler. Because I didn't receive an outpouring of love as a youth (which actually would have given me a whole new set of issues), I grew up thinking giving tenderness to women would only mean I wouldn't get it back. I decided I needed to find peace with my mother before I could welcome another woman into my life.

But I've welcomed a woman. I've found my soul mate. Maybe I'm spoiled. Maybe Maria doesn't count as a woman because it's so easy to love a 94-year-old. It's easy to tell people. There's no shame in it. No embarrassment. It's like saying you're in a love with a puppy.

I may be scared of losing Maria but I'm not scared of her ever leaving me. Someday I'll love someone my own age, and someday this girl from New Jersey and the issues I have with my mother will be as irrelevant as yesterday's weather.

But for now, I have my woman. I'm right where I'm supposed to be.

## December 4, 2010

(Francis and Nelly in Vancouver)

*"I would tell you not to get angry with your spouse, and not to fight them. Don't dwell on who's right and who's wrong. Just be good to them, and show them love, no matter what. That is the only way to make a marriage work."*

I journeyed, I fell, I got back up again, and now I'm back. I'm back with my woman. I'm comfortable, sitting with her. Just sitting. And enjoying. And being grateful.

Francis, Luise's son, came to visit this afternoon for a few days from Montreal. Perhaps Chuck described him best when he said, "Francis makes Tom look like an Asshole." Francis is 76, a tiny man with a full head of slicked back jet-black Al Pacino hair with a white streak down the middle.

He's seen quite a bit in his life. You already know his father, Victor, was executed in 1946, when Francis was twelve years old. And I've mentioned how he found his governess in Vienna with her head stuck in an oven one morning.

"All I remember is the oven, and seeing her hunched over. After that it's all a blur."

And just last year in early September, Francis went to the Toronto Film Festival with his mother-in-law. Suddenly she felt sick to her stomach. The doctor told her she had pancreatic cancer and three months to live. She died at the end of November. You'd never know he'd endured all this tragedy from the genial smile permanently pasted on his face.

The weather gods gave us a beautiful week. It'd been years since Francis's last meeting with his beloved aunt. They sat in deck chairs and laughed about old times.

"Maria is the last of her generation," he told me in the kitchen as we prepared roast beef sandwiches for lunch, while Maria, wearing her lime-green bathrobe and a white cap, sat by the pool admiring her poplar trees.

"Boy, were the Germans impressive," Francis went on. "They put on quite a show."

I told him how I remembered Maria telling me about the people in the streets rejoicing at Hitler's arrival in Vienna in 1938. It confused her at such an impressionable age.

"Hitler promised them food, employment, everything. And on top of all that, they had lost the first war, so I think the people were eager to feel a part of something great."

Francis left without saying goodbye to Maria. I know it was because he felt it might be his last time seeing her. It would have been too difficult to give his final farewell to a woman who's been so important in his life.

"A chapter is closing," he said to me in the doorway before getting into his cab. It was the first time he'd said anything without a smile.

*December 8, 2010*

*"They don't know how strong I am."*

Maria had gone down for a nap around two, and I was in the den reclining in Fritz's chair watching so-bad-they're-good movies on Showtime, which were so good they helped me stave off a nap of my own. The sound of rustling pulled my attention to the video monitor, where I saw Maria heave herself up using the trapeze bar Jim had built for her last year. She sat up in bed, emitted a loud groan followed by a whimper, then plopped back down on her back, out of breath. I got off my Showtime ass to investigate.

When she noticed me standing at the door she lightly patted the bed sheets. With a voice so weak it startled me, she said, "Gregor," and paused to catch more of her breath. There was a fear in her eyes and a panic in her voice I had never seen from her. She had no strength to continue so she gave up and stared out the window at the pool. I stroked her hair and asked if she slept.

She opened her mouth like a baby bird and said, "I don't want to go back to sleep because I'm afraid I'll never see you again."

I felt her arms. They were hot, but she was shivering. I called Tom. He didn't answer. I looked back at her and her eyes were closed. I rubbed her cheeks and she opened them and said, "I love you."

I tried Tom again, all the while continuing to hold her hand to keep her awake. Nothing but ringing. My heart was pounding.

I dialed a third time. *Finally.* He was at Costco buying groceries. I started to speak, and then I couldn't. My voice stopped working. Eventually I was able to form words.

"I think Maria's dying."

I hung up and fought off tears while I turned my head toward the backyard to hide them. But she caught me. She smiled at me as if she were proud that they were for her. I decided to sob in front of her for the first time ever, like Poldi did.

*Hurry up, Tom.*

My gut told me to call everyone I knew who loved her. Peter. Jim. Margie. Petra. Sheila. Randy. Francis. Plácido. Maria Harris. Bill Tandler. Ronald Lauder. Names flooded into my head like a typhoon. I was calm as I dialed each number, but when I heard a voice on the other end I couldn't speak no matter how hard I tried. *Fuck.* I was the caregiver. I wasn't supposed to lose control.

I left mostly messages, imagining them being checked and the person on the other end being stunned, which filled me with more desperation. Between calls I maintained calm eye contact with Maria as best I could, and she looked into my watery eyes and smiled again. She smiled and stared at me so long I thought she was going to die right there in my arms with a smile on her face.

I ran to the window in the front bathroom and pressed my nose against the glass, pleading with Danalda Street to produce Tom's Harley. No Mr. Davidson anywhere.

I returned to her room and sat on her bed. She rolled her head toward me and whispered, "Don't be nervous that I croak—you've made my last years a pleasure."

I told her everything would be okay, and I choked up because she had always said that to everyone. But I knew I lied to her. Deep down I had a feeling she wasn't going to be okay.

Moments later the soft, soothing rumble of Tom's Harley reverberated through the walls and the floor like the foot massage machine at Brookstone. I leapt up to greet him as the front door swung open. He took her vitals as if it were any other day. Her temperature, normally at a cool 96, was at 100, and climbing. She didn't even have the strength to sit up on her own.

"She's developing pneumonia," Tom whispered softly. He called Curtis and left him a message to get to the house immediately. I couldn't help but think about her Aunt Adele, and how she got sick suddenly and died within three days.

Maria stretched out her hand and held mine, and looked at me.

"When you make it to heaven they're going to kick everyone out and let you stay."

I showed her my weary eyes that had had about enough torture for one afternoon. If she died right there at least she'd see I wasn't perfect. I wasn't always strong. I was weak.

As sun gave way to moon, Maria laid in bed as delicate as a daffodil. Her eyes fluttered open and closed. I stroked her hand, and she suddenly looked up at me, and with a volcano of energy said, "Go like this."

I turned my head to show her my profile.

"Fabulous. Just fabulous," she whispered.

*She wants to play the games we used to play.*

As I paced the hallway I received a text from Peter that he and Margie were flying in first thing in the morning. Jim suddenly barreled through the front door. I couldn't look him in the eyes. He ran into her room and threw himself on her bed.

I kept sending texts to Petra, calling her every five minutes. Tom called David, who was already on his way to the house to work his usual night shift.

LaDonna, Jim, Chuck, David, Tom and I sat in chairs in a semi-circle surrounding Maria's bed as she lay there breathing in, and out... in, and out. *A living funeral.* Tom put on a CD of Plácido and boosted up his stereo. Within a split second we were in an opera house. Maria's eyes flitted open and she whispered, "Plácido." But then she fell back into her trance. We all sat there in pained silence watching it all unfold, staring at a woman we all knew only came once in a lifetime. Donna sat in a chair in the corner of the room bawling like I'd never seen her do. It was an especially bad time for her. Her sister was dying of cancer and given a year to live, her mother just turned 88 and wasn't doing well, and now... Maria.

Suddenly Petra arrived and joined the somber semicircle. Jim lay next to Maria humming her a hymn. Then he felt her forehead.

"Your forehead is really warm, Mom."

Maria forced out a smile. "Cuz I'm smart."

Donna laughed through her tears.

Chuck reached out his hand, his mother clasped it, and she said with as much enthusiasm as she could muster, "Well, Chuckie... I'm 91. I guess I've had a good run."

Chuck yelled, "Mother... You're not 91, you're 94!" She turned to me and winked in spite of it.

Not feeling great about his timing to be honest, Chuck said, "Do you still like me?"

Maria responded, "I have to check my calendar."

Suddenly Maria's eyes filled with purpose as she scanned the room made up mostly of men, and said, "My goodness. For a woman who's crazy about men... this is the room to be in."

Now everyone laughed through their tears.

Curtis arrived. He did a few standard tests on her, and made it all seem okay in the bedroom. But then we met in the hallway. He waited for us all to huddle around. "I give her three days." He lowered his head. "And that's being optimistic." I spent a few minutes on the back terrace wondering what I was going to do without her.

"That royal marriage in England—when is it?" she asked as I wandered back into her room a few minutes later. "It's not for another few weeks," I told her.

It seemed to take a load off her shoulders. She turned to Donna. "Donna, darling. Come here." Donna went to sit next to her. "Are you going to do your hair tomorrow night?"

Donna erupted into tears and, as she does so well, laughed them all away. She couldn't muster anything other other than a nod.

"And Chuck is wearing a tux?" Donna nodded again. Maria lay there content that her little Chuckie would wear his tux to a cocktail party.

After Curtis left, the tension in the house gave way to an acceptance we were forced to find peace with: Maria was probably going to die within the next few hours. *What a life.*

Petra got up to leave, and I walked out with her into the hallway. Her shoulder turned into a pillow for me to cry on, and she told me Maria would live in our hearts forever. It was the first time Petra and I had ever shared intimacy.

The clock struck midnight, and Maria had grown more incoherent. Everyone had left the house save Tom, David and me. All three of us sat in the kitchen in silence watching her on a monitor lying in bed alone staring at the wall. A hospital, by the way, was out of the question.

Chuck insisted his mother die in her own home. No disagreements from anybody, especially Maria.

I fetched a pillow and a blanket and made my bed on the living room couch. David took the foldout bed in the den, and Tom retired to his room. Before I closed my eyes to sleep I logged onto Twitter and tweeted, "I love you, Maria."

I had never said these words to her directly. But I sent them out into the world. It was a restless night for all of us. I lay in my bed imagining every waking moment could be the moment she could stop breathing for-ever. I envisioned the morning. We'd all get up to an eerily silent house, meet each other in the hallway and tiptoe into her room. Tom would lift her lifeless arm to take her pulse, and he'd look up at us, look down, and pull out his cell phone. I checked the monitor around 2 am. I heard light breathing. I exhaled and slammed my head back down.

At 3 am I awoke to rustling coming from her room. I ran into the den to wake up David, who was already up, intently watching the room monitor. With our shirts off and in our underwear, we met Tom in the hallway and convened in her room.

Maria took one look at her scantily clad caregivers towering over her bed, and said, "Now I can see why there are homosexuals."

David sat next to her. Maria rubbed his cheeks, then crinkled her nose and touched it, and said to him, "See? I have a cold nose. That means I'm a hot dog."

It was hard to leave her, even if I was a room away. Tom returned to his, and David and I sat on the edge of his bed in the den. We watched the monitor in silence. Then it came. She said it in a low tone and to herself, with an uncanny defiance...

"They don't know how strong I am."

The hairs on our bodies shot up. We sat there watching, waiting, like two cheetahs hiding in the brush. I felt David swivel his head toward me as I remained fixated on the monitor.

"You wrote that down, right?" I didn't answer, and he didn't need me to. We continued to stare, unable to move or speak. Then David got up to get water. I sat glued to Maria for at least five more minutes. *They don't know how strong I am.* I closed my eyes and fell asleep.

The morning sun shook our hearts awake. The Three Caregivers met in the hallway and eased into her room. As we stood over Maria's bed her eyes opened, and she was a child awaking to a brand new world. Tom took her temperature, and her blood pressure. *Normal.*

"Shall we have breakfast, my loves?"

And she lifted herself out of bed to put on her robe and slippers.

*December 16, 2010*

*"I want you to be my Gregor, and I want you to stay with me forever."*

Was it all a dream? It may as well have been. And to top it off, Maria's arthritis pain is suddenly gone. Tom's hypothesis—one he admits he's just throwing out there—is that her flirtation with death was a result of the steroids given to her to relieve the arthritis pain. But now that the steroids have worn off and her illness appears to have vanished, there is no logical reason why she hasn't gone back to complaining of arthritis pain. You can't explain miracles.

Peter and Margie flew in this morning just in time to meet with a gentleman from hospice, who had been called during the chaos last week. Maria seems on the road to full recovery, yet hospice looms like a mother bear watching over her cubs. Jim texted me this morning: "Make sure you don't tell my mother they are from hospice." I replied I was already ahead of him.

As expected, the hospice doctor spoke about death casually. "We believe there is a beginning and an end. Our job is to make the transition as comfortable as possible."

It was more than a little creepy to hear it said so matter-of-factly, knowing Maria was getting stronger every day.

The Comeback Kid snaps her fingers and ten people are at her beckon call. In the last couple years I've come to know firsthand that love is more powerful than medicine. I would even argue this on a nationally televised panel, because I've felt it with my heart and I've seen it with my eyes. Love healed this woman: the love she gives, and the love she's given.

Maria's grandson Phil showed up at the house this afternoon. Maria joked, "Now I know how to get you here!"

He brought his oldest son Avrick and his guitar to give Maria her own bedroom concert. At one point during his performance Avrick was adjusting his suit, and Maria exclaimed, "You remind me of Fritz, the way you adjust your sleeves!"

Lisa came over with her flute, and played Mozart and Chopin and Bach and Brahms, while Maria lay in her bed.

Christmas is just around the corner, and I don't want to leave Maria. I told her I was headed to San Francisco to visit my brother. She asked me if I was driving, and I told her I was flying, and she said, "Cuz you're an angel."

At the end of the night I sat on Maria's bed as she lay there holding my hand and looking at me. "I want you to be my

Gregor, and I want you to stay with me forever." *Oh, you silly girl,* was my expression, but then I raced into the hallway bathroom and let out a bucket of tears into one of the pink hand towels. I went to get her a glass of water, and returned.

"Come closer," she said softly.

I stood over her and we looked at each other for a long time.

"Sit."

I sat. I couldn't look at her.

"Do you know that I'm going to be up there looking down on you for the rest of your life?"

I nodded, staring at the wall.

"Do you know that I'll be making sure you find the woman of your dreams, that everyone is good to you, and that you achieve everything you ever wanted in life? Do you know that?"

I nodded again. I offered her the water to pull the attention away from my tears.

She took one look at the water and said, "No, darling... fish fuck in it," and she pushed it away. She waited for me to stop crying and be amused, and when she got what she wanted she winked at me and took the glass.

*December 24, 2010*

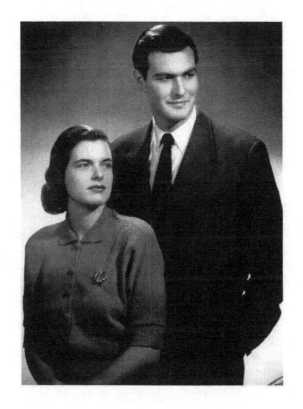

(Peter and Sheila in 1955)

*"Chestnuts are like pregnancy, when they're here they're here, and you can't do anything about it."*

Even as I was enjoying my Los Angeles family, I still felt the pull and love of my Washington, DC family. David and Tom kept me abreast of Maria's recovery while I was in San Francisco.

She continues to gain strength. There were a few issues while I was gone. A nurse sent over to shower her was a problem. According to David—who would sooner eat a can of worms than say something bad about anyone—the nurse was a nightmare. Aside from rushing through her duties as if she were a barista making a Cappuccino, she was devoid of any elegance or charm. It's beyond belief how the care industry can employ such people. I know, I know, they're underpaid. But no one is forcing them to be nurses.

———◆———

I returned to Los Angeles in time to meet Poldi's son Peter Bentley, and his wife Sheila, who arrived this morning from Vancouver to spend the day with Maria. As soon as I touched down at LAX I rushed to the house. I was excited to meet yet another fascinating link in the Bloch-Bauer chain.

A tall, robust man with a movie-star jawline just like his father, Peter spoke in a Godfather-esque whisper. He was only one of three people still alive who had met Maria's father. Maria lit up like a disco ball hearing Peter talk about what he remembered of him. She brought up all her chestnut stories again, and how Gustav would always make sure to take her to the main park in Vienna, through the little pathway filled with the aroma of roasting chestnuts. "Chestnuts are like pregnancy, when they're here they're here, and you can't do anything about it." We all understood what she meant. Few foods could ever excite Maria like chestnuts.

Weeks ago Maria told me that Poldi had been pulled over in Canada one day in the sixties by an unmarked cop car. Poldi had been racing the guy for miles thinking it was just another daredevil with a need for speed, but the car suddenly slowed, darted behind him, and started flashing his lights. Poldi got a whopping speeding ticket.

Peter told a story about his own run-in with the law. About ten years ago in Los Angeles he was also stopped for speeding.

"License and registration," the officer said. Peter reached for his papers.

"Where are you from?" the officer asked. "Vienna. I just moved here from Austria," Peter responded.

As Peter handed him his registration the cop eyed him suspiciously. "So which one is it, Vienna or Austria?"

Another time, Peter was driving along Sunset Boulevard in Hollywood one weekend afternoon and stopped at a red light. A convertible pulled up beside him. It was Dean Martin.

Dean leaned over and asked Peter, "Wanna play some golf?"

He had recognized Peter from the Bing Crosby Invitational the year before, where he met him and Poldi.

"So I went and played a spontaneous round of golf with Dean Martin."

While Maria, Peter and Sheila chatted in the living room, I drove to the German Deli to buy six fresh veal cutlets to make Wiener Schnitzel for dinner. Early in the evening we all sat and watched as Maria, who insisted on making everything herself for once, shuffled around the kitchen fumbling through drawers and cabinets to find a large pan. She put butter in it and turned up the heat, and then took out three small plates and laid them on the counter in front of us. On the first plate she cracked two eggs, on the second she poured flour, and on the third she poured breadcrumbs.

"See, you have to just slice the cutlet through like this," she said as she picked up a cutlet and dragged it through the egg, then through the flour, and finally through the breadcrumbs. The pan was searing hot as she tossed the first one in, and it fizzled and sizzled to all of our delight.

"You try now," she said to me, and I finished the remaining five, while she made her famous "four-vinegar" cucumber salad.

Peter and Sheila had a flight to Vancouver early in the morning. Maria ended their short stay with her usual spirit and optimism, but there was none in theirs. They surely sensed just as Francis did, that it would likely be their final goodbye.

# 2011

**January 24, 2011**

*"Come live with me."*

Maria took a tumble last night. I wasn't there. I got a phone call. After she had gotten out of the shower, Tom went to the kitchen to warm up a bowl of soup for her. Seconds later he heard a loud thud, and then a scream. He ran to her room and found her lying on the floor in the bathroom doorway. Apparently on her way out of the bathroom she stepped on a brush and fell. Chuck ran in and they somehow were able to lug her onto the bed. She was screaming in pain. It sounded so awful that I never wanted to hear about it again.

It turned out to be a night of falls. Jud took a nasty one around the same time. He got out of his standing wheelchair to open the fridge, lost his footing, and did a face plant right into the kitchen floor. If he wasn't wearing his helmet he would have cracked his skull open. I left a message for Mimi with my prayers, and rushed to Maria's house.

When I entered Maria's room she squinted at me like she was impersonating Peter's box turtle, trying to figure out who I was until I sat beside her and gave her a hundred kisses. I asked her how she was feeling, and she said, "I didn't know I had a back until last night."

It was a chore for her to talk so I told her to just lie there.

I rubbed her wrists. She looked at me and asked, "Do you want to walk with me down the street to visit Ferdinand?"

I told her I wanted to, and she smiled. After a moment her eyes focused on a pillow, then she looked at me, then back to the pillow, and said, "You two look alike."

She was all over the place. I left her to rest. I sat in the den but I didn't cry. Something inside me was letting her go.

An hour later I was still in Fritz's chair when I watched Tom make his way into her room and sit next to her on the monitor. He told her how much she meant to him, how his life changed since he met her, and how he admired her for being the matriarch and giving her family a life very few could ever enjoy. Then he said: "You're everything I want to be."

Getting her to use the bathroom was an ordeal. It took three of us to lift her up. She cried out in pain. When we made it inside the bathroom she took one look at the toilet and said, "Is this where I give my speech?"

When she situated herself on the toilet seat we all waited
for the speech that never came. The fall must have really rattled
her insides.

Danalda Drive is now a nursing home. Tom is operating a
pharmacy out of his room, and nurses and visitors constantly
flood the hallways. Maria has lost more of her short-term
memory. If I leave the room for more than a half hour, I walk in
for the first time.

"Come live with me," she said to me upon one of my re-
entrances. I laughed at how cute it was, and thought about how
Jim, who has been wanting to live with his mother for years now,
would have been jealous if he had been eavesdropping.

Today we were having trouble with another nurse. She
meant well and was polite, but she wasn't aware of how pushy
she was, and it was making Maria uncomfortable.

"Come here, Mama," she said over and over again. "Let's
go, Mama. Okay, Mama."

Finally Tom had to tell her to stop calling her Mama, and
to give you an idea of how much it was annoying Maria, *Maria*
told her to stop—albeit very tactfully.

At one point the nurse's back was turned, and Maria,
making sure I was getting a load of what she was about to do,
lifted her middle finger and pointed it at the nurse, whose back
was turned. Suddenly the nurse turned around to face us quicker
than we had expected, and Maria quickly moved her middle finger
to her cheek and acted like she was itching it.

"Got an itch, Mama?" the nurse asked obliviously.

Maria and I looked at each other and smiled. So many
moments like this we've shared.

God must have sent us the next nurse, April, who is Tom's
friend. Maria took an immediate liking to her, asking her, "Do you
have a boyfriend?"

April responded, "No, do you?" Maria laughed harder than
she had in days. The laughs eventually turned into coughs, and
April left her to rest.

Later while making dinner I was watching the monitor,
and Chuck walked in and sat next to her on her bed.

"I don't want to live like this, Chuckie."

"Mother, if you're ready to check out, you check out, okay? No one's gonna blame you for that."

Maria's birthday is fast approaching. "What's coming up?" she asked me. I told her ninety-five. She nodded her head and said, "That's a nice number," as if she was up for the challenge.

I put the feelers out to Richard again to see if Plácido might be in town and able to come by the house. Nope, of course he won't be in town, he may as well have wings and be called Virgin America. Supposedly Plácido will be sending Maria a birthday gift.

David set up his computer near her bed on a table and played *Rigoletto* over and over again. Like a crying baby calmed by a lullaby, at the sight and sound of the opera Maria completely forgot about her back pain.

Later she said to Chuck, "David took me to see *Rigoletto!*"

David sent out an email later with the subject line, BETTER THAN MORPHINE, making his case that when it comes to Maria, watching opera is more effective than medication.

God bless Hubertus Czernin's sister-in-law, Gertraud Czernin. When Gertraud's mother died about ten years ago, Maria told her she'd be her new mother. And now Gertraud is being a mother to Maria. She's been here every single day for hours on end helping make soup, holding Maria's hand and speaking German (she says it's important for Maria to hear her native language), and even painting Maria's nails. Gertraud and I have bonded like never before.

At one point today Maria said to me, "Are you and I going to play like we used to?"

I looked at her and couldn't find any words. I forced out a faux smile. She turned to stare into the backyard until I got up and left. She knew the answer.

**January 30, 2011**

*"You're the only good thing about the end."*

It's our three-year anniversary today. We set up an air mattress next to her bed, and even on nights I'm not scheduled to work I've been sleeping in her room because it makes her feel safe, and I can jump right up and help her instead of having to run all the way down the hallway from the den. Plus, Tom has been up all day and night and any chance to give him a rest is good for everyone.

"You're the only good thing about the end," she said to me this morning as I lay on my bed watching her lying in her bed. I took the opportunity to try and tell her how I really felt.

"You are the light of my life," I said. I couldn't bring myself to say any more. She squeezed my hand and we looked at each other. With that one look, everything that I wanted to say but couldn't was said. Our hearts are one.

The mail arrived. I have a friend named Marcella who lives in Cologne, Germany, who had met Maria this past summer (it also turns out Klimt has been one of her favorite artists since she was a child), and has been sending care packages ever since. Today she sent an early birthday bundle, rife with chocolate, a Mozart CD (I told her he was Maria's father's favorite composer), and a lovely card. I filmed Maria thanking her on video, uploaded it to YouTube, and sent Marcella a private link.

I was thinking today that this job started as one hundred percent caregiving, fast became one hundred percent companionship, and now it's one hundred percent of both. I've been learning all about Roxinol (Morphine), Larazapan (Vicodin), and Ambien. We've had no choice but to administer these regularly because Maria's entire lower body is in pain. She has bedsores on her heels, a rash on her stomach, and possible blood clotting in her legs. Hospice still looms.

The ducks crash-landed into the pool this morning for the first time in months. I snapped a photo and brought it to the bedroom.

"It's the two males again," she was delighted to point out.

Gertraud walked through the door today bearing fresh strawberries. Then Peter arrived. Margie is due any minute.

Peter sat on her bed, and she said to him. "I'm waiting for an angel." His presence warms the house.

We're all doing our best to give her a sense of calm. Everything is drawn out right now. Minutes feel like hours, hours feel like days. Will she make it to 95? Only time will tell.

*February 6, 2011*

*"Did you pack?"*

It's been three weeks since the fall. She's gone two and half days without food or water.

In my rose-colored world, no one I loved, love, or will love, dies. But death is an unavoidable force right now. Peter's best friend Jerry, who came down with Peter, told me today about death, "You never get used to it, but you start to understand it. And it will change your life."

Jerry has seen a lot of death. Both his parents died when he was a teenager, and his wife died of cancer at 39. Why is it that the people who have seen the most death in their lives are the most good-humored? Francis. Gerta. Jerry. *Maria.*

Visitors seem to be making their final rounds. Bill Tandler, the grandson of Julius Tandler (the renowned Austrian physician and politician), drove down from San Francisco. He entered her room holding flowers and a card, and at the sight of him Maria threw up her arms and said, "Well I don't believe it!" She hadn't had that energy in days.

Bill sat next to her on the bed and we cleared out of the room. He read his card aloud to her. It was so touching that they were able to see each other one last time.

Stephen Lash called me this morning to say he was in town and wanted to say hello. He hadn't heard about the fall. I kept his visit a surprise. When he entered her room she straightened up her posture and finger-combed her hair. He sat next to her on the bed and kept her spirits up as he's always done so effortlessly. I don't know what Stephen's relationship to his mother is, but he treats Maria as if she were his.

He walked out with sunken shoulders and got into his cab idling on the street. My phone dinged as I stood at the doorway to see him off. It was a text from Margie, who had just landed and was on her way to the house.

"Please tell my mother I love her and we have loved each other since I was born."

I told Maria before I even finished reading the text. She mouthed a thank you and I felt relieved I had carried out Margie's wishes.

I sat with Maria all day. On one occasion when I got up, she said, "Don't leave me."

I sat back down and held her hand and kissed it. She pulled it close and warmed it with the last breaths in her body.

"What can I do for you?" I asked.

"Just be here with me."

*Love may heal illness, but it can't heal age. It can't stop time. Why can't I come to grips with this?*

We sat in silence for a few minutes. She looked out her sliding door and into the sky.

"I'll never forget you," she said. Then she turned to me and asked with a sudden eagerness, "Did you pack?"

"For Austria?" I responded back. "Of course I packed." This brought a blazing euphoria to her face.

"Do you want to go with me?"

"Yes," I said. Then she let my hand go and closed her eyes. This was the last conversation I had with Maria Altmann.

———◆———

It's 2:00 pm. Tom is taking a shower and April is in the den on the phone. Peter and Jerry are taking a walk around the block. I text Peter: "I think she's close." Thirty seconds later he runs into the house. I hand him a glass of water and follow him to her room. I stop and stand at the door. He sits on her bed.

Her eyes slowly open and he helps her sip the water. She sees me standing there, and she struggles to crane her neck over Peter's shoulder. We lock eyes. She smiles and waves. I wave back. *Goodbye.*

*February 7, 2011*

It's 4:44. I've been standing in the doorway since 2. She sleeps soundly. Chuck, Jimmy, Peter and Margie gather together and surround her bed. A CD player on her bedside table plays *The Best of Plácido Domingo*. Jerry sits in a chair holding her hand, counting her breaths. Three seconds apart... five seconds apart... seven seconds apart... nine seconds apart...

She lets out one final gasp...

Dear Friends and Loved Ones;

At 4:45 this afternoon Mutzi's Angel arrived, on time. The Angel will take her to her father, Gustav, and husband, Fritz, to name few among many.

The passing was beautiful and peaceful. Mutzi was in a sleeping coma for the last few hours, and passed through the veil easily. Above her, the wall shimmered from sunlight reflecting from the pool. The room was filled with the voice of Plácido, singing Ave Maria. A golden daffodil lay on her pillow.

LOVE, PETER

## February 8, 2011

Dear Loved Ones;

We opened our show tonight with a dedication to Maria. Just a few short words to let her know that we were thinking of her and that she will never be forgotten. While we were speaking about her, the studio lights flashed on and off several times. This is something that has never happened in the two years we have been doing this program. We weren't looking for it, nor expecting it, so it really caught us off-guard. It wasn't until after we finished the show that it really began to sink in for us. Of course we can all interpret this in many ways, but we find it to be very special.

Please forward to anyone who has love for Maria.

Our love,

David and Karen

*February 9, 2011*

Elisa came in this past Thursday morning, the day after Maria was taken, not having heard the news, ready for another day of work. Peter pulled her aside and told her. In three years I never saw her get emotional about anything, but learning of Maria's death made her weep uncontrollably.

"Por toda mi vida, nunca me olvidare a Maria," she said. *For all my life I will never forget Maria.*

And I'll never shake the image of Jerry's face as he looked up at me after she took her final breath. It was one of the most heartbreaking and tender exchanges I'll ever experience with anyone. A man so poised, so polished, so happy-go-lucky... a man who had seen so much death and despair in his life... uncontrollably breaking down and crying into my shoulder like a baby.

I got out of bed this morning and turned my phone on, and as I watched the screen illuminate, it occurred to me it was the first time I turned my phone off since January 30, 2008.

Good night.

*February 11, 2011*

Today I drove around Beverly Hills to honor Maria.

Dr. Hartenbower pulled me into his office. A 30-year relationship had come to a close. "What a lady," he said. "And in all my years as a doctor I've never seen the level of care that you gave her."

At Maite's salon, everyone, even the customers, all swiveled around in their chairs to offer condolences. They had already read about the news. One lady said, "We were all lucky to know her."

I told the German deli on Olympic and Doheny their sausage contributed to her pleasure in her final years, and I went into Vons Grocery Store on National, the store where Maria and I shared our first shopping trip, and typed in her phone number in the electronic machine.

As the young man handed me the receipt for my peach he smiled and said, "Thank you, Mr. Altmann."

He'll never know why my eyes got all watery as I grabbed it.

I talked to Elisa again today. "Before you come to Maria," she said to me, "She had caregiver, and she treat Maria like baby. 'Do this, do that,' she tell her. Maria no happy. But you come to her, and she start smiling and laughing. You change her life."

*February 17, 2011*

My funeral cherry was popped today. I invited Archie and Anne, who are now a full-on item, and Andrea and Doug, who had all caught a glimpse of the woman I experienced on a daily basis.

I reminded Archie that Maria always loved saying his name out loud so melodramatically—"Aaaaaachie!"—and that she always said in amazement, "A Jewish man named Ahhchie... I think I've heard it all!"

Of course I reminded Doug about the barbecue and how much she couldn't get enough of his profile.

Karen and I reminisced about how she would call David during a shift, and David would hand the phone to Maria so Karen could hear a soothing voice before she went to bed. Karen could never wait to tell me what delightful things she and Maria spoke about on the phone, doing her best impression of Maria's Viennese accent. And I'm so grateful that through our many script-writing sessions at the house toward the end, Andrea got to experience Maria the most out of any of my friends. "Where did you find Andrea, she's so lovely."

The funeral was packed with around 150 people. I knew or met about half of them. Relatives, including Maria Harris and Peter Bentley, travelled all the way from Canada and Austria. There were some really great eulogies. Today being my first funeral, I had nothing to compare it with, but everyone I spoke to—including Chuck, who doesn't mince words even when it comes to his own mother—said it was one of the best they'd seen.

Jim gave a heartfelt speech, followed by Alana's courageous one, Margie's beautiful one, capped off by a brilliant one from Randy's mother, Barbara Shoenberg. She said what we were all thinking and feeling: "A giant door has closed."

Margie pulled me aside after the speeches and said, "You were my mother's last great love."

This will stay etched in my mind forever.

When the service ended the funeral procession migrated 300 feet to the burial, where twenty angel-white doves were set free. Chuck told me later that he went to a funeral years ago with Maria, where they freed doves.

"Ooh, Chuckie, I want doves at my funeral," she told him. She got her doves. Andrea snapped a photo of me releasing one named Maria.

# February 18, 2011

I had two to-dos today. One was to buy a new dish scrubber. I'm a guy. I keep underwear too long, I let the dust pile up on my bedside table until it looks like New York in January, and I let dish scrubbers go until the bristles are as hard and dirty as a tree branch.

For my other to-do, I showered and put on my khakis and my powder blue cashmere sweater. I drove the 405 Freeway South to the Howard Hughes Parkway exit, took two rights and pulled into a parking lot, waving to the man in the windless booth who recognized me from last week.

I walked down a small cement path and up a grassy hill, stopped above a large, flat stone, and looked down to read in the lower left portion: "Fritz Altmann, 1908-1994," and on the lower right, "Maria Altmann, 1916-2011."

I sat down on the damp grass and soaked in my first ever visit to a graveyard. First I made sure Maria knew I was wearing the same cashmere sweater she bought me last year. I introduced myself to Fritz even though I'm sure she already told him about me. Then I wished her a happy 95th birthday. I pulled out my phone and read aloud the poem I read to her on her 94th at Jim's house. My voice quivered as I read it, remembering the lines that made her cry.

When I finished I took a moment to find the right words, because I didn't want to make a fool out of myself on my first visit. I told her part of me wished I had told her I loved her while she was still alive, but that I knew it was always written all over my face. I paused and lowered my head, mustering enough courage to say it for the first time.

"I love you."

I stood up and brushed the grass off my backside, stuffed my hands in my pockets, and walked to my car. I was off to buy my dish scrubber.

*Epilogue*

## THE GOLDEN TRIP

### July 14, 2011

The thought of escaping somewhere other than the gym with my iPod nudged me out of bed with an extra sense of wonder this morning. I left my apartment in the Little Armenia section of Hollywood, and within seven minutes I was at the foot of the Los Feliz end of the Santa Monica Mountains. I decided to forgo my hike to keep a nice, quiet bench company. A few moments later I was suddenly overtaken by an inspiration: *I need to go to Vienna.*

Why it had taken five months to put into action the last thing I told Maria before she died—that I had "packed" for our trip—is something I will never know. But it was clear I needed to go home and pack for real. A rush of adrenaline shot through me.

I ran like a high school student expecting his college acceptance letter from Yale in the mail, logged onto the web and studied a map of Europe, ran my finger along all the countries I wanted to visit, and booked a plane ticket to Geneva, Switzerland on August 11, returning September 1. My itinerary: Geneva to Salzburg to Vienna to Prague to Berlin, in 21 days. All cities I'd never visited. I gave myself three weeks to go off and do as I pleased, to spend as much or as little time in each city I chose to visit.

My friend Meng suggested I "Couch-Surf"—a way of connecting to people around the world who would give up their couches free of charge. I sent out a flurry of "Couch Requests" to women spanning Central and Eastern Europe.

Since Maria's death I've searched for a chance to really feel her with me. She's been with me every day since February. But I've craved moments I could say, "Okay, *that* was from

Maria." If they were out there, I wanted to feel these sensations very badly. Maybe I'd discover them in Europe.

I couldn't wait to go. I bought a book of German phrases at the Barnes and Noble down the street from Maria's house. The book had a "Terms of Endearment" section. Reading through it brought Maria back to life sitting across from me in the kitchen, saying things she always used to say to me with such unbridled tenderness... Mein Schatz...Mein Galibtis... Mein La-Zona.

## Frankfurt

I flew from LAX to Philly, and from Philly to Frankfurt. The moment I stepped off the plane at the Frankfurt airport a sudden surge of loneliness took hold of me. It was clear for the first time that I was alone on this trip and if I wanted to enjoy it with someone, it was up to me to find someone.

But first things first: my ticket indicated my connecting flight would be on US Air from LAX to Frankfurt, then on Swiss Air to Geneva. I checked the flight menu. No Swiss Air flights to Geneva.

I found a lady at the counter and asked about the mysterious nonexistence of my flight. She glazed over the information on my ticket and slid it back across the counter.

"Call the airline."

Then she turned and started a conversation in German with her co-worker. I had been dismissed.

I could have used another cold German like I could have used a hole in my backpack, but when I ran down a nearly deserted corridor somewhere in the filthy and unfriendly Frankfurt airport, there sitting in front of me were two cold-looking Germans. I showed one my ticket. He looked at it for a few seconds, glared at me, and handed it back.

"Passport," he ordered.

I gave it to him. He casually thumbed through a few pages, leered at me then back at the passport, and then exchanged a few words in German with his friend sitting next to him.

As they bullied me with their eyes, I started to believe that maybe I wasn't Gregor Collins. Maybe I was an American spy on a covert operation to bring down Germany, and they were on to me big time. Then he had enough of me. He returned my passport and my ticket, and that was that.

I was as frantic as I was the day I was trying to get Maria to the endocrinologist. I flagged down a lady in a motorized cart and threw her a look of desperation, knowing that I was in danger of missing my flight. She slowed down and smiled. And the entire world smiled.

"You look lost," she said, and I handed her my ticket.

She called Swiss Air, and while she was on hold she asked me what brought me to Germany, and if I had family out here. It turned out Swiss Air bumped me onto a Lufthansa flight without informing me. She pointed me to the right gate, and I found my cramped window seat minutes before takeoff. *Ahhhh.*


## Geneva

My dad awaited me in Geneva. He'd moved there in 2008 with his wife Tea, and their five-year-old daughter Annika. I hadn't seen them since they left Washington, DC. It was clear my trip wasn't only a chance to be closer to Maria: it was a chance to be closer to my family.

As I walked out of my gate and into the airport I saw my dad before he saw me. He was still balding, still athletic, and still had that familiar pleasant disposition. As I neared him I noticed some new gray hairs around and above his ears—it was the only thing that reminded me of Father Time. When he saw me he flashed his placid smile.

Annika darted behind him before I could wave to her. I'd only met her once, when she was two, but from what my dad was telling me she didn't remember the meeting. For all intents and purposes she was seeing her "brother in California" for the first time. To her heart and her soul I was her flesh and her blood, but to her touch and her eyes I was a big tall stranger towering over her and embarrassing her: she had no idea what to do or say other than blush and hide behind our dad.

By the time we got to the car, though, she turned into Ms. Loquacious, telling me about her horseback riding class, her gymnastics class, her French lessons, her swimming lessons, her amazing trampoline skills, and on and on. And she listened when I spoke. She acknowledged what I was saying, and occasionally even applied it to her own life. If I said something funny, she would stare at me for a few seconds in amusement, then laugh and shake her head and say, "Oh, Gregor, you're so silly."

And she was already fluent in French. I don't know many things cuter than a little girl who speaks French.

We drove through the peaceful pastures and sweeping sunflower fields surrounding their condo in a French-speaking suburb called Collex—a mere five hundred yards from the French border.

I took my first picture of the trip outside their place.

Everything was so quiet and clean—and the air! To say I wasn't in smog-filled Los Angeles anymore would be an understatement. I've never seen a cleaner airport, a cleaner neighborhood—a cleaner country—in my life. Until somebody tells me otherwise, Switzerland is the cleanest place on earth.

The three of us had an action-packed couple of days.

Annika led me around her neighborhood, knocking on doors and taking me to the houses where some of her friends lived. She seemed to have more to talk about with the parents than her friends. We also went to a carnival downtown, where we rode bumper cars and ate lots and lots of ice cream and chocolate.

We stopped at an abandoned church and I told her about a faraway land called California.

But my real adventure awaited me. "This way," Annika said as she guided us to my train track, her tiny frame bouncing up and down, her little pigtail bobbing left and right. She was interested in everything and everyone along the way—the same fearless curiosity Maria exhibited everywhere she went. It did my heart good to see Dad happy with his little partner-in-crime. At 64 he was more like Annika's grandfather. This was a delightful reminder of Maria and her dad.

## Salzburg

My cabin aboard the twelve-hour train ride to Salzburg was basically a medium-sized closet with six beds folded up against the wall. A couple of shorthaired ladies in their fifties entered, and said "Bonjour" to my "Hello." Suddenly they started pointing in unison out the window and looking at me as if I was supposed to do something.

Dad and Annika were standing on the track trying to get my attention. I waved and blew Annika kisses.

"Merci," I said to the ladies, who appreciated my acknowledgment of their act, and from that moment on we all spoke the language of love.

Two minutes later two cute twenty-something German girls walked in. When introducing themselves they spoke French to the ladies and English to me. Making an effort to show that I, the Dumb American, had some culture, I proudly rattled off a few phrases in Spanish. They both responded back in perfect Spanish. I fell in love with one of them. She was tall, curvy in all the right places, brunette, quick-witted, and had a warm smile. She just got married to a young doctor. *Those young doctors.*

The comic energy was in full bloom when the giggling girls, despite speaking fluent French, purposely left it up to the Frenchies and I to figure out our bed situation. I'd point to myself, then a bed, then make the "sleeping sign," which seemed clear to me this meant the bed I pointed to would be the bed in which I intended to sleep. But it only resulted in confused looks. And instead of replying back with the hand gestures I was giving them, the ladies spoke back to me in French, as if I'd been speaking French to them the whole time. We were all a mismatch made in heaven, and it was making the German girls roar with laughter. There's nothing sexier than a sexy girl with a sexy laugh.

The train en route to Vienna arrived in Salzburg at 6 am. The ladies on the bottom bunks were counting French sheep, and I whispered goodbye to the girls on the top. The doctor's wife looked down at me sensuously, lying there half asleep in her baggy sweatpants and nothing else. God, I wished I could just slip into her bed and forget the rest of my trip.

But God wasn't listening, thank goodness. The sun was rising as I exited the train, and with the doctor's wife still on my mind I thought about how grateful I was that I was single when I met Maria, and remained that way until the end, and if it was any other way I would never have written this 376-page love letter.

I stopped on the track to breathe in the Salzburg air, and peered in the distance at the massive alpine vistas I'd only seen watching *The Sound of Music*. As they sat there full of such poise and majesty, my eyes became Maria's eyes. The year was 1935, and I was seeing the mountains as she saw them with Fritz. *I'm here, Maria... can you believe it?*

A text from Brigitte—my first Couch Surfer—led me to a bus and to a bike path about twenty minutes from the station. I had been instructed to look for a girl on a skateboard. There she was, racing toward me. I waved at her, but she didn't wave back, instead she coasted past me, pointing off somewhere and shouting, "My place is the one with the garden. I'll be back later!"

Then she skated madly down the path and disappeared. I pulled out my phone and looked at her address, checking for numbers on the sides of the buildings. No luck. When I noticed every single apartment in sight had a garden, I wanted to strangle her.

I found an older woman walking by with a small dog.

"Sprechen sie English?" I asked her, and showed her the address. She furrowed her brow. I showed a young guy, and he wasn't any better. What a ridiculous, brow-furrowing predicament I was in. Brigitte wasn't responding to my texts, I had no clue when she would return, I was tired, thirsty, and my phone was running out of juice.

I slumped on a bench in a nearby park, so stunned I couldn't think straight. Friendly faces walked by with their kids and their dogs and I stared back at them with death. I was practically dying of thirst, and I looked around for a store, a fountain, a lake, anything, considering the worst-case scenario to be that I'd have to drink my own urine to stay alive. But I needed a filter for that.

Ding! A text from Brigitte. "Call this number," it said.

The number belonged to her boyfriend, who was at the apartment. I called it.

"Be right out," he said, as if I were an inconvenience.

Fifteen minutes later he showed up on a skateboard and led me to the apartment, which was a few feet away. He never asked a single question about me. But at least I had a place to sleep.

He took me to my room and showed me what I'd travelled halfway around the world to see: a couch to surf. But as quickly as we entered he was leaving, and like his wonderfully communicative girlfriend, he couldn't tell me where he was going or when he'd be back. He was out the door before I realized I didn't ask for a key. Now I couldn't even leave if I wanted to. But sleep was all that mattered. I sprawled out on my very own couch. Three hours later I woke up to an even emptier house.

I wandered into the kitchen. There was a brownie on a baking sheet, and I wolfed it down. *The least they could do was give me a brownie.* I stepped onto the back porch. A German Shepherd puppy appeared at my feet. His water bowl was bone dry, so I filled it, and he finished it in less than a minute, and looked up at me like, "I'm gonna need another fill-up." I filled it again, in fact I refilled it two more times and he was still going strong. It was four o'clock. I had been alone at the house since ten, with no key, no friends but this nameless dry-throated puppy, nowhere to go, and nothing to do. I looked out at the mountains again. *Are you there, Maria?*

I decided to write them a break-up note. This was my fifth draft, and I hoped they wouldn't root around the trash and find the other four.

Hi there;

I guess I had a different idea of what couch surfing would be, so
I'll be leaving you. I have no key, and I have no idea where you
are or where to go. I gave your dog water and he drank for five
minutes. He's probably still drinking. Have fun skating around
Salzburg.

Gregor

I laid the note on the couch and said goodbye to my furry friend,
and as I broke free from the chains of that dark and desolate
apartment, I headed into the unknown with the only certainty
that anything was better than that.

I sat on that same park bench, free as a bird but still lost.
Lisa Schuler suddenly popped into my head. If my memory served
me correctly she lived on the outskirts of Salzburg. I'd met her
two years before with her mother, Stephany, at a lunch at Maria's
house. In 2006, on the heels of Maria's Supreme Court case win,
Lisa, who had friends in high places, invited Maria to Salzburg to
stay at the Schloss Leopoldskron (see "Max Reinhardt" in the *Cast
of Characters* section).

I didn't have Lisa's number, but I had Stephany's, and
luckily Stephany answered her phone. I reminded her who I was,
and told her I was in Salzburg and wanted to call her daughter.
Thirty minutes later Lisa picked me up on the way to a dinner
party.

I decided not to go into detail about my Couch Surfing
experience because I didn't want to be angry around such a sweet
woman in such a beautiful city. I told her my sleeping
arrangements fell through and I'd need to find a hotel.

Then she said: "That'll be difficult because the Salzburg
Festival's going on."

My heart snapped awake when I heard "Salzburg Festival,"
ignoring the bit of news that made my situation sound even more
dire. I told her Maria's father took her there when she was fifteen.
We talked about Maria for the rest of the ride.

(Lisa)

I'm not sure who was more charming, Clemens, his wife Helen, or their three precocious kids, but they all welcomed me into their home unconditionally. The first question I was asked was, "What are you drinking?" I asked for a gallon of water. Then a margarita.

During dinner Clemens leaned over to me and asked, "Where are you staying tonight?" I laughed. I was having so much fun I'd honestly forgotten about it.

"Here's the thing about that," I said, and it was all he needed to hear to offer me a room. I was too embarrassed to say yes right there, so he told me to think about it.

(Clemens and Helen)

Clemens is a photographer and a painter, and Helen is an architect. My kind of people. I bonded with a supercool Austrian filmmaker named Michael who used to live in Hollywood, and a really welcoming German guy named Nicholas and his eccentric wife, who both seemed to defy the "cold Germans" to which I'd become accustomed.

Later we headed to a bar in downtown Salzburg, a stone's throw away from the flat in which Mozart was born. Clemens, Helen, Lisa and I sat drinking the best beer I've ever had, although everyone said, "Wait'll you get to Prague."

At one point Clemens brought up the Salzburg Festival, and told me that as we spoke, Don Giovanni was playing in the *Steingasse*—the opera house across the street. It was due to end any minute. I looked at the giant opera house doors ready to burst open and imagined Gustav holding Maria's hand as they walked through them to find their seats. Then it occurred to me that if I had never met Brigitte I never would have met Lisa, never would have met Clemens and Helen, and I never would have been sitting across from that opera house feeling like Maria knew exactly where I was.

At 11:30 Clemens suddenly sprang from his chair.

"They're coming!" he exclaimed, and darted toward the front to see if there was an open table so we could get a better look.

Droves of operagoers swarmed out the giant doors in classic tuxedos, top hats and ball gowns, a la the 1920s. Clemens stood and watched them like a kid watching Shamu at Sea World.

The rest of the night I regaled my friends with stories about Maria. Later lying in bed I replayed the whole night in my head, feeling myself sitting outside freshly-showered and shaved in one of the world's most precious cities, speaking to new, riveted faces about a woman I loved so dearly and they found so utterly fascinating... and I honestly couldn't imagine a more life-affirming evening. It may have been the greatest evening I've ever had.

I spent my last day walking around the city. First, Lisa brought me to her former place of work, the stunning aforementioned Schloss Leopoldskron, a beautiful private palace situated on one side of a small lake right outside Salzburg.

I snapped a photo as I walked out onto the terrace. It looked like a painting.

I made sure to visit the Hotel Sacher to try the *Sachertorte*, a rich chocolate cake Maria told me I just had to try if I was ever in

Salzburg. I traversed the steep Honensalzburg Fortress, one of
Europe's oldest preserved medieval castles, and bought a wurstel
from a guy manning a cart on one of the dirt paths leading into
the castle. I was certain Maria knew I was sitting down with my
dollop of mustard devouring it.

On the way back to the house I bought a few prints of the
city of Salzburg from an Asian man holding his brush in one hand
and taking my money with the other. And I stopped in a souvenir
shop and chuckled to myself when I saw little round chocolate
candies called "Mozart's Balls." Maria had always joked about
them. I smiled as I bit into one. I also bought an umbrella I
couldn't resist that was decorated with *The Gold Portrait.*

The next morning I stood in an empty kitchen holding my
new umbrella, my one bag, and a bouquet of flowers that I left for
Helen and Clemens. The whole house was asleep. That's when I
received a text from Couch Surfer Helena.

"Something's come up and I can't host you tonight."


## Vienna

I sprinted to the train station to find a coffee house with Wi-Fi,
and sent emails to a dozen Couch Surfer potentials. The first rain
I'd seen began to fall as I rushed to my train holding my Klimt
umbrella still in its plastic, fielding stares from people indubitably
thinking, "I wonder why he doesn't use it." *I would never use your
wife to shield myself from the rain, Ferdinand.*

The train opened its doors and I sat in a seat next to a
window, definitely on edge, but thinking about how grateful I was
to have connected with Lisa. As I said goodbye to the misty
mountains I regretted not having enough time to climb, my phone
rang.

A tiny voice said: "Ees thees Gregor?"
Meet last-minute Couch Surfer Viktorija Budreckaite.

Turns out her weekend had freed up seconds before she got my request. I was to meet her at the Stephansplatz Square in five hours, which was feasible considering I was due to be in Vienna in four. When I arrived at the square I found a café and bought a nice, tall glass of beer, my backpack and my Klimt umbrella enjoying a well-deserved rest. I ogled at the massive Stephansdom Cathedral, which my travel book indicated was the most important religious building in Vienna. Then a brunette in dark shades tender-footed through the door, and being sure it was Viktorija I jumped up and gave her a hug. I could tell from her kind eyes that I'd found someone who would be more than just a Couch Surfer host. She was the first person I'd ever met from Lithuania.

Viktorija and I weaved in and out of the horses and carriages waiting to give people tours of the city. I told her that Maria—whom I had briefly alluded to earlier at the café—used to feel so sorry for the horses that would "slip on the ice like a pretzel" during the winter. Walking through the cobbled alleyways made me imagine Maria as a child walking ahead of me, her little shoes clicking and clacking on the uneven square concrete stones.

Viktorija's flat was on the top floor of an Art Nouveau building. I looked out her window and could barely see the gothic tips of the sky-high Stephansdom Cathedral in the distance. If I had to choose who was more elegant—Maria or her beloved Vienna—I'm not sure I could decide, since their beauty and grace seemed to so mirror one another. As the sun set we sat on her porch, drank wine, and toasted our happen-stance friendship.

The next morning I told Viktorija I had a mission: to find the Fifth District, where Maria grew up in a house on Elisabethstrasse. It took us an hour to walk through districts one through four, and finally we found written in tiny letters on the side of a building: Fifth District. But I had no idea where Elisabethstrasse was, or what part of it Maria called home. We stopped at the corner and wondered which direction to go next. That's when my phone rang.

Jimmy was inviting me on his boat on Monday for my birthday. He had no idea I was in Europe, let alone Vienna, footsteps away from where his mother grew up.

"Walk to the Strauss Statue," he said. "She grew up in that neighborhood." I mouthed *Strauss Statue* to Viktorija, and we walked in that direction.

We found the statue in the main park in Vienna. Could this have been the actual park where Maria used to buy chestnuts from the chestnut roasters? The thought delighted me. She always used to say that if she were to start a business this late in life, she would line Rodeo Drive in Beverly Hills with chestnut roasters. We found Elisabethstrasse, and walked down a portion of it. That alone was enough for me.

*We may never have been able to go to Europe together, Maria, but we're clearly here together now.*

When we returned home, Viktorija—who I had been thanking profusely all afternoon for being so willing to help me complete my mission—made a delicious chicken and potato dinner, a giant salad with mushrooms and carrots and tomatoes, and afterwards a plate of cantaloupe that we nibbled on while we drank white wine and looked down at the horse-drawn carriages below.

———— ◆ ————

I'd received an email a few weeks ago from a guy named Guenter, a Vienna native. He had stumbled on my profile on the Couch Surfing website and happened to notice a picture of Maria and me taken on my birthday last year at Ruth's Chris.

"I'm never on here," he said, "but I saw your picture with Maria Altmann, and I just had to write—you're lucky to have met her."

He invited me for coffee when I was in town. I hadn't heard from him since. Tonight when I checked my email there was a note from him wondering if I was here. I told him I wanted to meet him at the Stepansdom Cathedral, "Right near the horses."

I stand nearly six foot three in my big brown hiking boots, and Guenter towered over me like a building. He looked to be in his late thirties, with a well-manicured goatee and a cream-colored Indiana Jones hat which he dutifully removed to shake my hand. His wise smile faded quickly, though: he wanted to get down to business. He had a mere afternoon to show me around his native city, and that wasn't nearly enough time.

I couldn't help but tell him the "horses slipping on the ice" story. His softening at my first mention of Maria comforted me. He already knew all about her. It was obvious I hadn't just met any old Couch Surfer. No, this was a very special, very brilliant man who had knowledge of art and history far beyond most people I'd met in my life. He worked at the "Museumsdorf Niedersulz," the largest, open-air museum in lower Austria.

As we walked through the medieval core—the area around the cathedral—I thought about how many times he must have walked around his city and how often he'd shown what he was about to show me today... yet he had an eagerness and curiosity as if experiencing everything for the first time.

*Look how proud he is of your city, Maria.*

By the time lunch rolled around we had walked through most of Vienna, and he had given me a history lesson from the year 1200, to the Hapsburgs, to Emperor Franz Joseph, to the Holocaust, to present day. He seemed to have a compelling story to tell me about every building we passed. All day I chimed in with things about Maria: "Maria's niece Nelly is married to a Hapsburg," and, "Maria spoke at length about Emperor Franz Joseph and what a tragic family life he had," and he would nod with a knowing smile.

The last item to check off my list was the Belvedere Museum. It was about a twenty-minute walk from the Stephansdom Cathedral.

On the way up the stairs into the museum, I said, "I was reading a travel book on the plane and found the name of someone I'd like to meet here." I read Guenter the name off my phone. "Dr. Agnes Husslein."

He stopped, and politely stepped aside to allow a group of people to continue up the stairs. When we stood there alone he leaned close to me, trying not to laugh.

"Gregor, asking for Agnes Husslein at the Belvedere would be like asking for Barack Obama at the White House."

I had somehow overlooked that Frau Husslein was in charge of the entire museum, a museum considered one of the most prominent in all of Europe. I still threatened to ask for her because I liked how it got under his skin.

The museum was as impressive as I had imagined. There were a fair amount of Schieles (in whom I had taken great interest during my short stay in Vienna), some Kokoschkas, a few Renoirs, a van Gogh, a couple Monets (Maria's favorite painter), and the largest collection of Klimts in the world, including "The Kiss," which was far more stunning in person.

We ended our day at a quaint restaurant that, according to Guenter, served "the best Tafelspitz (boiled beef) in town." He insisted on treating me.

*Thank you for Guenter, Maria.*

It was my final evening in Vienna, and I had a bus leaving for Prague first thing in the morning. As I sat in a coffee shop below Viktorija's building fiddling on my brand new MacBookPro, I heard the word Budapest come out of the mouth of a Viennese man sitting next to me talking with his friend. This prompted me to look up a map of Europe and see how close it is to Vienna. It was a mere three-hour bus ride.

It was Sunday, August 21, the day before my birthday, and thanks to the stranger sitting next to me, I cancelled my bus to Prague and replaced it with one to Budapest. *Birthday in Budapest.* It had a ring to it.

I bought another ticket to Prague Tuesday morning. I figured one day in Hungary would suffice. I couldn't be dilly-dallying—I still had two more countries to visit in seven days, before I had to be back in Geneva to catch my flight to Los Angeles. But there was just one problem: I had nowhere to sleep in Budapest. For some reason I wasn't worried.

### Budapest

I left at 5 am for a 7 am bus. When I arrived at the stop I sat on my bag on the sidewalk.

I noticed a young guy lying on his back on the grass smoking a cigarette. I walked over and learned his name was Gyorgy, and that he was Hungarian, and we bonded over the bus being a half hour late. His English needed work but I understood everything. I told him it was my birthday, and he jumped up to give me a great big hug. "Congratulations! Thees ees good, Gregor!" Within ten minutes we were best friends, and sat next to each other on the bus. He was fascinated I was an actor, and wanted to know everything about me. Then he asked where I was staying, and I told him about my plan to find a bar to hang out at until my bus to Prague left in the morning. He insisted I stay with him.

When we arrived in Budapest we walked to the metro to take a train to his flat. As we entered our car a tall, tan, voluptuous girl wearing a colorful sundress walked in and sat down next to us. I couldn't take my eyes off her. Gyorgy kept gesturing for me to talk to her.

I was in no shape to meet a girl, let alone a cute one. I hadn't showered since yesterday morning, my beard was getting to the "homeless" point, and there I was sitting on a dirty train in dirty clothes eating a giant three-day-old sausage Gyorgy handed me out of his bag. I smiled at her, and she smiled back. I told her I was in Budapest for the first time, and that I usually looked more presentable. She spoke English well. I introduced her to Gyorgy, and they spoke Hungarian. Our stop came. I told her we had to go, but it was her stop too, so she got off with us.

As we walked together along the busy track I handed her my business card.

Gregor Collins
Actor
www.gregorgcollins.com

She admitted I was the first American she had ever met in her life, let alone the first actor. She was overwhelmed with firsts. We parted ways.

As Gyorgy and I left the station I couldn't stop staring at all the Hungarian women. I had never seen such naturally beautiful women in my life!

When we arrived at his flat he showed me the couch and disappeared into his room. Gyorgy had been on a sleepless seven-day hiking trip through the Austrian Alps with a few of his Viennese friends, and I hadn't gotten a good night's sleep since Saturday. I fell into a coma until the ring of my cracked iPhone woke me two hours later. It was the girl from the train. She suggested dinner, and she wanted to bring along a friend for Gyorgy.

On our way to meet the girls, Gyorgy took me to meet another girl—his mother—who lived in a flat downtown. She didn't speak English, so her son translated for me.

He told her the exciting details surrounding our chance encounter. She was delighted. She made me a glass of freshly squeezed orange juice in her tiny kitchen, and, as if we were entering another apartment entirely, she led me into a stunning Victorian living room with old master paintings lining the walls, giant, ornate oriental rugs sprawled out on the floors, and antique tables and shelves on top of which lay porcelain dolls of all shapes and sizes. We were in another world. Another era.

She would pick up a doll as if it were a newborn baby, fluff and straighten the trousers on the little boy or the dress on the little girl, and proudly explain the history behind each one, sometimes forgetting that I couldn't understand a word she was saying. Gyorgy explained her whole life she'd been repairing and restoring dolls for people all around the world.

"Koszonom," I said to her on the way out, and she smiled and said, "You're welcome."

We met the girls at a Middle-Eastern restaurant. The friend was tall, charming, and spoke perfect English. The place was tiny. We had to duck as we were led to our table, because the ceiling was so low. If Guenter were with us they would have had to make a hole in the roof for him. After dinner the four of us danced the night away to American hip-hop at a club right in the middle of Pest: Budapest is actually made up of two cities, Buda, and Pest, something I didn't know. Gyorgy and the friend were getting along well, but he had a girlfriend, so he kept his distance from her. Since in a way this night was in honor of my visit, he didn't want to ruin it by telling her he was taken.

The whole day and night I'd been reminding everyone I had a bus leaving for Prague in the morning, as if I secretly wanted to be convinced to stay. It was eating me up inside. I didn't want to wake up from the dream.

So the dream continued. We closed the club and cabbed it to Gyorgy's building, and climbed onto the roof that overlooked all of Budapest. Eventually we split off into pairs. The girl in the colorful sundress and I were left alone on a bench, with not a person in sight and not a sound nearby. I put my arm around her, and she leaned her head against my chest. We sat there both trying to make sense of our meeting.

I threatened her again with my bus, and she looked up at me. The flash of her big brown eyes made me realize our time together was worth more than a bus ticket. I told her I wanted to wear my birthday suit with her, and after I explained what that meant and that it was actually my birthday, her eyes—just like Plácido's did when I told him I was Maria's caregiver—couldn't contain their excitement.

My shackles loosened. The night was now our oyster. As I looked into the horizon like Leo into the Pacific, I felt like the King of the World.

The next day she and I walked arm-in-arm around the city. We made sure to visit the legendary Hungarian baths, walking around in our bathing suits visiting the various steam rooms and showers, holding hands as if we were a couple. With every passing hour it was clear our time together was waning, and we both knew it and felt it.

Nearing dusk, Gyorgy stole me away from her, insisting he drive me somewhere alone. Ten minutes later we both stood on a beach staring down the stunning Danube River.

"Thees is one of my favorite places," Gyorgy said. We stood and admired the view for a few moments, and then we hugged and he wished me luck. It was the second most meaningful farewell of my life. He dropped me back at her house.

The morning came, and a sadness we both refused to acknowledge swept over us as we lay in bed together. She walked me to my bus.

As it idled in the street I looked into her eyes, and in that moment I knew I had the power to tell her I wanted to leave Los Angeles to be with her. *Screw acting. Screw Hollywood. Screw everything I've ever known.* But instead I looked up at the busy flow of cars on the overpass.

As her head rested on my shoulder, thoughts flooded through me. That I wasn't even planning on going to Budapest, that I met Gyorgy, and that if the bus wasn't late I never would have met her in that train car. I thought about Maria, and how I was sure she knew I was in Europe and had led me to a beautiful girl with a beautiful heart, and how happy that makes her. And I thought about how the magical moments in life are always the ones that are unplanned.

I kissed the girl in the sundress goodbye, got onto the bus and found a seat by a window. As we pulled away I cried down the Danube.

## Prague

Prague was littered with tourists, and it wouldn't have been tolerable if we weren't in one of the coolest cities I'd ever seen.

But even in such a cool city, my heart was still in Budapest. The trip could have ended here, and I would have felt content.

I couldn't resist plunking my bags down and having a beer outside the hostel before I checked in.

A girl from Australia and a guy from Japan became my travel buddies. We took a guided tour around the city.

During the tour we passed an opera house in the center square, and the guide gave us a great anecdote about Mozart's "Marriage of Figaro": he had premiered it back in Vienna to tepid audiences. Shocked and offended at the lukewarm reception from his hometown, Mozart brought it to Prague, to this very opera house at which we were now admiring, where he received raucous applause and standing ovations. From that point on he held a special place in his heart for Prague. After the concert he called the reception "The happiest moment of my life."

We also got an education on Czech's most famous writer, Franz Kafka. I took special interest in this because if I had a penny every time someone asked me, "Have you read *The Metamorphosis*?" after hearing my name, I could afford to buy up all the Klimt umbrellas in the world.

## *Berlin*

My final Couch Surfer was Monika Berlin.

Her flat would have been tricky to find, so she volunteered to pick me up at the bus station in downtown Berlin and take me there. She spoke perfect English, and a seasoned Couch Surfer, evidenced by a giant poster she had on her hallway wall with hundreds of "well wishes" from former surfers.

She told me in the car that in all her years of hosting she could only remember having real trouble understanding one guy—a "surfer dude" from California.

"He would say an entire sentence and I'd be like... huh?"

I told her I was a Couch Surfer, not a surfer. She laughed.

In the morning Monika and I walked to meet a tour group in front of the Brandenburg Gate. We saw things like the last remnants of the Berlin Wall, "Checkpoint Charlie," and a slew of Jewish memorials. I was grateful that she humored me with monuments she's surely seen dozens of times.

A German filmmaker I met months ago on Facebook named Daniel Boheme had randomly seen *Night Before the Wedding*, and sent me a note saying he liked my acting work and had me in mind for a role in his new film. I mentioned I'd be travelling through Germany and we arranged a meeting.

Watching Daniel was like watching a squirrel. Every few minutes he would disengage from our conversation, raise his head to listen for a sound or observe a detail at the café like a fork dropping or a busboy cleaning a nearby table, then reengage with me with renewed intensity.

"Sorry, I have heightened senses," he said as he peered at me from his keen eyes—eyes only a born filmmaker could own. We parted ways promising to keep in contact about his film.

On my final day I went to the museums. There are a group of them clumped together on what's dubbed "Museum Island." I decided on the Pergamon Museum, which housed, among many other amazing artifacts, the original Ishtar Gate, built in 575 BC, once considered the seventh Wonder of the World. I posted it on Facebook. There was a feeding frenzy of likes and comments.

In the late afternoon I took the train to the airport. The cheerful conductor came through to snap our tickets. In the States he would likely have been down on his job. The passengers would have treated him as lower class. But in Europe there seems to be a sense of honor about everything, and everyone, no matter who you are or what you do. A human being is a human being. It reminded me of how Maria used to say that before Hitler no one seemed to care what status, race, or religion you were. It was irrelevant.

I sat next to an actual human being from Bordeaux—a polite, 20 something French girl. I always figured only grapes lived there.

———◆———

*Dear Maria,*

*Before my trip I thought you might wonder if I'd be in Europe, but now I know that you knew I was there and you took good care of me. You sent me the lady in the motorized cart, the girls on the train to Salzburg, Lisa, Helen and Clemens and all their friends, Viktorija, the telephone call from Jim, Gyorgy and his mother, the girls from Budapest, Guenter, Monika, Daniel, and all the beautiful people in between. You wanted to ensure my trip left me with indelible memories, and lifelong friends.*

*I thought you should know something else, which I have a hunch you already know, but I'm back in LA helping care for Chuckie, while he recovers from another back surgery. I'm giving him pills and making him meals—does this sound familiar? You should also know that he speaks about you in present tense, in fact he's often not even aware he's doing it.*

*Sure, he can be difficult, we both know that, but it's like I'm still caring for you, the way he looks at me or what he says to me sometimes. And he refuses to admit that he inherited any of your best qualities... some things will never change.*

*Ever since you left I've been busy with the script I'm writing with Andrea, and another film I did with David called "Goodbye Promise"—it had that dog, Snowball, you thought was so cute.*

*This year I've done some of the best creative work of my life. My creativity holds so much more meaning than it ever did without you. But I do miss you. Guess what I miss the most (aside from your smile that lit up rooms around the world for nearly a century)? Our chats in the kitchen. That kitchen was our oyster.*

*I stumbled on this quote recently from Alexander Smith: "Love is the discovery of yourself in others." When I found it I couldn't wait to tell you about it. I used to think God dropped the ball; that He should have arranged our meeting when we were both young and had our whole lives ahead of us. But I've realized that you didn't come into my life to be my love interest—you were here to interest me in love; to show me who I truly am, and who I could truly be. You were here to honor me and to trust me, and to be my stalwart friend. And I was here to return that to you tenfold. Someday I'll find the perfect woman who can love me like you loved me. And I know you'll be proud.*

*The success of my trip to Europe reminds me of how you lived your life—enjoying and appreciating each moment and every person along the way, and always expecting good around every corner. You truly lived as if everything was a miracle. And you loved and forgave everyone, even those who didn't deserve it.*

*I often think about how you lived nearly your entire life not knowing I existed, and I not knowing you existed. And the universe could have kept it that way. But one day at the end of your life and at the beginning of mine, it decided we should meet. And now look at us. In just three years look at what we've accomplished together, and look who we've become through each other. I cry tears of joy.*

*All the greatest artists in history had it right: There is no greater subject to consider, no greater reason to be granted a life, than to love. Your life was love. You set the bar. Now for the rest of my life I will try and live up to it.*

*—Your Caregiver*

# Cast of Characters

The final section includes all known individuals who have had any influence on Maria since she was a child. Many of the famous names were regular guests at the Bloch-Bauer residence and at Adele's salon. To make referencing easier, the names listed under each category—Family, Friends, and Famous—are in alphabetical order. Please note that "Family" may in some cases double for "Famous" (and vice versa), and many of her "Friends" were like "Family." I've included comments from Maria about each of them. For most of the famous names, I've included a quote from them as well.

## FAMILY

### Bernhard Altmann (1888-1980)
Fritz's older brother. Credited with introducing and popularizing cashmere and argyle in America on a mass scale starting in 1947.

> *Maria: "He was a genius, and I think this distanced him from Fritz. Fritz resented that he always had to rely on Bernhard for money and work. So Fritz never gave him the proper respect, and I think it ate Bernhard up inside."*

### Chuck Altmann (1940)
Maria's oldest son. Worked as a Systems Engineer at IBM for 25 years. Has two sons named Philip and Kenny. His wife, Donna, aside from everything else she does for everyone in the family, teaches computer classes to seniors.

> *Maria: "Chuck has never told a lie. Even as a kid, he always told the truth."*

### Cecil Altmann (1934-2008)
Bernhard's son. Has a daughter, Calixte, who lives in New York and is married to former Jimi Hendrix and The Who manager Chris Stamp (brother of actor Terrence Stamp).

> *Maria: "After Fritz died, I told Cecil, 'Well, Fritz is up there looking down on us,' to which he replied, 'More like looking up at us.'"*

### Garret Altmann (1978)
Maria's grandson (from Jimmy). Lives in Alaska. Ranked top ten in the nation in mogul skiing in 2001, but suffered a career-ending knee injury while filming a Warren Miller ski film.

> *Maria: "Am I crazy or did Garret mail us a salmon last year?"*

### Jim Altmann (1955)
Maria's youngest son. Remodels homes. Specialty: fireplaces. Lives in Agoura Hills with his girlfriend, Jesell, a realtor, and his three children, Gregory, Alana and James.

*Maria:* *"It's going to hit him the hardest when I croak."*

### Kenny Altmann *(1976)*
Maria's grandson (from Chuck). Worked in marketing at Yahoo. Lives in San Francisco. Recently married a girl named Hilary, and for their honeymoon they embarked on an eight-month-long, around-the-world-trip.
> *Maria:* *"He's very funny, and full of the Devil."*

### Marguerite Emily Altmann *(1947)*
Maria's only daughter. The "Emily" comes from Maria's governess, Emma. Lives in Hawaii. Works in real estate with her husband, Myron.
> *Maria:* *"We used to talk every day on the phone together. It was rare that we missed a day."*

### Peter Bernhard Altmann *(1945)*
Maria's second oldest son. Retired bus driver. Lives in Tacoma with his wife Donna, a former bank manager.
> *Maria:* *"Out of all my children, Peter is most like my father."*

### Philip Altmann *(1971)*
Maria's grandson (from Chuck). Works as a lawyer in the entertainment industry. Lives in Calabasas, CA with his wife, Tonya, a pediatrician and author of *Mommy Calls*. They have two boys, Avrick and Colin.
> *Maria:* *"He's a wonderful father. He should have been an actor."*

### Fritz Altmann *(1908-1995)*
Maria's husband of 58 years. Dachau Concentration Camp survivor.
> *Maria:* *"Both Fritz and my brother were the amateur golf champions in Vienna, and so they decided they each have a very young sister and a very young brother, and why*

*shouldn't they meet? So they arranged for us to meet at a party, and we fell in love after that. Before long all Fritz had to do was walk through a room and I was pregnant. My friend would say, 'Didn't he at least stop for a second?' And I would say, 'He didn't need to.'*

### Tina Angelotti *(1975)*
Maria's Personal Trainer. Head Fitness Instructor for The Krav Maga National Training Center in Los Angeles.
> **Maria:** *"Every week she manages to come up with new atrocities."*

### Nelly Auersperg *(1930)*
Luise's daughter (Maria's niece). Scientist. Sister of Francis. Lives in Vancouver with her husband, Hans Hapsburg — a prince and a descendent of The House of Hapsburgs, one of the most powerful family dynasties in Europe between 1452 and 1740.
> **Maria:** *"She ran all over town trying to save her father's life (Victor). She was with him all night before they killed him, and she was only about sixteen. I can't imagine the turmoil she must have gone through at such a young age."*

### "Adele Bloch-Bauer 1" *(1907)*
Painting featuring Maria's Aunt Adele (sometimes referred to as *The Gold Portrait* or *The Lady in Gold*). Took Klimt three years to finish. Hitler changed *Adele Bloch-Bauer 1* to *The Lady in Gold* so the name was non-Jewish. Current residence: Neue Galerie in New York. Austria's loss of the painting reportedly costs their economy millions of dollars per year.
> **Maria:** *"The Getty Museum in Los Angeles was interested in acquiring it around the time Lauder was—they had more than enough money to buy it—but the man who was in charge of that department was found to be a crook. Apparently he had stolen money, or something like that, so he was fired and the deal fell through. It would have been nice to have paintings I grew up with just around the corner."*

### Adele Bloch-Bauer (1883-1925)

Maria's aunt. Married to Ferdinand. Daughter of a banking family. Hosted many of Europe's leading artists, musicians and intellectuals at her salon in Vienna. The only model painted twice by Klimt. Died of meningitis at the age of 42. The night of her death, Ferdinand's two German Shepherds sensed trouble, alerted him at his bedside, and led him down to be with Adele in her sickbed, who died in her sleep only three days after she took ill.

> **Maria:** *"For Adele her marriage to Ferdinand was more out of respect than love. She enjoyed the intellectual opportunities it afforded her. Ferdinand loved her very much. She was striking and elegant, but very introverted. She was sort of a tortured woman. She had dark hair and was very frail, and had a crippled finger which she always tried to hide—you can see how it just lays there in the portrait. She always had a gold cigarette holder in her hand and I remember she always wore this long, white dress. She had an incredible urge for knowledge, and was extremely bright and self-educated. Sort of a modern woman living in the world of yesterday. She was a socialist, on the side of the people and the poor. She left a lot of money to social worker organizations. She tried to have kids but none lived beyond infancy. Two were stillborn, and one died during childbirth. My mother had five, and I think this made her a little bitter... I mean how could it not?"*

> **Chuck Altmann:** *"One thing you don't hear is that Adele had severe migraines her entire life, and that's ultimately what killed her. For a while in her forties my mother had consistent migraines, and there was a stretch where she was frightened she would die young, like Adele. But they went away, and never returned."*

> **Adele:** *"If fate has given me friends who are intellectually and ethically exceptional, I attribute these friendships to but one of my qualities: ruthless self-criticism. I always was and will remain my own harshest judge." (from the book Portrait of Adele Bloch-Bauer, for sale at the Neue Galerie in New York).*

*Ferdinand Bloch-Bauer* (1864-1945)
Maria's uncle. Married to Adele. Sugar magnate. Commissioned
Gustav Klimt to paint two portraits of his wife (*Adele Bloch-Bauer
1* and *Adele Bloch-Bauer 2*). Owned one of the most prominent
art/sculpture collections in Europe, valued at around five million
Czech Korunas in 1934. The collection included painters Rudolph
von Alt (Hitler's favorite painter), Ferdinand Georg Waldmuller,
Friedrich von Amerling, Josef Danhauser, Franz Eybl, Peter Fendi,
Friedrich Gauermann, August von Pettenkfen, Emil Jakob
Schindler (Alma Mahler's father), Eugen Jettel and Carl Moll, and
sculptors Auguste Rodin, Constantin Meunier, and Georg Ehrlich.

> **Maria:** *"After Adele died, Ferdinand turned her room into a
> shrine. When we went to his estate for brunches on Sundays,
> I remember peeking inside her room because no one was
> allowed in there, and there were fresh flowers strewn
> everywhere around the bed and around the paintings. The
> Nazis took away everything my uncle had worked for in
> life."*
>
> **Ferdinand:** *"In Vienna and Bohemia, they stripped me of
> everything. Not a single keepsake remains. Perhaps I will get
> the two paintings of my poor wife and my own portrait...
> otherwise I am completely impoverished and may be able to
> lead a modest life for a couple years, if one can call killing
> time living." (In a letter to friend/painter Oskar Kokoschka
> in 1941, from the book Portrait of Adele Bloch-Bauer, at the
> Neue Galerie in New York).*

*Gustav Bloch-Bauer* (1863-1938)
Maria's father. Czech. Lawyer.

> **Maria:** *"As you know, the cello to him was everything.
> When a child was born, he would say, 'Look, he has cello
> hands!' He was friendly with many of the top musicians, like
> Leo Slezak, and Johannes Brahms—if Plácido and Pavorotti
> were in Vienna at that time, my father would have known
> them. He was adorable. Our butler loved him so much. And
> so after he would hear my father play the cello in the other
> room, he would feel he had to compliment him on it—'Herr*

*Bloch-Bauer, the way you handled that one medley'—as if he were knowledgeable about the cello! It was so sweet. Everyone wanted to be nice to my father. When the Nazis came, my father said to me, 'What do you mean the Germans are our enemies? They were our friends!' He died at just the right time, before they really got serious."*

### Leopold "Poldi" Bloch-Bauer (1905-1986)

Maria's oldest brother, with whom she had the closest relationship. His son, Peter Bentley, and his wife, Sheila, live in Vancouver.

> *Maria: "We were very close, but he kept his emotional distance, even with me. I don't think anyone ever really knew the real Poldi."*

### Luise Bloch-Bauer (1908-1998)

Maria's only sister. Lying in a hospital bed at age 89, after hearing that the passing of the Restitution Law in 1998 made it possible for Maria's case to move forward, according to her granddaughter Maria Harris, her final words were: "That's gonna take a good lawyer."

> *Maria: "I could never kill an animal. It's unthinkable to me. And my sister could do it without batting an eye. She was a big gambler. We were on a ship once, and I left her alone to gamble, and I went off and read an entire book, came back, and she looked up at me from the slot machine as if I were crazy. She said, 'What, back so early?'"*

### Therese Bloch-Bauer (1877-1957)

Maria's mother. Adele's sister. German. All four of her brothers died in their thirties: three died of tuberculosis, and one died of bullet wounds suffered during a duel.

> *Maria: "She was the 'typical lady of Vienna'—did nothing but entertain guests and saw to it her children got a good education. I always laugh about this—my mother could do any accent flawlessly. My father had gone alone to a mask ball, and she snuck in later dressed as a French maid with a*

*mask. She went up to my father and started flirting with him. He had no idea it was her. Blushing and stammering, he said to her, 'I'm married, I'm sorry.' After midnight she took off her mask, and said to him, 'Well I'm afraid we have to go home now.' He was completely shocked!"*

## FRIENDS

**Lily De Britto** *(1911-2010)*
Maria's friend of nearly 80 years. Lived in Brentwood. Survived by her two daughters Jackie and Lilo, and her 94-year-old sister, Gerta, who lives in New York.

> **Maria (weeks before Lily's passing):** *"She can cook, that's about it."*

**Petra Kaun** *(1940)*
Maria's accountant and friend of over 50 years. Also worked the books for Lily. Car, animal, and plant enthusiast.

> **Maria:** *"Petra saved Jim's life. When he was a baby, he was playing near the pool, and had somehow found his way into it. She dove in after him. I have Petra to thank for my Jimmy."*

**Peter Koller** *(1920-2006)*
Maria's best male friend. Swiss. Architect.

> **Maria:** *"Peter had this fabulous nose. Not quite as fabulous as yours, but close."*

**Mark Koller** *(1958)*
Peter Koller's son. Lives in Palm Springs. Sells high-end audio equipment.

> **Maria:** *"Mark got me into trouble one day. Fritz had recently passed away, and a friend was consoling me at my house. Suddenly Mark, who was staying in a room at the time for the summer, and very handsome, happened to walk out of my room with his shirt off—he had just finished playing tennis at the club down the street. When my friend saw him standing there without a shirt, she quickly gathered her belongings and ran out the door! She must have thought I was already making my rounds with the local young men!"*

**Edith Metzner** *(1919-2010)*
Maria's childhood friend from Vienna. Lived down the street in
Cheviot Hills.
> **Maria:** *"We played dress-up together as kids—I was always
> the fairy princess, and she was always the wood-chipper."*


**Lynn Emma Raschke** *(1880-1938)*
Maria's governess in Vienna. Worked at the Bloch-Bauer
Household for 35 years.
> **Maria:** *"There are two people I consider the greatest loves of
> my life: my father, and Emma. She had no friends, nothing
> that really made her happy. I was all she had. I loved her
> more than my own mother."*


**Maria Reitler** *(1913-2006)*
Maria's best female friend, who also had a husband named Fritz.
Financed a few Hollywood films, including Fritz Lang's, *Hangmen
Also Die.*
> **Maria:** *"The Reitlers were also very close friends with the
> Slezaks. When Hitler took over Vienna, Maria and her
> husband, who were both Jewish, were stranded in their
> house, and Leo Slezak, who as you know was the top opera
> star in Europe at the time and was the opposite of Jewish,
> would come and stay there as long as he had to, to make sure
> the Nazis didn't harm them. They would never have done
> anything to Maria's family as long as Leo was there
> protecting them."*


**Randol Shoenberg** *(1966)*
Maria's lawyer. Son of Barbara Shoenberg. Has the rare
distinction of being the grandson of two eminent twentieth
century composers (Erich Zeisl and Arnold Schoenberg). Active
President of the Los Angeles Museum of the Holocaust, and
member of the Los Angeles Opera Board.
> **Maria:** *"The Klimt case wasn't the first time a Shoenberg
> represented me. Of course I tell you this now in utter
> embarrassment. About 30 years ago I was in Robinson's May*

*and I had this sweater I wanted to buy and there was this huge line. I grew impatient because Margie's in-laws were in town and I needed to get home to make dinner. So I walked right out with the sweater. Just as I was out the doors, I felt a gentle tap on my shoulder, and it was a security guard, telling me I can't do these sorts of things. Well I wanted that damn sweater! So anyway, I called Randy's father, who was a judge, and he spoke to the security guard, and it was all worked out on the phone. They were very kind and I apologized, and that was that. Now, you're probably going to say 'She's not only an old bag, but she's a sweater thief!'"*

**Ronald Shoenberg (Randy's father):** *"My whole life I've been 'Arnold's Son,' and now I'm 'Randy's Father.' I can't seem to win!"*

**Father Sweeney** *(1933-2010)*
Priest. Longtime friend of the Altmanns.

    **Maria:** *"He always said to me, 'If I wasn't a priest, Maria'... and I always said, 'I know, I know, Father!'"*

## *FAMOUS*

**Raoul Aslan** *(1886-1958)*
One of the most popular Austrian theater actors in the early
1900s. Good friend of Fritz.

> **Maria:** *"I had a crush on Aslan when I was a little girl,*
> *before I met Fritz. I had no idea he was gay. He simply*
> *wouldn't touch a woman. Well... maybe he was right."*
> **Raoul (in a conversation with Gustav Gründgens, the**
> **favorite actor of Hermann Göring):** *"Mr. Gründgens,*
> *you're the greatest German actor, I am the greatest German*
> *actor. You're a homosexual, I am a homosexual. But one*
> *thing you should never forget: My family comes from*
> *Konstantinopel via Thessaloniki to Vienna. And you, Mr.*
> *Gründgens, you are from Düsseldorf."*

**Johannes Brahms** *(1833-1897)*
Influential German composer and pianist sometimes credited as
the third B behind Bach and Beethoven. Maria's father got to
know him well during various opera gatherings.

> **Maria:** *"One evening my father and a friend were invited by*
> *Brahms to see one of his live cello concerts. In the middle of*
> *it, my father leaned over to his friend, proudly pointing at*
> *the stage, whispering, 'This movement coming up is very*
> *difficult,' to which his friend replied, 'I wish it were*
> *impossible.' My father assumed everyone should love opera!"*
> **Johannes:** *"A symphony is no joke."*

**Pau "Pablo" Casals** *(1876-1973)*
The first great cellist. Widely considered the greatest of all time.

> **Maria:** *"My father was given the opportunity to meet Casals*
> *at a luncheon, so he brought with him a framed picture of*
> *Casals playing the cello. He was as excited to meet him as I*
> *was to meet Domingo for the first time. 'Mr. Casals,' my*
> *father said, and Casals said, 'Call me Pablo.' He gave him*
> *the picture, and Casals asked, 'What shall I write?' And my*
> *father, who was understandably a little star-struck, couldn't*

*come up with a suggestion. So Casals wrote, 'To my dear colleague, Gustav.' The picture is right over there in the hallway. You've seen it, haven't you, my love?"*
**Pablo:** *"Each person has inside a basic decency and goodness. If he listens to it and acts on it, he is giving a great deal of what it is the world needs most."*

### Count Hubertus Czernin (1956-2006)
Investigative journalist from Vienna. Made it possible for Randy and Maria to launch their lawsuit. His brother, Johannes, is a respected nuclear scientist and teacher at UCLA, and Johannes's wife, Gertraud, is an artist. They live in Pacific Palisades, CA.
    **Maria:** *"He was such a kind and sweet man."*
    **Randy:** *"Mr. Czernin was a hero to me. He committed his life to exposing unspoken truths about Austria and its Nazi past."*
    **Hubertus (in 2006, weeks before his death and days before Lauder bought the Gold Portrait and had it shipped to New York):** *"I would much prefer to see the paintings in New York. Probably more Austrians would see them there than in Vienna."*

### Plácido Domingo (1941)
Director of the Los Angeles Music Center.
    **Maria:** *"I have a great love for him, as you well know. But I wouldn't want to be married to him."*
    **Plácido:** *"I am never wrong when it comes to my possibilities."*

### Emilie Floge (1874-1952)
Top fashion designer in Europe. Klimt's closest friend.
    **Maria:** *"She handmade my mother's wedding dress for her wedding. I still see it in front of me for some reason! Dark, maroon velvet, with a little black pin stripe going down the shoulders. It was exquisite."*

**Rita Georg** *(1900-1973)*
Popular German opera singer and actress.

> **Maria:** *"Rita was married for many years to my brother,*
> *Charles. She was what you called a Soubrette, which referred*
> *to a female in an opera, who was always the very flirtatious*
> *and naughty one. She would tell me about a man she was*
> *with, and I'd ask her, 'How was he?' And she'd say, 'Ugh!'*
> *And then she'd make her fingers go like this, so as to*
> *indicate the size of his... you know. She was an attractive*
> *little thing, and loved my brother very much. At Charles'*
> *funeral, I looked at Rita's hand and it sort of laid there, limp.*
> *They said she suffered a stroke during the service. It had*
> *become difficult for her to live without Charles. She died a*
> *couple years later, one might say of a broken heart."*

**Hermann Göring** *(1893-1946)*
Son of a judge. Drug addict. Art lover.

> **Maria:** *"In Vienna, Randy met the actual Gestapo who took*
> *all my jewelry—which was Adele's jewelry—in 1938. A man*
> *by the name of Landau, which is a Jewish name—I'm not*
> *sure if the name was real or not—told Randy that all the*
> *jewelry went to Göring's wife. I didn't feel as bad because I'd*
> *heard his wife did some good for people. She had a lot of*
> *Jewish friends and supposedly helped hide some of them."*
> **Hermann:** *"Every educated person is a future enemy."*

**Paul Henreid** *(1905-1992)*
Austrian actor and director who starred in such films as *Now,*
*Voyager,* and *Casablanca.* Has two stars on the Hollywood Walk
of Fame: one for film, one for television.

> **Maria:** *"He was so elegant and had such a radiant career,*
> *and died an unhappy man. You see, he made a big mistake.*
> *He called his grandson's fiancé a Proletariat. He said to him:*
> *'How could you want to marry such a Proletariat?' His*
> *grandson never forgave him for that. 'If you ever write me*
> *again,' he said to Paul, 'I will not reply. If you ever send me*
> *money, I will not accept it.' And they never spoke again. This*
> *really devastated Paul. He really loved his grandson. He tried*

*to make amends with him but he ignored all his calls and letters. One day I saw Paul walking along Olympic and Doheny, and I barely recognized him. He was hunched over and looked like a broken man. I couldn't bring myself to even say hello at that point. I just knew he would have been embarrassed to see me. He died a couple years later. I think the grandson was wrong not to forgive him. A very tragic end to a good life."*

**Paul:** *"I never felt Lee Strasberg could act, and I fail to see how someone who can't act can teach acting."*

### Lena Horne *(1917-2010)*

Acclaimed American singer and actress who lived on the same street as the Altmanns when they first moved to Los Angeles (along with Bogart and Bacall), just above Sunset Boulevard on Horn Avenue.

**Maria:** *"Chuck says he touched tongues with Lena's daughter when they were both 5 or 6, and as you know he doesn't lie, so I don't doubt they did."*

**Lena:** *"I really do hate to sing."*

### Emperor Franz Joseph I *(1830-1916)*

Crowned Emperor of Austria at age 18.

**Maria:** *"He died just a few months after I was born. His kids went to the same swimming pool to which I went. I used to see them there all the time. They were very normal and friendly, but boy, were they ugly. How does that happen? You have two good-looking parents, and the kids turn out ugly. Anyway, he had a tragic life. Just horrible. His brother was executed, his wife was murdered—she was on a ship to Geneva with her Ladies in Waiting, and was stabbed to death... and his son, Rudolph, committed suicide with his mistress because he could only marry royalty and they could never be together. It was like a real-life Romeo and Juliet. Supposedly they were both lying in bed, and he shot her, and sat there for an hour or so watching her, and then shot himself."*

**Gustav Klimt** *(1862-1918)*
The first Austrian artist to delve deep below surface appearances
to become a key transitional figure between Impressionism and
Expressionism. Painted portraits of Vienna's leading ladies of
society, including Alma Mahler, Adele, and Emilie Floge. Not until
the 1960s and 70s did he begin to become popular with the
younger generation. Obsessed with the female body. Allegedly
fathered eighteen illegitimate children. Had a Far Eastern
influence, especially in his later work. His father was a gold
engraver, most likely inspiring him to paint *Adele Bloch-Bauer 1*
and *The Kiss*, which he completed during his "Golden Phase."
Many of his works have been lost over time, two notable ones
being *The Golden Apple* and *Wally*, which were destroyed in a fire
in Vienna in 1945.

> **Maria:** *"He was not into beauty. I mean, my Aunt Adele
> wasn't the most attractive woman. He made his ladies look
> far more beautiful in his paintings. All the women he
> painted and courted were different and distinctive in some
> way. He liked imperfection."*
> **Gustav:** *"If you can't please everyone with your deeds or
> art, please just a few."*

**Hedy Lamarr** *(1914-2000)*
Austrian-born American actress. Major MGM contract star.

> **Maria:** *"I knew her well, we ran in the same circles in
> Vienna. The first time I met her was at a ball in 1937. I
> remember vividly—she had on this stunning sapphire blue
> sequin dress. She was gorgeous... but as stupid as a goose.
> She believed anything you told her. All that stuff about her
> helping invent wireless communications or whatever they
> say, isn't true. When you're beautiful, I guess you can make
> anyone believe anything!"*
> **Hedy:** *"I am a very good shot. I have hunted for every kind
> of animal. But I would never kill an animal during mating
> season."*

### Ronald Lauder (1944)

American businessman, philanthropist, and art collector. Bought his first painting at age thirteen—a Schiele—from money he received from his Bar Mitzvah. Founded the Neue Galerie in New York on November 16, 2001, with late business partner Serge Sabarsky.

> **Maria:** *"Mr. Lauder called me personally to buy the painting. He flew in from New York and came to my house. He was very nice. A man of his stature could certainly get away with being arrogant, but he was anything but. He told me that when he was sixteen he had seen my Aunt's portrait in Vienna with his mother, and he dreamed of owning it one day. On the day it arrived in New York from Vienna, he ordered the entire block cleared and guarded, and had it delivered at five in the morning, just to be sure it made it safely."*
>
> **Ronald:** *"The Gold Portrait is our Mona Lisa."*

### Alma Mahler (1879-1964)

Prominent socialite in Vienna around the turn of the twentieth century. Considered a brilliant pianist and composer. Dated, married, and/or inspired many of the "geniuses" of the time, like composer Gustav Mahler, architect Walter Gropios, novelist Franz Werfel, and painter Oscar Kokoschka.

> **Maria:** *"I had met Alma in her forties at our house. She used to be very beautiful, but by then had let herself go. I had heard she would go to the airport carrying a large thermos, and the airport security would ask her what was in it, and she would respond, 'It's my tea,' and it was of course filled with liquor. I knew her daughter well—Manon. She died of polio at eighteen. I remember hearing a rumor at the time that Alma put a snake in Manon's bed, to kill her so she wouldn't have to suffer anymore."*
>
> **Alma:** *"God granted me the privilege of knowing the brilliant works of our time before they left the hands of their creators. And if I was allowed to assist these knights for a while, then my existence is justified and blessed!"*

**Gustav Mahler** *(1860-1911)*
One of the leading Austrian composers of his generation.
> **Maria:** *"Supposedly Mahler met Alma Mahler during a visit to my Adele's salon. They were there often together."*
> **Gustav:** *"Destiny smiles upon me but without making me the least bit happier."*

**Zubin Mehta** *(1936)*
One of the premier conductors of Western classical music today.
> **Maria:** *"Barbara Shoenberg, Randy's mother, lives across the street from him in Brentwood, and a couple of years ago she invited me over to have lunch at his house. He was so charming. Boy, was he charming. He said to me, 'Maria... if only I had met you forty years ago.' And I of course was thinking the same thing."*

**George Minne** *(1866-1941)*
Belgian artist and sculptor.
> **Maria:** *"He made these wonderful sculptures for my parents, and we had them in our house growing up. We gave two of them to the Neue because they had spent so much money on the portrait and we didn't want them to have to spend any more."*

**Ezio Pinza** *(1892-1957)*
One of the most popular Italian opera singers and actors of his time.
> **Maria:** *"He was the basso in Europe at the time. My father took me to my first festival in Salzburg when I was fifteen, to see him sing. It was Mozart's Don Giovanni, and of course Ezio was playing Don Giovanni. I remember it like it was yesterday—Ezio had on these white satin pants that ended at the knee, and I said, 'Daddy, he has such beautiful legs!' And my father grumbled, 'What business of yours are his legs?' As if his legs were his sexual organs!"*

### Giacomo Puccini *(1858-1924)*
Italian composer whose operas *Madama Butterfly* and *Turandot* are among the most frequently performed around the world today.

> ***Maria:*** *"A friend of my mother was dating the Italian ambassador at the time, and so my mother would get invited to these lavish parties, where Puccini would be playing the piano for all the guests. You could go right up to him and request a song! Can you imagine?!*
>
> ***Giacomo:*** *"Art is a kind of illness."*

### Max Reinhardt *(1873-1943)*
Jewish theater director who spent nearly twenty years living at the Schloss Leopoldskron, a palace in Salzburg where he staged plays and glamorous receptions for prominent individuals in the world of art and culture. The palace was considered the birthplace of the Salzburg Festival. The Nazis confiscated the estate in 1938 as Jewish property, and Max would never be able to see it again. He died in exile in New York.

> ***Maria:*** *"I visited Vienna after our case, and I stayed with some friends at the Reinhardt Mansion. It was gorgeous. They gave me Max's room to sleep in! I felt like a queen!"*
>
> ***Max:*** *"I believe in the immortality of the Theatre, it is a most joyous place to hide, for all those who have secretly put their childhood in their pockets and run off and away with it, to play on to the end of their days."*

### Karl Renner *(1870-1950)*
Influential Austrian politician who headed the first republican government in Austria in 1918.

> ***Maria:*** *"Karl, Julius Tandler and Adele were all very good friends. Tandler and Renner passed through our house often. These were brilliant men that I couldn't fully appreciate because I was so young."*
>
> ***Karl:*** *"Little kids understand more than they are able to express; with adults it's the other way around."*

*Arthur Schnitzler* *(1862-1931)*
Prolific Austrian author and dramatist. Along with fellow
Austrians Egon Schiele, Oskar Kokoschka, Gustav Klimt and
Sigmund Freud, he made significant contributions to the portrayal
of the unconscious psychology of sexuality and aggression in bold
new ways.

> *Maria: "We would all drive out to the country with Arthur
> and his son. Arthur had a crush on me. The way he looked at
> me and flirted with me, and I was so young! I absolutely
> loved his writings as a teenager. He was my favorite
> childhood author. His stories were so sweet and romantic. He
> was a womanizer, but his stories were fabulous."*
> *Arthur: "Tolerance means excusing the mistakes others
> make. Tact means not noticing them."*

*Erich Zeisl & Arnold Shoenberg* *(1905-1959/1874-1951)*
Erich—father of Barbara Shoenberg, grandfather of Randy
Shoenberg. Fritz's best friend. Scored films such as *Lassie Goes
Home* and *The Postman Always Rings Twice.*

> *Erich: "The two things I hate most are Hitler and the sun."*
Arnold—father-in-law of Barbara, grandfather of Randy. Often
called "The father of modern music." A pioneer of atonality.

> *Arnold: "I owe very, very much to Mozart; and if one
> studies, for instance, the way in which I write for string
> quartet, then one cannot deny that I have learned this
> directly from Mozart. And I am proud of it!"*

*Leo Slezak* *(1873-1946)*
Walter Slezak's father. Ranked in the top one hundred greatest
voices of all time.

> *Maria: "I remember my father telling me he was with Leo
> one day and saw a woman looking through the window of a
> bra shop, and Leo went up to her and said: 'You don't need
> one of those, I'll hold them up for you.'"*

### Walter Slezak *(1902-1983)*

Son of Leo. Austrian actor who appeared in numerous Hollywood films such Hitchcock's *Lifeboat*, Robert Wise's *Born to Kill*, and *Treasure Island*. Also played the Clock King in the *Batman* TV series. Committed suicide at age 81.

> **Maria:** *"Walter was constantly trying to get me into bed. 'I could do things to you that you would really enjoy,' he would say, and, 'I would eat you up with salt and pepper.' But he knew better than to ever do anything fresh with me."*
>
> **Walter:** *"You have to work years in hit films to make people sick and tired of you, but you can accomplish this in a few weeks on television."*

### Richard Strauss *(1864-1949)*

Leading German composer who had a profound influence on the development of music in the twentieth century.

> **Maria:** *"My father's favorite composer was Mozart, and Strauss was a close second. He was another regular at my aunt's salon, so my father would always take the opportunities to pull him aside and talk to him about music."*
>
> **Richard:** *"Do you believe I am ever, in any of my actions, guided by the thought that I am 'German?' Do you suppose Mozart was consciously 'Aryan' when he composed? I recognize only two types of people: those who have talent and those who have none."*

### Joan Sutherland *(1926-2010)*

One of the most accomplished female opera singers of the twentieth century.

> **Maria:** *"My brother Charles told me one day he had an affair with her in London one summer. I said, 'Sure, right.' I didn't believe him. So he told me to go to a show she was doing and go backstage and tell them 'I'm the sister of Charles Bloch-Bauer and I'd like to see Joan.' So, reluctantly, I did. 'I'm the sister of Mr. Bloch-Bauer,' I said to them backstage. A few moments later Joan came running out. 'How is my Charles??!!' I couldn't believe it. She was so nice. And tall. She towered over me, and I'm five-foot-eight!"*

> **Joan:** *"You can listen to what everybody says, but the fact remains that you've got to get out there and do the thing yourself."*

## Julius Tandler *(1869-1936)*

Respected physician, social democratic politician, and professor in Vienna. Close friend of Adele.

> **Maria:** *"I met Julius a few times in my teens, with my mother. He used to say to his classes... 'Which human body part increases to ten times its size when stimulated?' Appalled, a female student stood up and said, 'I refuse to answer such an inappropriate question.' So he asked the same question again, and the same student stood up and said, 'I'm going to go home and tell my parents how sick you are!' Finally a male student stood up, looked around nervously, and said, 'The body part that increases to ten times its size when stimulated is the womb in the time of pregnancy.' Mr. Tandler smiled and said, 'Very good.' Then he turned to the disturbed female student and said, "As for you, young lady, you are going to be very disappointed one day!"'*
>
> **Julius:** *"If you build palaces for children you tear down prison walls"*

## Danny Thomas *(1912-1991)*

Popular film and television actor, best known for starring in the television sitcom, *Make Room for Daddy*, and *The Danny Thomas Show*. Founded the St. Jude Children's Research Hospital. Friend/neighbor of the Altmanns.

> **Maria:** *"Such a kind and decent man. But his wife? The only time in my business life I ever cried or had a reason to cry was when I dealt with that bitch. I had ordered her a special outfit from Italy—it was of the highest quality, and exactly what she requested—and I walked over to her house and showed it to her and without even trying it on, she scoffed, and said, 'I would never wear this. I'll give it to my maid.' I was walking back across the street and I broke into tears. She treated me so horribly! Chuck used to play basketball with*

*their butler, and he said all the hired help adored Danny, and hated the wife. Well I don't like most women, but you know this, darling."*

**Danny:** *"Success in life has nothing to do with what you gain in life or accomplish for yourself. It's what you do for others."*

## Arturo Toscanini *(1867-1957)*

One of the most acclaimed musicians of the late nineteenth and twentieth centuries.

**Maria:** *"As you know my husband just devoured anything to do with opera. He had such a passion for it. Well he noticed Toscanini's mother sitting near the front row at an opera, and he went up to her during intermission and talked with her for several minutes. She liked him so much that she said, 'I'm going to introduce you to my son.' So Fritz and Arturo spent a whole afternoon together chatting about music. Fritz was beside himself. He said it was one of the most thrilling moments of his life."*

**Arturo:** *"When I was young, I kissed my first woman and smoked my first cigarette on the same day. Believe me, never since have I wasted any more time on tobacco."*

## Otto Wagner *(1841-1918)*

Prominent Austrian architect.

**Maria:** *"He and Klimt would come to my aunt's salon together."*

**Otto:** *"What is impractical can never be beautiful."*

## Franz Werfel *(1890-1945)*

Austrian novelist, playwright, and poet. Husband of Alma Mahler.

**Maria:** *"He lived across the street from us, so he would occasionally show up at our house with Alma and their son."*

**Franz:** *"Religion is the everlasting dialogue between humanity and God. Art is its soliloquy."*

***Berta Zuckerkandl*** *(1864-1945)*
Austrian art critic. One of the few critics who continuously defended Klimt's "degenerative" art in her column "Art and Culture".

> **Maria:** *"She and my aunt shared a lot of the same friends, and were both well-known personalities in Vienna."*
> **Berta:** *"On my divan, Austria comes alive."*

## *Photograph Credits*

# *Acknowledgments*

My most important thank you goes to the Altmanns, especially the four kids and their significant others—Peter and Donna, Chuck and LaDonna, Margie and Myron, and Jim and Jesell. Thank you for trusting me to care for your mother. I am eternally grateful for your unwavering, unconditional love and support throughout my brief stay on Danalda Drive. I will always consider you family.

A dear thank you goes to the beautiful Tom Trudeau for your friendship and love over the years, and for introducing me to the person who would change my life. I thank the original night caregiver, Chris Haskell, for always bringing Maria an endless supply of childlike wonder, and an extra special thank you to David Branin, for being nothing short of superhuman when it came to caring for a woman who did nothing but care for others. Thank you Anne-Marie O'Connor, for all your help and guidance, and to both Stephen Lash and Steven Thomas, for treating Maria like a mother, not a client.

This book would never have been what it is without the heart and skill of editor Jessica Swift, who believed in it enough to take it on and treat it like her baby. If a book could ever have a soul mate, it would be you, Jessica. And thank you to book designer Sara Dismukes for your professionalism and craftsmanship, and for being so patient with someone who is not. Thank you Joanne Shwed, for being the first person to read my manuscript and to offer valuable direction, and thank you to copyeditor Shakirah Dawud, who made me look good (or at least not horrible) for the presses. I thank writer/publisher Rita Mills for all your unsolicited advice during the days leading up to the book's release, and I thank Allison Kiessling for hours of free counsel on website design.

Thank you to Guenter Fuhrmann for our chance meeting in Vienna in 2011, for being the best tour guide I've ever had, and for your friendship ever since. It's my turn to show you a good time in Los Angeles.

I thank my Mom, my Dad and his wife, Tea, and Christian and his wife/new mother, Suki, for always being there for me.

Lastly I'd like to thank you, God, for taking good care of Maria, and, of course, for making sure she gets a nice, comfortable chair.

Made in the USA
San Bernardino, CA
05 April 2015